A HISTORY OF MONTANA IN 101 OBJECTS

A HISTORY OF MONTANA IN 101 OBJECTS

Artifacts & Essays from the
MONTANA HISTORICAL SOCIETY

Introduction by KIRBY LAMBERT

Photography by TOM FERRIS

MONTANA HISTORICAL SOCIETY PRESS
Helena

Front cover photograph: Square & Compass Branding Iron, ca. 1899,
Gift of the Montana Stockgrowers Association, x1967.08.07

Cover and book design by Diane Gleba Hall
Typeset in Warnock Pro

Printed in Great Falls, Montana, by Advanced Litho Printing

Distributed by Farcountry Press, 2750 Broadwater Avenue, Helena, MT 59602
(800)821-3874

ISBN 978-1-94052-796-3

Library of Congress Cataloging-in-Publication Data

NAMES: Ferris, Tom, 1959– photographer. | Montana Historical Society, issuing body.

TITLE: History of Montana in 101 objects : artifacts & essays from the Montana Historical Society / Montana Historical Society ; photography by Tom Ferris.

OTHER TITLES: Artifacts & essays from the Montana Historical Society

DESCRIPTION: Helena : Montana Historical Society Press, [2020] | Includes bibliographical references and index. | Summary: "History of Montana in 101 Objects: Artifacts and Essays from the Montana Historical Society highlights the Montana Historical Society's collections. The book features objects from the museum and archives. Each object is accompanied by an essay that explains the historical significance of the object"—Provided by publisher.

IDENTIFIERS: LCCN 2020043600 | ISBN 9781940527963 (paperback)

SUBJECTS: LCSH:
Material culture—Montana. | Montana—Antiquities. | Montana—History. | Montana—History—Pictorial works. | Material culture—Montana—Pictorial works. | Montana—Antiquities—Pictorial works. | Montana—Social life and customs—Pictorial works. |Montana—Social life and customs.

CLASSIFICATION: LCC F728 .H57 2020 | DDC 978.6—dc23

LC record available at https://lccn.loc.gov/2020043600

THIS book was made possible in part by the generous financial support from the following institutions:

The Borick Foundation

The Liatis Foundation

Montana's Cultural and Aesthetic Projects Trust Fund, a trust funded by a percentage of severance taxes paid on coal mined in Montana

My Cabin
in Montana 1866.

THIS book is dedicated to the generous donors who, since 1865, have provided the collections that the Montana Historical Society holds in trust for all people of Montana.

◈

Contents

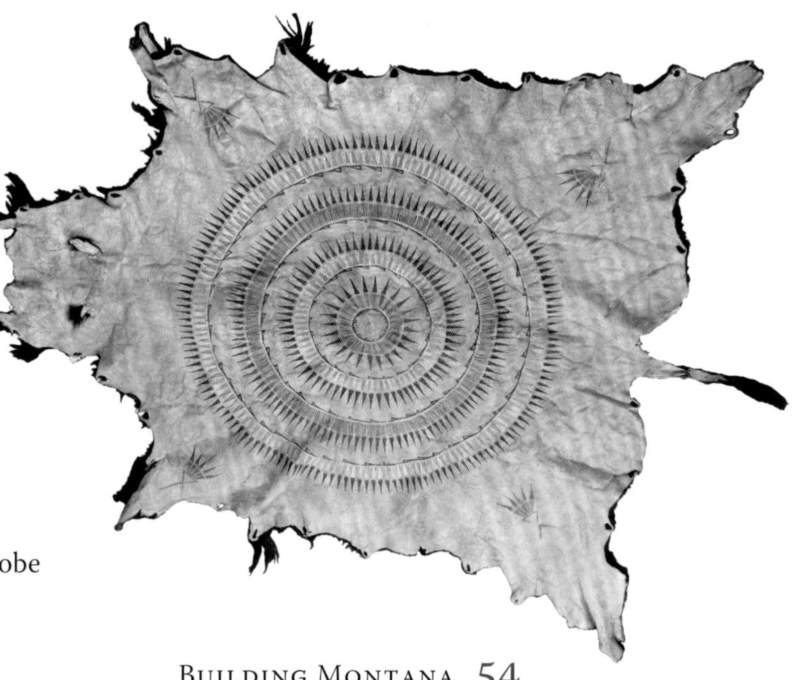

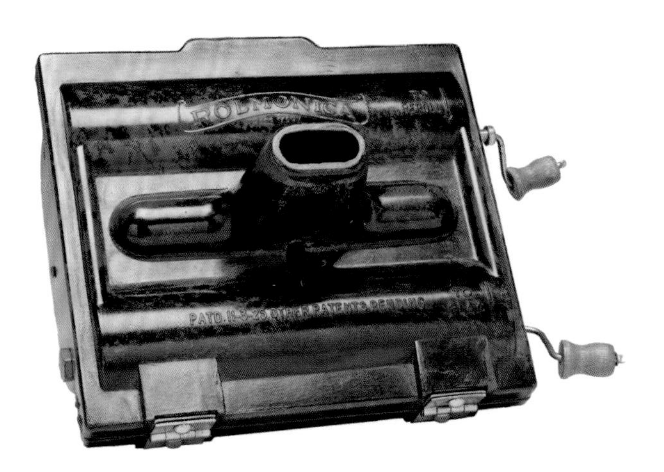
ROLMONICA

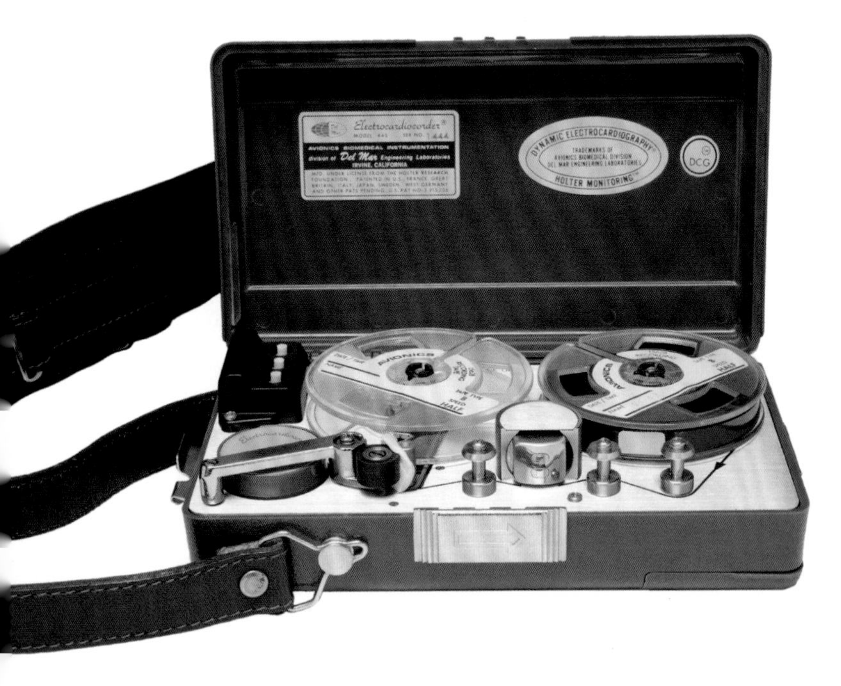

Electrocardiocorder
AVIONICS BIOMEDICAL INSTRUMENTATION
division of Del Mar Engineering Laboratories
IRVINE, CALIFORNIA
DYNAMIC ELECTROCARDIOGRAPHY
TRADEMARKS OF
AVIONICS BIOMEDICAL DIVISION
DEL MAR ENGINEERING LABORATORIES
HOLTER MONITORING
DCG

Acknowledgments

◈

A PROJECT of this scale truly takes a village, and many individuals contributed greatly to this effort. We would like to thank:

Stephenie Ambrose Tubbs, for bringing the inspiration
and letting us play along

Tom Ferris, for his excellent photographs, and Kendra Newhall,
for coordinating the collections' photography

Diane Gleba Hall, for her remarkable talent as a book designer

Editors Molly Holz, Caroline Patterson, Randall Williams,
Laura Ferguson, Martha Kohl, Micah Fields, Diana Di Stefano,
and Jeff Bartos, and proofreader Ann Seifert,
for creating cohesion out of chaos

Bruce Whittenberg, MHS director from 2011–2020,
for his support and enthusiasm

All our MHS colleagues—past and present—whose work
preserving these collections, and the stories that they tell,
makes projects such as this one possible

A HISTORY OF MONTANA IN 101 OBJECTS

HITTIN' THE HIGH SPOTS
IN MONTANA
Irvin Shope

Introduction

"Appropriate, Curious, and Rare"

◈

As this is the only cabinet of a permanent public society preserved for the whole Territory, it is hoped that whatever is appropriate, curious, and rare will be preserved therein, and no longer scattered abroad.

–*Contributions to the Historical Society of Montana*, 1876[1]

In many respects, the Montana Historical Society serves as Montana's memory. Objects from the past comprise its heart and soul. Individually, these items offer fascinating glimpses into the lives of earlier generations. Together, the stories told by the hundreds of thousands of items held by the Society intertwine to form a rich tapestry that illustrates our shared past. *A History of Montana in 101 Objects: Artifacts & Essays from the Montana Historical Society* features only a select few of the "appropriate, curious, and rare" gems from the Society's vast collections. Together, the artifacts in this book help us better understand who we, as Montanans, are today and how we got here.

The Montana Historical Society (MHS) was founded fewer than eight months after Montana became a territory.[2] In December 1864, the newly convened Legislative Council, meeting in Bannack, approved the idea of creating an organization to "collect and arrange facts in regard to the early history of this Territory, the discovery of its Mines, incidents of the fur trade, &c., &c." Five weeks later—following the requisite political wrangling—the House concurred. Governor Sidney Edgerton signed the Society into being on February 2, 1865, thus creating one of the earliest organizations of its kind in the American West. As MHS editor Vivian Paladin noted, "No other state in the Union can boast that its first legislators displayed better foresight than this."[3] Or, as the *Big Sandy Mountaineer* less concisely observed:

> When one pauses to consider all the problems that confronted those pioneer lawmakers—problems of establishing law and order as well as finding ways and means of putting a new territory into successful operation—it is a matter of wonder that they had time to think of starting a historical society. But they did—and by that very act gave the society and the work it was contemplated it should do an importance in Montana affairs that present day citizens should not forget.[4]

Montana Highway Department Promotional Flyer, 1938, 8½" × 11". Irvin "Shorty" Shope, illustrator. Gift of Charles Diggs Greenfield Jr. and Ann Greenfield Jancic, 1986.11.32

Like the Indigenous record-keepers depicted by Maynard Dixon (1875–1946) in his 1917 oil painting *Blackfeet Historians*, the Montana Historical Society serves as Montana's memory, preserving the past for the benefit of its citizens, present and future. 17¾" × 11⅜". X1964.10.01

The act of incorporation signed by Governor Edgerton identified twelve distinguished citizens who, along with "their associates and successors, are hereby made and constituted a body politic, under the name and style of the Historical Society of Montana." The founders held their first meeting on March 25, 1865, at a mercantile store belonging to Walter B. Dance and James Stuart in Virginia City, which by then had become the young territory's capital. At a second meeting held at the same location one month later, attendees elected officers and voted to admit fourteen additional members.[5] With the foundations of MHS in place, the *Montana Post* reported, "There will now be an opportunity for all our citizens . . . to contribute such facts as may be of interest to the present and future inhabitants of this country. . . . It is for our people now to say whether they will preserve the early history of Montana in an enduring form, so that after times may know the thrilling drama here enacted."[6]

Over the next century and a half, MHS slowly evolved into a fully realized, modern institution widely acclaimed for the quality and significance of its collections. While initial efforts focused on manuscripts, maps, books, and newspapers—items then recognized as holding the greatest value for future researchers—over time its collections expanded in both size and scope. Today, the Society collects all types of materials relevant to the history and culture of this place we call home. Acquiring and caring for the physical remnants of Montana's past remains among its core functions, but MHS has continually moved toward broader public inclusion and engagement.

As with any organization, highs and lows marked the Society's development. In 1873, MHS wrote and adopted a constitution, "modeling itself on venerable private societies in the East."[7] The constitution limited official membership to the original twenty-six "corporators," admitted a small number of specially selected "corresponding" and "honorary" members, and created the office of librarian to oversee the collection.[8] That same year, President Wilbur Fisk Sanders moved the collections from Virginia City to his law offices in Helena, where, on January 9, 1874, they were destroyed in a fire that devastated Montana's Queen City. By 1887, however, the collections had been rebuilt to the extent that MHS opened its first "public rooms" in the newly erected Lewis and Clark County Courthouse. Here, as reported by the Helena Board of Trade, visitors could spend "a pleasant hour . . . examining relics and early newspapers and talking about the old days." The report further observed that "few States and Territories, if any, have so complete and perfect a record of early exploration and adventure."[9]

As the century closed, MHS transformed from a private gentlemen's club into a public institution. In March 1891, the Society became a state agency, turning its collections—and, two years later, its governance—over to state control. By 1900, the Historical and Miscellaneous Department of the Montana State Library, as it had been renamed, boasted "a large number of manuscripts and diaries, for the most part original matter of inestimable value, as they furnish the records of the settlement and early history of the state as written by actual participants in the events recorded . . . [as well as] a highly interesting and rapidly expanding

The founders of the Montana Historical Society held their first organizational meeting on March 25, 1865, inside this building, which was, at the time, a mercantile owned by Walter B. Dance and James Stuart. This photograph of an unidentified group of people posed outside the structure was taken about 1880. 956-356

Between 1887 and 1902, the Society exhibited its collection in "public rooms" located in the Lewis and Clark County Courthouse, which also housed other offices of Montana government. The Lowe Printing Press No. 2 (see page 58) is prominently displayed. 952-762

Cases filled with Indian artifacts and taxidermy mounts line the walls of MHS's displays in the basement of the state capitol, 1928. Miss Ishikawa and her belongings (see page 220) can be seen at the end of the hall on the right. L. H. Jorud, photographer. 952-804

collection of the flora, fauna, metals and minerals of Montana and many relics of the tragedies and thrilling and romantic occurrences in its early history."[10]

When the state capitol was completed in 1902, MHS moved into the west end of the ground floor. A decade later, with the expansion of the statehouse, it relocated again to the new east wing. Almost immediately, however, librarian Laura Howey lamented the inadequacy of the space and called for the construction of a deliberately designed, dedicated home for the Society. This sentiment was repeated frequently by Howey's successors after the highly capable librarian, the first "chosen for relevant experience rather than pioneer kinship," lost her job due to gender discrimination.[11] In 1907, Montana's attorney general ruled that the MHS librarian was a public official and thus subject to the state's constitution that officeholders be eligible voters. Since women in Montana did not gain suffrage until 1914, both Howey and the Society suffered the loss.

In the mid-twentieth century, the dream of a building for the Society became a reality when "a trend toward progressivism and professionalization materialized in state historical societies nationwide."[12] In 1941, the legislature approved a bond to fund a new building, but that effort was stalled by the United States' entry into World War II; lawmakers subsequently increased that bond amount in 1945 and again in 1949. That same 1949 bill also expanded the Board of Trustees to provide for increased representation statewide, changed the organization's name back to the Historical Society of Montana, "defined the duties of the librarian, established the society's collecting parameters, and emphasized the need to promote the study of Montana history through lectures, museum exhibits, and publications."[13] These efforts were backed by, among others, history faculty from the State University in Missoula and the State College in Bozeman. As noted by former MHS librarian Robert M. Clark, "Professors replaced pioneers as the most interested parties."[14]

Finally, in 1953, MHS moved into its very own headquarters across the street from the state capitol. The Montana Pioneers and Sons and Daughters of Montana Pioneers donated land for the site, and veterans' organizations helped provide furnishings. Consequently, the new structure was named the Veterans and Pioneers Memorial Building, and these groups were provided office and exhibit space on the third floor. Expansions followed in 1970 and 1986, but by the beginning of the twenty-first century, MHS once again needed more room to exhibit and care for its growing collections. The 2019 Legislature voted to support the construction of the Montana Heritage Center, a 66,000-square-foot addition.

Almost as significant as the new building was the hiring of K. Ross Toole in 1951 as the Society's first official director, tasked with overseeing the operations of the now multi-departmental organization. The ideal candidate, he had "a pioneer pedigree, academic credentials, and the moxie to promote the importance of Montana history to the legislature and the public."[15] Toole hired Smithsonian ethnologist Dr. John Ewers, who had formerly worked on the Plains Indian Museum in Browning, to design the exhibits at the Society's new headquarters. He also

After years of waiting for a facility of its own with sufficient space for its growing collections, the Society took up residence in its new, International-style headquarters across the street from the state capitol in 1953. Catlin's Studio, photographer. PC 001 HELE-MHS

recruited artists—both nationally recognized and locally available—to create a series of then state-of-the-art dioramas for the main level's Formal Museum. As its name suggests, the basement-level Informal Museum exhibited objects from the Society's collection in a less structured fashion. In 1969, the Informal Museum was replaced with the immensely popular Territory Junction, an 1880s street scene lined with replica building fronts stocked with artifacts appropriate to the era. The Montana Homeland exhibit, created for the state's upcoming centennial, took over the space occupied by the Formal Museum in 1988.

One of Toole's primary challenges in reorganizing the museum's operations was tersely summarized in a letter he wrote to a disgruntled would-be donor who had inquired about gifting a piano to the Society:

> Now if we had unlimited space I would certainly take your piano. But we already have four pianos and this year alone we have been offered twelve more pianos. If I had accepted them, we would have a piano museum, not a historical museum. And our problem is not merely with pianos. . . . You see we simply had to make up our minds whether we wanted a meaningless hodge podge of relics that did not tell a cohesive, chronological story, or whether we wanted a real museum. We chose the latter.[16]

Artist Gardell Dano Christensen applies the finishing touches to the buffalo jump diorama (see page 12) that would become one of the most popular displays for schoolchildren and other visitors after the opening of the Society's new building in 1953. MHS B06

The completion of the new building, coupled with Toole's vision for the museum, ushered in a new era in collecting. After 1953, MHS attracted new, sizable, and nationally significant art collections, including works from Montana's "Cowboy Artist" Charles M. Russell, sculptor Robert M. Scriver, cartoonist Stan Lynde, and the Poindexter Collection of Abstract Expressionism. Likewise, the

Governor Forrest Anderson joins young museumgoers Sue Morgan (left) and Meg Duffy (right) at the 1969 grand opening of MHS's Territory Junction exhibit. Behind the counter of the "Fullerton General Store," curator Bob Morgan cuts a plug of tobacco. MHS B11 TerrJct

Research Center benefited from the addition of major donations ranging from the F. Jay Haynes and L. A. Huffman photograph collections to the Amos and Margaret Booth Teakle Range Life Memorial Collection and the Anaconda Copper Mining Company records.

In 1951, Toole also launched the Society's new periodical, *Montana The Magazine of Western History*. The magazine's predecessor, *Contributions to the Historical Society of Montana*, had been an important—albeit infrequent—publication amounting to ten volumes over a sixty-year period beginning in 1876. Published quarterly, *Montana* was designed to appeal "not only to the scholarly and academic reader, but to people everywhere who have developed a full-blown love for Western history, who like the color and drama of the subject but who like it straight, readable and without Hollywood distortion of fact."[17] By the end of the decade, MHS had also launched the Western Press of the Historical Society of Montana, which later became the Montana Historical Society Press.

In 1969, Montana's legislature designated MHS as the keeper of the official state archives, charged with caring for the permanent records of its government. The

During the second half of the twentieth century, the Society acquired a number of remarkable collections, including the Haynes Foundation Collection of materials—photographs, documents, art, and three-dimensional objects—relating to Yellowstone National Park and the Northern Pacific Railway. In this image, Black soldiers from the 25th Infantry Bicycle Corps pause for a photograph atop Yellowstone's iconic Minerva Terrace during an 1896 excursion from Fort Missoula. F. Jay Haynes, photographer. Gift of Mrs. Isabel Haynes, Haynes Foundation Photograph Collection, H-03614

resulting "vigorous raids through [other] agency offices in the 1970s" soon doubled the size of the Society's collections.[18] In 1977, the State Historic Preservation Office (SHPO) moved from its organizational home within the Montana Fish & Game Commission to the more philosophically aligned Historical Society. This development not only established another division at MHS—it also provided the Society with greater opportunities for statewide outreach. While museum and research efforts depend on gathering collections for preservation, SHPO's efforts are directed toward preserving Montana's history on-site at original locations.

Today, MHS is organized into six operational programs, two of which hold the collections that first come to mind at mention of the Historical Society. The first, the Museum, cares for and interprets approximately 60,000 objects pertaining to Montana's past, among them historical, archaeological, ethnological, and cultural artifacts as well as works of fine art. The second of these, the Research Center, is home to the Society's Library, which collects published written material such as books, periodicals, and maps, now numbering more than 50,000 items, including 95 percent of all newspapers ever published in the Treasure State; its Archives, which houses unpublished written material including diaries, manuscripts, business and governmental records, and letters, totaling more than 35,000 linear feet; and its Photograph Archives, which maintains more than 550,000 still and moving images.

The Society's four non-collecting programs help share Montana's past—and the importance of understanding that past—with the broadest possible audience. MHS's Publications program produces the prize-winning journal, *Montana The Magazine of Western History*, as well as award-winning books. The State Historic Preservation Office works with property owners, tribes, and local communities to identify, document, preserve, and celebrate Montana's historic buildings, sites, and places. The Outreach and Interpretation Program engages patrons—both young and old, and in-house visitors and distant learners alike—in studying Montana's colorful past. All the while, Centralized Services handles the necessary business and administrative functions that keep the whole institution operating smoothly.

Together, these six programs spent the year 2015 celebrating the Montana Historical Society's 150th birthday. *A History of Montana in 101 Objects* grew out of that commemoration. Helena historian Stephenie Ambrose Tubbs first suggested the idea, and so enthusiastic about the project were MHS staff that we asked if we could not only publish the book but play an active role in its creation. With her agreement, we convened a panel of authors representing the Society's various divisions to do just that.

◈ ◈ ◈

THERE are, of course, countless books devoted to Montana history. Here, however, we seek to tell the Treasure State's story from a different vantage, using artifacts to guide our journey through the past. Our approach to this work is informed by the words of the Smithsonian Institution's Richard Kurin, who observed that "a well-chosen, authentic museum object . . . not only bears witness to history, it is also part of it—it was *there*, at that time, at that place. Objects have the power to connect us in a direct, visceral, sensory manner to other times and places in ways words do not."[19] As British Museum director Neil MacGregor succinctly stated, "Telling history through things is what museums are for."[20]

With that in mind, the first step in creating this book—and the one that ultimately proved the most difficult—was narrowing down the Society's immense collections to a manageable number of representative artifacts. Of course, the decision of which artifacts best illustrate Montana's history was not ours alone. Instead, those determinations took their initial shape long before this project began, when someone decided that, for whatever reason, a prized possession should be preserved in trust for future generations. The items featured in this book represent both a gift from our forebears as well as a concrete statement about what they valued as Montanans. Yet even with the curated field we inherited, our original "short list"

One of the many early relics collected by the Society to document Montana's formative years, this "souvenir" associated with the 1864 execution of notorious sheriff and outlaw Henry Plummer provides a visceral link to the Treasure State's past.
3"× ¾". X1982.01.44

contained more than five hundred items, each passionately championed by one or more of the authors. Short of producing a multi-volume encyclopedia, featuring five hundred objects was clearly impossible; so too, however, seemed narrowing the list given the depth and breadth of the MHS's holdings. The end result, sadly, was that many important topics and prized artifacts wound up on the metaphorical cutting room floor.

Ultimately, we tried to choose those artifacts that would best reflect the many different cultures, places, and eras that make up the Montana mosaic. Other considerations shaped the final list. Each item selected for the book had to be held in the Society's collections, and that decision was made with the knowledge that this requirement would prevent the coverage of some important topics. In addition, artifacts to be included also had to be photographable. For example, we reluctantly omitted items, such as a fragile Nez Perce–style dugout canoe as well as a bow made of bighorn sheep horn and covered in snakeskin, because photographs could not adequately convey their beauty, complexity, or significance.

Despite the difficulties of this process, eventually a list of 101 items emerged. Some choices, like the Kessler Banner, were obvious due to their singular place in Montana history. Others, including the USS *Montana* silver service, were chosen for their exceptional beauty and remarkable craftsmanship. Several artifacts—including Father Ravalli's carved skull and crossbones—made the cut due to their uniqueness, while certain items—like Amanda Perälä Kraftenberg's loom—were chosen to represent the warp and weft of daily life. Among the selections, too, were items that illustrate aspects of our shared heritage, like the arrival of mail service or the construction of drivable roads, that we now take for granted, but which represented monumental transformations in the lives of Montanans past.

The book's objects have been grouped into eleven thematic chapters, yet another struggle given that many fit equally well in multiple categories. Nevertheless, we committed to this approach rather than a chronological organization because we wanted to reinforce the idea that although specific details vary, many of the larger themes of life in Montana remain consistent over time. These objects reveal far more commonalities between us and our ancestors—and between one another—than we might at first suppose.

We hope that *A History of Montana in 101 Objects* provides a valuable contribution to the study of Montana history and that it illustrates the importance of material culture to understanding our past. It is also intended to be a celebration of the Montana Historical Society's role in preserving our shared heritage. Of course, we also hope you enjoy this book. And if you do, come see these treasures (and so many more) in person. Even in today's age of virtual reality, there remains no substitute for the real thing.

—Kirby Lambert

Notes

1. "Introduction," *Contributions to the Historical Society of Montana; with Its Transactions, Act of Incorporation, Constitution, Ordinances, Officers and Members* vol. 1 (Helena: Rocky Mountain Publishing Company, 1876), 11.
2. For more complete histories of the Montana Historical Society, see Robert Morse Clark, "The Montana Historical Society," in *Encyclopedia of Library and Information Science* (New York: Markel Dekker, Inc., 1985), 281–91; and Brian Shovers, "Saving Montana's Past: The Creation and Evolution of the Montana Historical Society and *Montana The Magazine of Western History*," *Montana The Magazine of Western History* 52:1 (Spring 2002), 48–59.
3. Vivian Paladin, "Historical Society Reaches Maturity," *The People's Voice* 21:35 (Aug. 5, 1960), 1.
4. "State of Montana Needs Historical Building," *Big Sandy Mountaineer*, Aug. 25, 1927, 3.
5. Membership was originally restricted to twenty-six. The original twelve men named in the founding legislation elected their fellow active members through unanimous ballot. In 1873, the Society expanded to include non-voting "honorary" members, who had to be Montanans, and "corresponding" members, who did not. Charlotte O. Van Cleve, a Minnesota historian and sister of founder Malcolm Clark, fell into this second category and was the only woman whose membership is documented during this early period.
6. *Montana Post*, Apr. 1, 1865, 2.
7. Clark, 282.
8. Ibid.
9. Helena Board of Trade, *Report for 1887* (1887), 24, 32.
10. "The State Library," *Progressive Men of the State of Montana* (Chicago: A.W. Bowen and Co., 1982), 1613.
11. Clark, 283.
12. Shovers, 51.
13. Ibid., 52. In 1963, the organization's name was once again changed, this time to the Montana Historical Society.
14. Clark, 285.
15. Under Toole's tutelage, MHS transitioned to the "museum model," a phenomenon that occurred in historical societies nationwide during the late 1950s and early 1960s. Shovers, 53.
16. K. Ross Toole to Helena Dawson Edkins, Oct. 14, 1952, Toole File, MHS Director's File.
17. Paladin, 4.
18. Clark, 286.
19. Richard Kurin, *The Smithsonian's History of America in 101 Objects* (New York: Penguin, 2013), 4–5.
20. Neil MacGregor, *A History of the World in 100 Objects* (London: Viking, 2010), xiii.

Before Montana

◈

Artifacts—from stone tools to a letter from an early fur trade post—speak to the twelve-thousand-year-plus history of "Montana" before Montana. Likewise, countless stories, rituals, and customs passed down through generations bear witness to this rich, complex, and vital past.

For millennia, the ancestors of today's Plains and Plateau tribes endured the oftentimes harsh elements to develop diverse cultures that thrived in the place we now know as Montana. While archaeological evidence indicates that humans have occupied this area for at least fourteen thousand years, each tribe has an origin story that situates it here from the beginning of time or a migration tale explaining a later entrance into the region. These oral traditions, passed down from generation to generation, offer glimpses into the human experience in Montana that predate any written records.

First Peoples adapted their lifeways over eons as Montana's environment evolved in response to a changing climate. Initially, they subsisted on now-extinct large game like mammoths, mastodons, and ancient bison. As these species disappeared, Indigenous peoples shifted their focus to hunting smaller animals, and plants became a more important food source. Tools, crafted from stone and bone, reflected these adaptations.

Approximately fifteen hundred years ago, cooler and slightly wetter conditions led to a significant increase in the number of bison on the northern Plains. This population surge, coupled with the invention of the bow and arrow, ushered in an era that saw buffalo, always important, become even more critical for Native peoples as a primary source of both food and the raw materials needed to craft tools, clothing, and other provisions. To harvest bison, tribal communities crafted tools like bows and arrows and utilized natural features on the landscape as *pishkuns* (buffalo jumps), where hunters hazed the shaggy beasts over cliffs. Some

Buffalo jump diorama, 48" x 72"; figures, 1955, by Gardell Dano Christensen (1907–1991), backdrop, 1988, by Dale Livezey (b. 1957). 1988.118.01

individuals worked on top of the jumps, driving the animals forward, while others below processed the kill. The introduction of guns and horses into the region during the 1700s dramatically altered these centuries-old lifeways.

At the turn of the nineteenth century, Euro-Americans began to venture into the region in ever-increasing numbers. Among the earliest were explorers like Thomas Jefferson's Corps of Discovery, who came in search of the fabled Northwest Passage, a water route by which it was hoped the fledgling United States could access the Pacific Ocean and the markets of Asia. Trappers—both free agents and representatives of fur companies—followed, seeking wealth in the form of beaver furs to meet the market demands of European fashion. Across North America, Indigenous men and women played key roles in the fur trade, which served as a catalyst for cultural exchange and intermarriage with non-Indians. The case was no different in Montana, especially after British and American fur companies established trading posts at strategically located points along major waterways.

By the 1840s, changing styles and the decline of the beaver population led to the emergence of bison robes as the new focus of the fur and hide industry. Over the next forty years, the large-scale commercial slaughter of these iconic animals

Indigenous peoples used carved steatite bowls like this one for cooking because they could be placed directly into hot coals. This particular style of bowl was used by the Shoshone in the higher elevations of today's Greater Yellowstone Ecosystem, where quarries provided the needed raw material for their manufacture.
5⅜" × 7½" × 6½". Gift of A. W. T. Anderson, x1964.29.01

brought them to the brink of extinction, coinciding with federal policy and military action intended to deny Plains tribes their primary source of subsistence and to wrest control of tribal lands. These developments had a devastating impact on the traditional lifeways of First Peoples.

Beavers mark their territory with a mixture of urine and castoreum, which they secrete from a pair of castor sacs located near the base of their tails. Early trappers used castoreum—which they carried in "scent pouches" like this one made of leather stitched with string, with a bone stopper, ca. 1885—to bait their traps. 2½" × 5". Gift of W. A. Clark, x1892.01.05

1. Ellison's Rock Petroglyph

no date, 31" × 13" × 31¼". Gift of Western Energy Company, 1988.14.01

◈

Petroglyphs (rock carvings) and pictographs (paintings) left on the landscape by Native peoples are among the most tangible and revealing links to understanding life on the northern Plains before Europeans arrived in North America. While these forms of rock art document dramatic historical developments, from technological advances like the invention of the bow and arrow to cultural transformations like those resulting from the acquisition of horses, they also reflect the most important milestones in the lives of their makers, such as a spiritual vision or ritual, a planned hunt, readiness for war, or a battle won. More than any projectile point or animal bone, prehistoric rock art can offer insight into the thoughts and value systems of its makers.

This petroglyph panel depicting a shield-bearing warrior came from Ellison's Rock, a sandstone outcropping near Colstrip. Before mining the area for coal in 1987, the Western Energy Company completely removed Ellison's Rock by dividing it into six different pieces. Panel Three was donated to the Montana Historical Society.

Archaeologists have classified Panel Three as Timber Creek–style, a style found at nineteen sites spread across southeastern Montana and northwestern South Dakota. The artist may have been of Crow/Hidatsa origin, and the petroglyph is between 350 and 2,000 years old. The large size of the shield depicted and the lack of horses or guns suggest pedestrian warfare. As horses became more readily available on the Great Plains after 1700, shield sizes shrank to accommodate riding. One interpretation by archaeologist and veteran rock art specialist James D. Keyser suggests that Panel Three's large central warrior was rendered first and the smaller human figures on the right and left came later, perhaps as part of a ritual passing on of the shield design.

The petroglyph's literal meaning may never be known, but comparative analysis of hundreds of shield-bearing warrior sites over the last fifty years provides clues to understanding shield symbolism and the significance of war deeds in establishing a warrior's status. Though northern Plains men gained respect for their hunting skills and generosity, war honors or "coups" determined membership in military associations, a man's position in society, and even his wealth and prestige. Deeds were ranked by relative difficulty or danger, and successful coups were recounted at dances and ceremonies, drawn on tools, garments, and tipi liners, and painted or carved on rock. Through these forms of memorialization, the record of a man's war honors served as his currency, following him throughout his life and affording him everything from material goods and marriage to leadership in times of war. *–CB*

2. Hagen Site Artifacts

ca. 1450–1525, below: bone awl, 3¾" × ¾"; opposite: (top) bone awl, 3½" × ¼"; (center) pottery fragment, 2⅓" × 1½"; (bottom left) chert projectile point, 2¾" × 1"; (bottom right) chert drill, 1⅓" × ½".

Gift of the Central Montana Historical Society, 1987.57

◈

In 1937, local archaeologist Oscar Lewis noticed scattered bones, ceramics, and stone flakes on a piece of land in Dawson County owned by Thomas Hagen, the mayor of Glendive. Lewis reported his findings to the Montana Archaeological Survey, and excavation began in 1938 under the direction of Lewis and William Mulloy and funded by the Works Progress Administration. Today, the Hagen Site, which dates to approximately five to six hundred years ago, is one of Montana's most important historic places and a designated National Historic Landmark.

Most archaeologists believe the site is associated with the early Crows, who broke from the more agrarian Hidatsas to eventually become bison hunters. While Montana's Native peoples generally did not occupy established villages or engage in agriculture, the Hagen Site contains permanent structures, forty-one bison-bone hoes and picks, and several squash or pumpkin seeds. The hoes, picks, and seeds suggest that the people were familiar with agriculture, but the remains of 341 bison suggest this was also a hunting-oriented site.

One of only two permanent village sites excavated in Montana, the Hagen Site features an earthen lodge, twenty cache or storage pits, and a circular platform mound. The earthen lodge, similar to lodges of the Hidatsas, had twelve support post holes and a hard-packed floor, indicative of its long use. The raised platform, forty-five feet in diameter, proved to be a ceremonial mound containing the skeletal remains—mostly mandibles and teeth—of forty individuals. Some mandibles appeared to have been deliberately broken with stone implements. Mulloy speculated that the platform corresponded with the Mandan tradition of placing skulls in a mortuary circle.

Most archaeologists agree that Hagen inhabitants were forerunners of the Apsáalooke (Crow) Tribe. The Hagen Site tells an important story of a people in transition. The artifacts pictured here include a sampling of the thousands of pottery sherds, bone implements, and stone tools scattered throughout the site.

Among a wide range of pottery styles discovered, cord-wrapped designs predominate. Such designs are rare in the Missouri River valley, and their presence here reaffirms Crow oral tradition, which traces the tribe's roots to a land of many lakes—likely the Great Lakes region—before other tribes pressured them into westward migration. Viewed in the context of Montana's Indigenous history, the Hagen Site may be a crucial tool in understanding a people's transition from woodland roots to bison culture. *–EB*

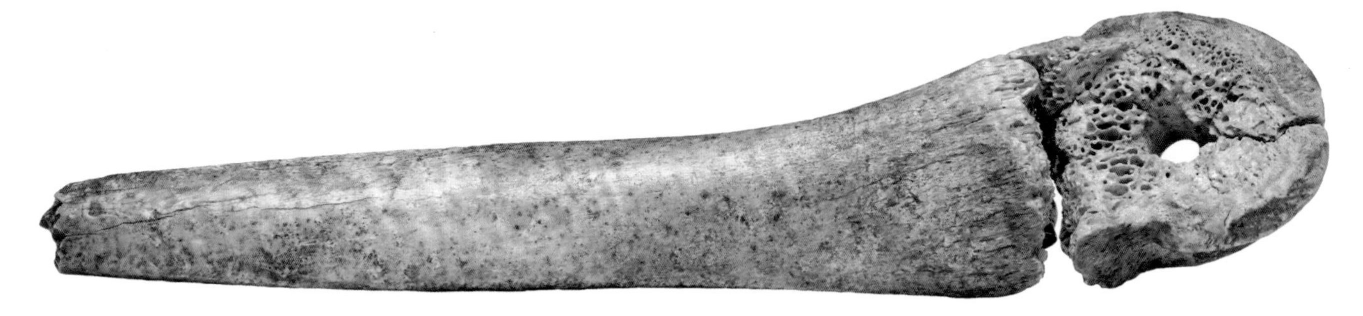

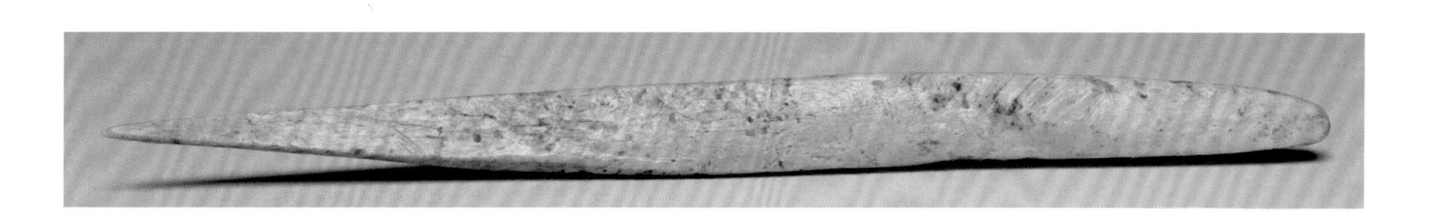

3. Amskapi Piikuni Elk Tooth Dress

ca. 1830–1860. Gift of William A. Clark, x1892.01.25

◈

According to an 1897 article in the *Helena Daily Independent*, this elk tooth dress dates to before 1860 and was originally owned by Marguerite Black Weasel (Maggie Wetzel), a Blackfeet survivor of the 1870 Baker Massacre and the wife of trader Joe Kipp. It came into the possession of Indian agent Major Rufus A. Allen during his survey of the Blackfeet Indian Reservation in the 1880s and was later held in trust by the Montana Historical Society until it could be acquired outright.

Conservators have estimated that the fifty-four-inch-long dress could date to as early as 1830. It consists of two expertly tanned hides, possibly from mountain sheep, sewn together with sinew. It was originally decorated with 192 elk "ivories" (eye teeth), some of which are now missing. Dresses of this length and style were common among several tribes of the Rocky Mountain and northern Plains region until the mid-1800s, and the eye teeth, which come from both bull and cow elk, would have been collected over many years' time. A single dress ornamented with fifty to three hundred elk cuspids would have been worth at least two good horses, suggesting that the use of elk teeth conferred social and economic status on the wearer. Men occasionally used elk teeth to decorate pipe bags or other ceremonial items, but they were typically used as clothing adornments on the dresses of women or girls. The first use of elk teeth as ornamentation was likely among the Mandans of the lower Missouri River region in the fourteenth century; from there, the practice seems to have spread to the Hidatsas, Cheyennes, Crows, Arapahos, Dakotas, Assiniboines, and Blackfeet by 1800.

In the second half of the nineteenth century, wool trade cloth became readily accessible to northern Plains tribes and began to replace elk, sheep, and deer skins as clothing material. Soon thereafter, the establishment of Indian reservations and the demise of large game animal populations by settlers made it difficult to obtain a large quantity of elk teeth. Today, both real and imitation elk eye teeth (usually carved from bone) are still used to decorate women's dresses and are often worn as part of traditional tribal regalia by Montana's Native peoples.

Major Allen's collection, which consisted of dozens of Blackfeet items, was described in the 1890s as "probably the most complete and interesting collection that has ever been gathered to illustrate the dress, ornaments, implements, and weapons of any single tribe of Indians within this state." As such it provides a valuable representation of the craftsmanship and material culture of the Blackfeet and their relatives. In promoting the collection to the public, the *Helena Daily Independent* declared, "It is desirable that . . . this collection, which is so closely identified with the beginnings of Montana history, be kept within the state for the present and future benefit of the people." When the Society's appeal to the legislature to acquire the Blackfeet items fell on deaf ears, Copper King William A. Clark purchased Allen's collection in its entirety and donated it to the Montana Historical Society. *–LF*

4. Assiniboine or Sioux Painted Buffalo Robe

ca. 1840–1850, 82" × 88". Originally loaned by George R. and Dorothy (Cosier) Milburn in 1967.
Donated by Janet (Milburn) Doughterty, Howard M. Cosier Collection, 2017.65.01

◈

Fort Peck trader Howard M. Cosier acquired this rare and magnificent robe in the 1880s. Robes showing images of personal exploits were generally created by men, whereas robes with geometric patterns—like the feathered circular patterns or multitiered warbonnet motifs seen here—were painted by women.

In this portrait, Pehriska-Ruhpa (Two Ravens) wears a painted buffalo robe similar to the one in MHS's collection. German artist Karl Bodmer sketched the Hidatsa chief at Fort Clark (now in North Dakota) in 1834. This aquatint, with engravings, was produced from Bodmer's original.
14½" × 20". X1970.27.11

This robe contains four concentric feather patterns decorated in blue, red, and brown pigment with white accents. Its corners are embellished with light orange details, and each feather is adorned with a red line that flares at the tip. Likely made between 1840 and 1850, robes of this kind were worn by men of several tribes of the upper Missouri—the Mandan, Hidatsa, Sioux, and Assiniboine.

Hides such as this were harvested in the winter when the buffalo's hair was the thickest. The hide was scraped of all flesh, tanned using the brains of the buffalo, then stretched and rubbed until soft and supple. The finished product was pliable yet extremely strong. The edges of this robe display the holes made when it was stretched and staked to the ground. The ears and the tail of the animal remain, and the rest of the head has been carefully stitched flat.

To create the decorations, the artist first pressed the design into the newly tanned robe, then applied colors made from berries, earthen pigments, and other materials. Some of the remaining spaces were covered with a "sizing glue" made from boiled hide scrapings, which allowed the hide to resist natural discoloration and wear.

While it is not possible to know how long the feathered-circle pattern has been in use, historian John Ewers writes in *Plains Indian Painting* (1939) that the design's popularity suggests it was "known to the Upper Missouri River tribes for many years." Of equal importance to us now, the care and craftsmanship with which this spectacular robe was created have proven crucial to its preservation. Today, its colors remain vibrant and fresh, and it is as soft and warm as it was the day it was made. *–JBO*

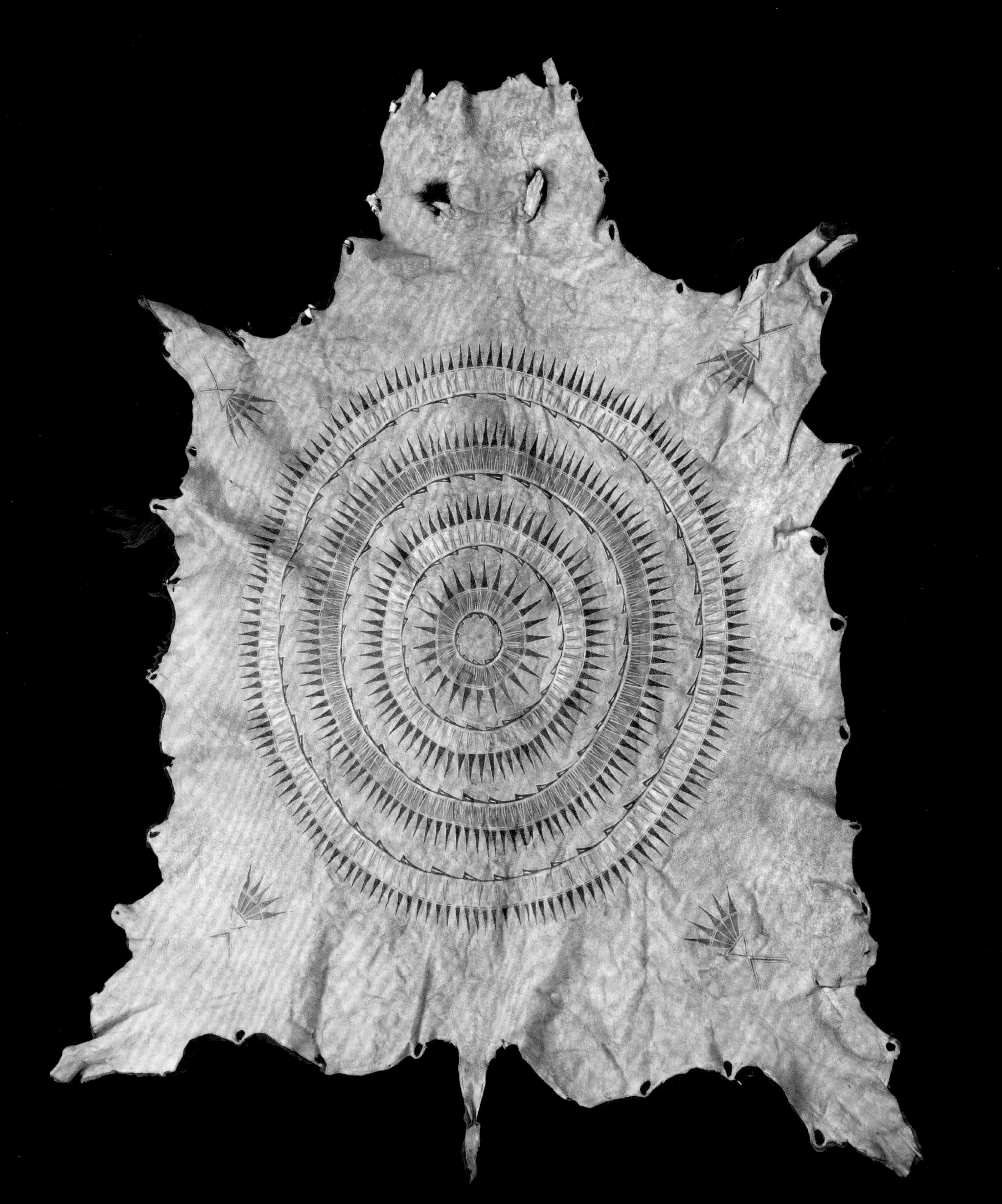

5. *Indian Hunters' Return*

1900, 35½" × 23¾", by Charles M. Russell (1864–1926).

Mackay Collection, x1954.02.01

STAYING warm in a region where temperatures regularly fall below zero for extended periods required great adaptability and resourcefulness. Charlie Russell's oil painting, *Indian Hunters' Return*, depicts a group of Blood Indians returning to camp after a successful winter hunt. Russell's deft imagery—the hazy campfire smoke in the air, the steaming breath of man and beast, and the pallid glow of the dying sun—conveys the bitter cold of a winter camp during the Plains Indians' halcyon "buffalo days."

Although each of Montana's Plains tribes had distinct cultural identities, they also shared commonalities, such as a dependence on bison as a primary food source, the use of portable tipis made of hides, and the movement of camps according to the seasonal availability of resources. This practice of patterning life according to seasonal rounds (moving from place to place to hunt migrating bison or to harvest ripening roots or berries) required an intimate knowledge of the landscape and its resources. Long before Plains tribes integrated horses into their economies in the 1700s, dogs pulling travois were the primary beasts of burden.

In early autumn, men gathered in a communal buffalo hunt to procure enough meat to feed their families through the cold months ahead. Women dried the meat, then mixed it with berries and fat to make pemmican—a dense, high-protein food that could be easily stored throughout the winter. In late fall, when the days grew shorter and the weather turned colder, extended families settled into winter camps situated along rivers and streams where grass and timber were plentiful and, ideally, ridges or bluffs helped provide shelter against frigid winds.

In addition to serving as a break against the wind and snow, the trees surrounding winter camps provided a source of fuel for the fires that Plains peoples used to heat their lodges and cook their food. Liners made of tanned bison hide were secured to the inside of the tipi poles, producing a second wall that offered insulation and helped draw smoke up through the hole at the top of the tipi. Additional buffalo hides, with the hair left intact and worn or used as a cover, served as the final barrier against low temperatures.

Although Russell arrived in Montana Territory too late to have witnessed such a scene in person, the St. Louis-born artist devoted his career to portraying an earlier time, or, as he termed it, "the West that Has Passed." Although he often romanticized his subjects, Russell was also a serious student of history, and *Indian Hunters' Return* has been lauded by ethnologists for the accuracy with which it portrays an important event from a bygone era. *–KL*

Indians, Dogs, Dogsled is another artwork in which Russell pays tribute to the traditional lifeways of Indigenous Americans living in northern climes. ca. 1920, 6" × 3¼". Gift of Antoinette Schillo Wilbur, x1969.02.01

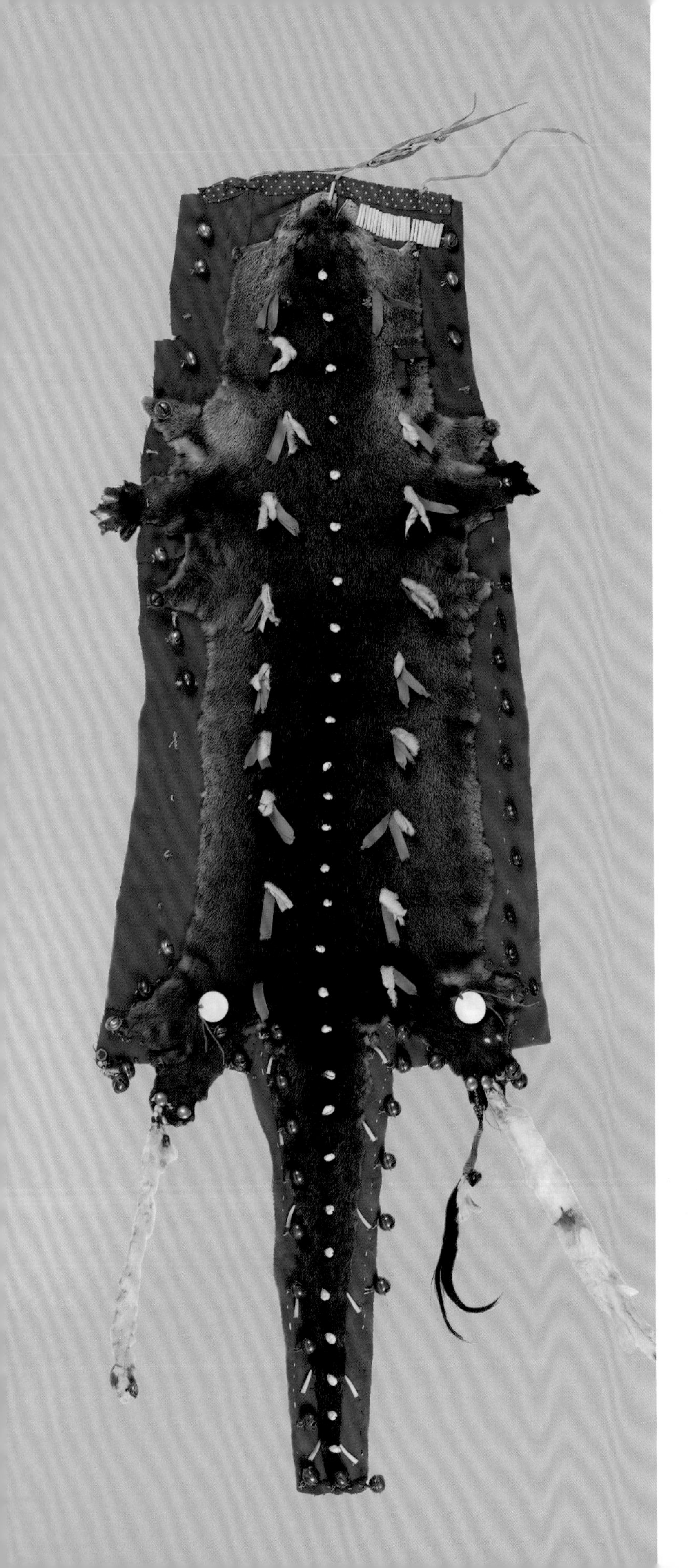

6. Qĺispé Otter Skin Horse Ornament

ca. 1888, 20" × 52", by Elizabeth Ashley (1876–1960).

Gift of Wiley Glenn Mountjoy and Opal Matlock Mountjoy, x1975.18.06

◈

One of a matched pair, this otter-pelt horse ornament was made by Elizabeth Ashley around 1888. She was a descendent of English and French fur traders and a member of the Upper Pend d'Oreille (Qĺispé) Tribe of the Flathead Reservation. Intermarriage between European fur traders and the Indigenous inhabitants of the Northwest was common long before widespread settlement of the region by non-Indians, and over the course of the 1800s, the Ashley family married into the Salish, Pend d'Oreille, Kootenai, and Spokane Tribes.

The otter pelt is sewn to a backing of red wool trade cloth and adorned with brass bells, cowry shells, and bits of pink and white ribbon. Two weasel skins hang from the otter's back feet, and a scalp lock is attached near one of them. The otter pelt would have been displayed just behind the saddle and its mate similarly displayed on the other side of the horse. In a tradition still practiced today, tribal members outfitted their horses with elaborate ornamentation for special occasions, such as parades, celebrations, and powwows. These adornments conferred honor on the rider and acknowledged the essential role of horses in Indigenous cultures.

The Pend d'Oreille, inland Salish, and Kootenai Tribes acquired horses in the mid-1700s from the Nez Perces and Shoshones, who had by then become successful horse breeders. In time, horses replaced dogs as beasts of burden, enabling people to travel farther and faster. By the late 1700s, Plateau and Plains tribes had become master equestrians, training horses for warfare, bison hunting, sport, and travel.

Elaborately beaded horse tack—like that displayed by Josephine Camille and her daughter Lucy Pierre on the Flathead Reservation ca. 1906—illustrates the importance of horses in both the practical and cultural lives of Montana's Indigenous peoples.
Morton J. Elrod, photographer. PAC 954-554

Horses were prized by all tribes, and by the 1800s were essential to their well-being and survival. They made it possible for tribes west of the Rocky Mountains to hunt bison on the plains twice a year, bringing them into contact with new trading partners like the Crows, as well as their adversaries, the Blackfeet. While horses increased tribal mobility and military prowess, they also became objects of raids between tribal groups, as young warriors earned honors by stealing these valuable animals.

The establishment of the reservation system severely curtailed intertribal trade, buffalo hunts, and wide-ranging travel, but horses retained their importance among all of Montana's tribal nations. Some, like the Crows and Cheyennes, became successful horse breeders, only to see their extensive herds culled mercilessly by the federal government in the 1920s. Despite such setbacks, tribes have maintained their esteem for horses and horsemanship.

Today, as in the past, horses are presented at giveaways for special occasions, such as naming ceremonies and weddings. At cultural events like the Arlee Powwow and the Crow Fair, they are paraded in full regalia—from beaded bridles and colorful headstalls to elaborately decorated saddles, saddle blankets, martingales, and other ornamentation—demonstrating the horse's enduring significance to Montana's Native peoples. *–LF*

7. Patrick Gass's Journal

1807, 4¼" × 6⅝". Locker 917.804 G21J 1807

◈

The first non-Indians to venture into what is now Montana were European and Euro-American explorers. Of these, the best-known today are Meriwether Lewis and William Clark—but they were not the first. The Lewis and Clark Expedition's legacy is due in large part to the fact that its members kept extensive journals that captured public imagination and informed future travels west. Lewis and Clark published their own journals, of course, and others followed, but the first member to publish his account

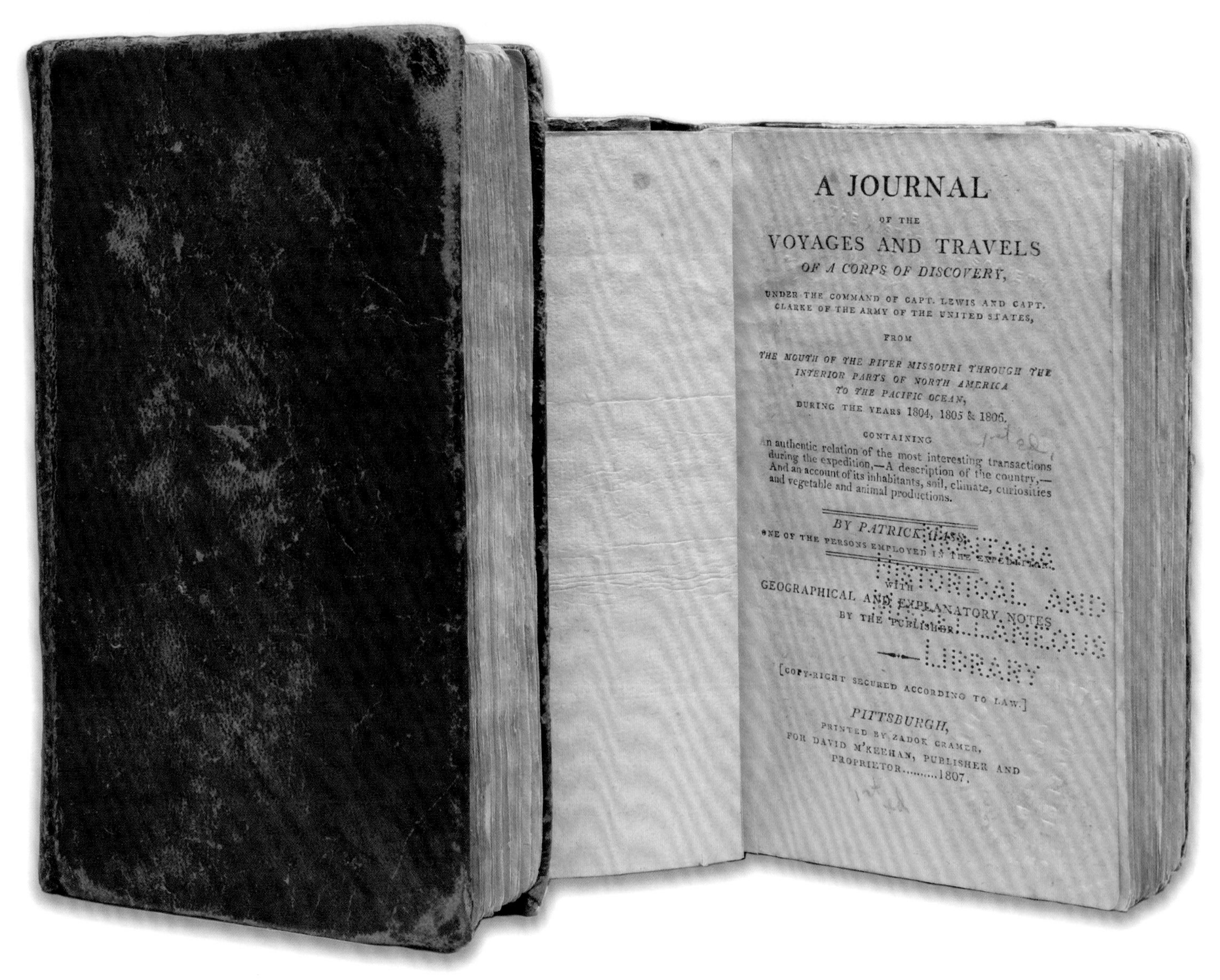
A JOURNAL
OF THE
VOYAGES AND TRAVELS
OF A CORPS OF DISCOVERY,
UNDER THE COMMAND OF CAPT. LEWIS AND CAPT.
CLARKE OF THE ARMY OF THE UNITED STATES,
FROM
THE MOUTH OF THE RIVER MISSOURI THROUGH THE
INTERIOR PARTS OF NORTH AMERICA
TO THE PACIFIC OCEAN,
DURING THE YEARS 1804, 1805 & 1806.
CONTAINING
An authentic relation of the most interesting transactions during the expedition,—A description of the country,—And an account of its inhabitants, soil, climate, curiosities and vegetable and animal productions.

BY PATRICK GASS,
ONE OF THE PERSONS EMPLOYED IN THE EXPEDITION.
WITH
GEOGRAPHICAL AND EXPLANATORY NOTES
BY THE PUBLISHER.

[COPY-RIGHT SECURED ACCORDING TO LAW.]

PITTSBURGH,
PRINTED BY ZADOK CRAMER,
FOR DAVID M'KEEHAN, PUBLISHER AND
PROPRIETOR..........1807.

upon the crew's return in late September 1806 was Patrick Gass (1771–1870).

Gass, a Corps of Discovery sergeant and carpenter, was of Scottish heritage and a Pennsylvanian by birth. He was recruited for the expedition by Lewis in 1804 from Captain Russell Bissell's command at Fort Kaskaskia, Illinois. Gass's journal, published in 1807 by Zadok Cramer of Pittsburgh, is a small volume with an unwieldy title: *A Journal of the Voyages and Travels of a Corps of Discovery, Under the Command of Capt. Lewis and Capt. Clarke of the Army of the United States from the Mouth of the River Missouri Through the Interior Parts of North America to the Pacific Ocean During the Years 1804, 1805 & 1806 by Patrick Gass One of the Persons Employed in the Expedition.*

Although Lewis granted permission to Private Robert Frazier to publish his personal journal, it seems to have come as a shock to him when Gass, with the help of David McKeehan, a neighboring printer, issued a prospectus for his book at a time when Lewis's own journals languished in his traveling trunks. A heated exchange of letters posted in the local papers indicated Lewis's dim view of Gass's forthcoming publication, alluding to "several unauthorized and probably some spurious publications now preparing for the press on the subject of my late tour to the Pacific Ocean by individuals entirely unknown to me." Lewis warned readers not to be taken in by this proposed version, claiming it would "depreciate" the worth of his own proposed three-volume account.

While McKeehan did take some editorial liberties with Gass's original account, the voice of the expedition's carpenter echoes throughout his journal. Gass makes keen observations on subjects others overlooked. As Carol Lynn MacGregor writes in her introduction to the 1997 reprint, "[R]eaders can see the beauty Gass saw in trees, rivers, plains and mountains, and his fascination with new sorts of people and animals, as the unknown unfolded each day for a working member of the Corps."

Gass was the third-oldest member of Lewis and Clark's corps. He lived longer than any other member of the expedition and was one of only two to be photographed. In his post-expeditionary life, Gass fought in the War of 1812 and later served in Washington, D.C., as a delegate on behalf of veteran pensioners. Although his original journal has been lost, the Montana Historical Society is fortunate to have a copy of the first edition, which reads on the inside cover: "Bought in Wheeling 10th Oct. 1807, R. Graham." The publication remains invaluable to Montana's history as one of the first written accounts of the northern Plains and the upper reaches of the Missouri River.

–SAT

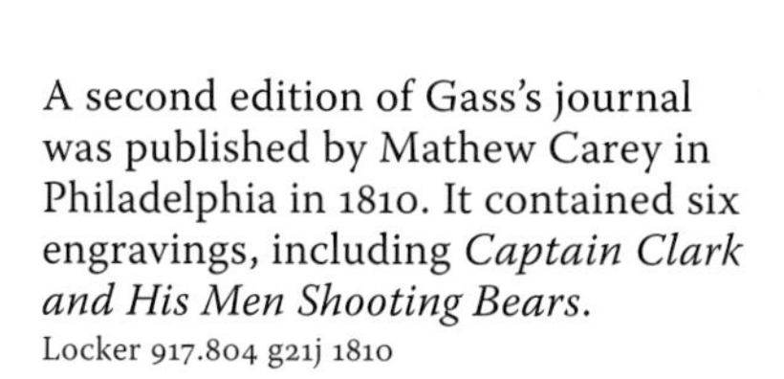

A second edition of Gass's journal was published by Mathew Carey in Philadelphia in 1810. It contained six engravings, including *Captain Clark and His Men Shooting Bears.*
Locker 917.804 g21j 1810

8. Pierre Menard Letter

1810, 8" × 10". Gift of Hiram Chittenden, Pierre Chouteau Jr. and Company Records, MC 4

◈

THIS four-page letter from Pierre Menard (1766–1844) to his brother-in-law, Pierre Chouteau Jr., is the earliest unpublished document in the Montana Historical Society's collection. Writing just four years after the Lewis and Clark Expedition returned east in 1806, Menard describes the difficulties of travel, hostilities with the Blackfeet, and competition with rival trading operations on the upper Missouri, offering a captivating glimpse into post-expedition Montana.

As a founding partner of the St. Louis Missouri Fur Company, Pierre Menard was among those seeking fortune on the upper Missouri after members of Lewis and Clark's Corps of Discovery returned with tales of a region filled with beaver and other fur-bearing animals, ready for the taking. Entrepreneurs in St. Louis embraced the prospect, but to achieve their goal they would have to contend with aggressive competitors working their way south from Canada, such as the Hudson's Bay Company and North West Company, as well as tribal nations intent on protecting their land and economy.

In the spring of 1810, guided by veteran frontiersman John Colter, Menard and company partners Andrew Henry and Reuben Lewis set out for the headwaters of the Missouri with a group of trappers. Upon arrival at the confluence of the Madison, Jefferson, and Gallatin Rivers, the men began construction of a fur trading post and sent out trapping parties. The operation struggled, however, and conflict with the Blackfeet resulted in the death of several trappers. Ultimately, the post was abandoned in June of 1810, and Menard returned to the Midwest. Although French-Canadian by birth, he later played an active role in Illinois politics.

The historical significance of Menard's letter is rivaled only by the fascinating story of its journey from the hands of Pierre Chouteau Jr. to the archives of the Montana Historical Society. While author Hiram M. Chittenden was researching his seminal work, *History of the American Fur Trade of the Far West* (1902), he presented a copy of his manuscript to Chouteau, who in turn made a gift to Chittenden of "an old missive made famous in the fur trade." Chittenden then donated the letter, written in French, and an English translation to the Montana Historical Society, ninety-two years after Menard penned the document. Menard's treasured dispatch, now held in the Society's Pierre Chouteau Jr. and Company records, illustrates the fierce competition for natural resources and commerce that came in the wake of Lewis and Clark's famed journey. –*RA*

Old Fort Benton—a mural in the Montana State Capitol painted by F. Pedretti's Sons in 1902—depicts two prominent leaders of the Montana fur trade, American Fur Company entrepreneurs Andrew Dawson (standing) and Pierre Chouteau Jr. (seated). Oil on canvas, 102" × 168". X1902.04.10

trois fourche du Mi sourie 25 avrill 1810

Monsieur
Pierre Chouteau Esqr

Monsieur et beau frere

Je matandoit Pouvoire vous Ecrire Plus favorable
que Jene suis amemme de le faire a present
Les prospect de vent Nos yeux il ha dix Jourre etoit
Baucoup Plus flateure quil le sont aujourdheui
un party de nos Chasseurre on Etez de fait Par les
pied Noire le 12 du present il ha heuf deux homme
de tuez tous leure Castore pilliez et Baucoup de piege
de perdez et Lamonition de plusieur de nos Chasseure
et 7 de nos Chevaux Nous avont Etez a leure poursuite
mait Malleureusemant Nous navont pas pus les rejoindre
Nous avon ramasse 44 piege et 3 Chevaux que nous avont
Ramené icij et Nous Esperont trouver Encore quelque
piege Set Maleureusse a faire a toute effet Decourage
Nos Chasseure il neveulle plus allee a la Chasse icij
il En partera se pendent de moins 30 qui sont tous de
gens a gage les 14 Lous et 16 Fransais il vont
a l'androit ou les autres on Etez de fait Jene leure donne

9. Jim Bridger's Hawken Rifle, Binoculars, and Case

ca. 1850, rifle 50" × 1½", binoculars 6½" × 5¼" × 2". Rifle gift of J. I. Allen, x1910.02.01; Binoculars and Case gift of Frank LaCox, x1968.28.01

As Americans moved westward during the first half of the nineteenth century, the St. Louis gunsmiths that armed them began to alter their rifles to better meet the demands of the new country. Based on the suggestions of returning explorers, guides, fur trappers, and traders, the gunsmiths shortened rifle barrels and made them heavier, strengthened the rifle locks, and increased bore diameters from about .40 caliber (as was common for the older-style Kentucky rifles) up to .53 caliber or even larger. Firearm technology changed in other ways during this period, and in the 1830s the percussion ignition lock almost completely replaced the flintlock. By the time emigration to California and Oregon peaked in the 1850s, so-called plains or mountain rifles had fully evolved into their characteristic form.

Brothers Jacob and Samuel Hawken were prominent developers and manufacturers of this new style of rifle, and the two worked as partners from 1825 until Jacob's death from cholera in 1849. The Hawken brothers stamped their rifle barrels "J & S HAWKEN," and after Jacob's death, Samuel Hawken continued the business in St. Louis, stamping his rifle barrels simply "S HAWKEN." According to Charles E. Hanson Jr., "uniform quality, accuracy and dependability made Hawken rifles the universal standard on the frontier." Explorers, emigrants, guides, and others who spent time on the western frontier prized these firearms. Among those admirers was Jim Bridger (1804–1881), the famed mountain man, guide, and scout.

Bridger was born in Richmond, Virginia, and came west from St. Louis in 1822 with the initial expedition of the Rocky Mountain Fur Company under W. H. Ashley. In 1830, he became a full partner in the company. In 1842, the beaver trade was failing, so Bridger started a trading post in partnership with Louis Vasquez on the Black Fork of the Green River in what is now southwest Wyoming. Westering pioneers valued Bridger's detailed familiarity with the country from the Missouri River to the Pacific and from New Mexico to Canada. In the mid-1860s, Bridger forged the Bridger Trail north from the Oregon Trail through Bighorn Basin to the goldfields of present-day southwestern Montana. Around the same time, Bridger also guided troops for the U.S. Army during its campaigns against the Native peoples of the central and northern Plains.

The exact date and circumstances under which Bridger obtained this rifle are unknown. We do know, however, that in 1866 he sold it to Pierre Chien (1829–1877) for sixty-five dollars at Fort C. F. Smith in southern Montana Territory. Chien, who was an interpreter for the Crow Tribe for thirty years, kept Bridger's Hawken until just before his death, when he gave it to frontier guide and scout J. I. Allen (1839–1929), who, in turn, donated it to the Society in 1910.

–VR

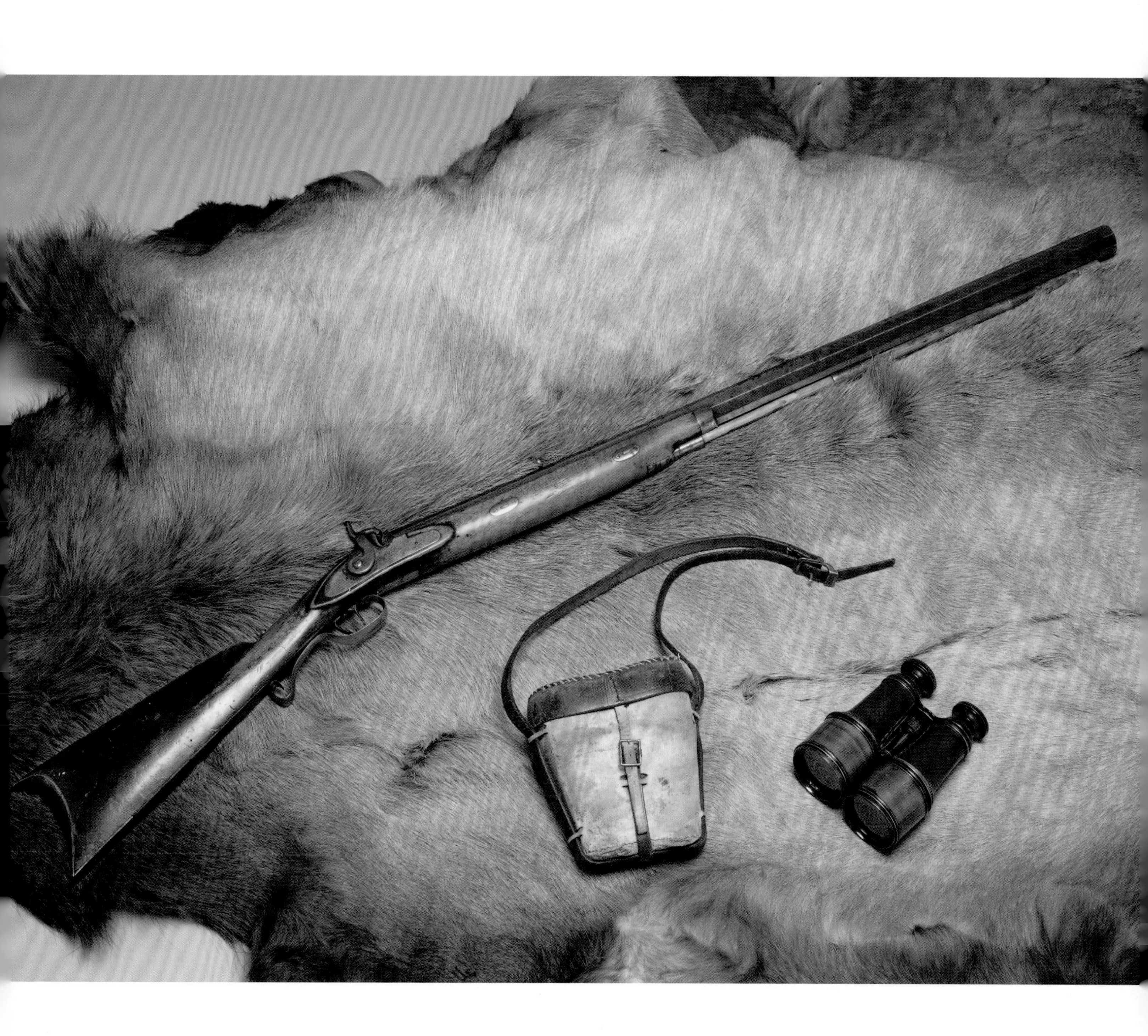

Bremen - Helena City
Montana =
Territory
U. S. Amerika.

Coming to Montana

◈

The explorers and trappers who ventured into this region in the early 1800s were soon followed by immigrants of a more permanent nature. The first Jesuit missionaries arrived in the Bitterroot Valley in 1841 at the request of the Salish, who had traveled to St. Louis to invite them back to their homeland. Thereafter, other missionaries—both Catholic and Protestant—followed, hoping to instill the Christian faith and an agricultural lifeway among the region's Indigenous peoples.

Major gold and silver strikes in the 1860s and 1870s brought fortune-seekers to the region in numbers far greater than ever before. Booming camps, populated mostly by young men from around the globe, sprang up seemingly overnight in places like Bannack, Virginia City, and Last Chance Gulch. Merchants, saloon-keepers, barbers, blacksmiths, and purveyors of entertainment joined the rush to "mine the miners," providing all manner of goods and services to these growing hubs of population. While the camps themselves did not always last, they helped catalyze great changes in the region that would unfold over the second half of the nineteenth century.

Among those developments were the creation of Montana Territory in 1864 and the formation of a new territorial government. While some sought to establish order on the frontier, others were equally devoted to lawlessness and illicit gain. When these two groups collided, vigilantes took matters into their own hands and delivered "frontier justice" as they defined it.

The first cattle had been brought to Montana in the 1840s to stock trading posts and missions, but ranching expanded rapidly to feed the influx of miners in the 1860s. By the 1870s herds were being driven north from Texas, giving rise not only to a cattle boom but also to the birth of the cowboy as one of America's most beloved folk heroes. The open-range era was short-lived, however, as

Immigrant's wooden trunk, ca. 1875, 3' × 2' × 2'.
2013.76.01

Mary Ann Thomas, pictured here in an early tintype, arrived with her Welsh-immigrant parents in Alder Gulch shortly after gold was discovered there. This photograph was reportedly taken in Virginia City in 1863, which, if correct, makes it one of the oldest extant photographs created in Montana. 3¾" × 5", C900-010

Immigrants from many nations came to the American West to help build the railroads. Here, Italian Northern Pacific crew members utilize traditional methods to bake bread in a makeshift earthen oven near Terry, ca. 1908.
Evelyn Cameron, photographer.
PAc 90-87 VP RR workers bread

nature had the last say during the winter of 1886–1887, known as the Great Die-Up for its devastating impact on the cattle herds of the northern Plains.

Ultimately, railroads would bring incredible numbers of settlers to Montana, but first, laborers had to lay the networks of tracks that traversed Montana to link the east and west coasts. These young, single men—often immigrants from such countries as China, Japan, Sweden, Norway, Italy, and Bulgaria—were subjected to poor living conditions while performing backbreaking and frequently dangerous work for low pay.

All those who came to Montana brought with them their own cultures, languages, and beliefs. They also carried personal possessions, from items small enough to fit easily into a pocket to wooden trunks loaded with reminders of home. As successive waves of newcomers worked to establish themselves in a new place, Montana's Native peoples struggled to protect their traditional homelands and ways of life.

10. Fort Benton Weathervane

ca. 1854, 23" × 16½". Purchased jointly by the Montana Historical Society and the Hornaday Committee, Fort Benton, Montana, 1995.46.01

THIS sheet-iron weathervane is nearly all that remains from the structure of Old Fort Benton, one of the first non-Indian settlements in the present state of Montana. Founded in 1846 by the American Fur Company, Old Fort Benton operated as a trading post for furs and bison hides supplied by local tribes. Its fourteen-foot adobe walls witnessed all manner of frontier commotion, from the commerce of fur traders to the movement of gold seekers, freight haulers, outlaws, and road builders who passed by on their way to fortune or failure.

The fort's overseeing agent, Major Alexander Culbertson, proved a competent frontier diplomat, obliging the Blackfeet's request for the fort to be relocated by replacing the original log structure with one built from Missouri River clay on the opposite shore. The completed fort consisted of two two-story blockhouses with portholes for defensive cannon or rifle fire, a trade store, a warehouse, blacksmith and carpenter shops, a kitchen, and a barn. Likely fashioned by the resident blacksmith, this eye-catching weathervane is shaped in the silhouette of a bison. In a sketch of the fort by pioneer Granville Stuart from 1866 (pictured here), the weathervane is plainly visible atop the kitchen's cupola, its presence representing the encroachment of Euro-American culture even among the vast expanses of the northern Plains.

While the old fort succumbed to the ravages of time and the harsh Montana climate in the 1880s, its weathervane survived. According to historian Ken Robison, the weathervane went on to grace the cupola of the Wetzel/Duer mansion in the town of Fort Benton, which served as a sanatorium from 1910 to 1916. With the assistance of the Hornaday Committee, the Montana Historical Society acquired the weathervane in 1995 from Greg Chastain of Georgia, who traced its provenance back to a former fort agent, Julius Falk. Somewhat worse for wear, missing one leg, and battered by sharpshooters, the weathervane symbolizes the decades of history it witnessed from its perch overlooking the "World's Innermost Port."

–*SAT*

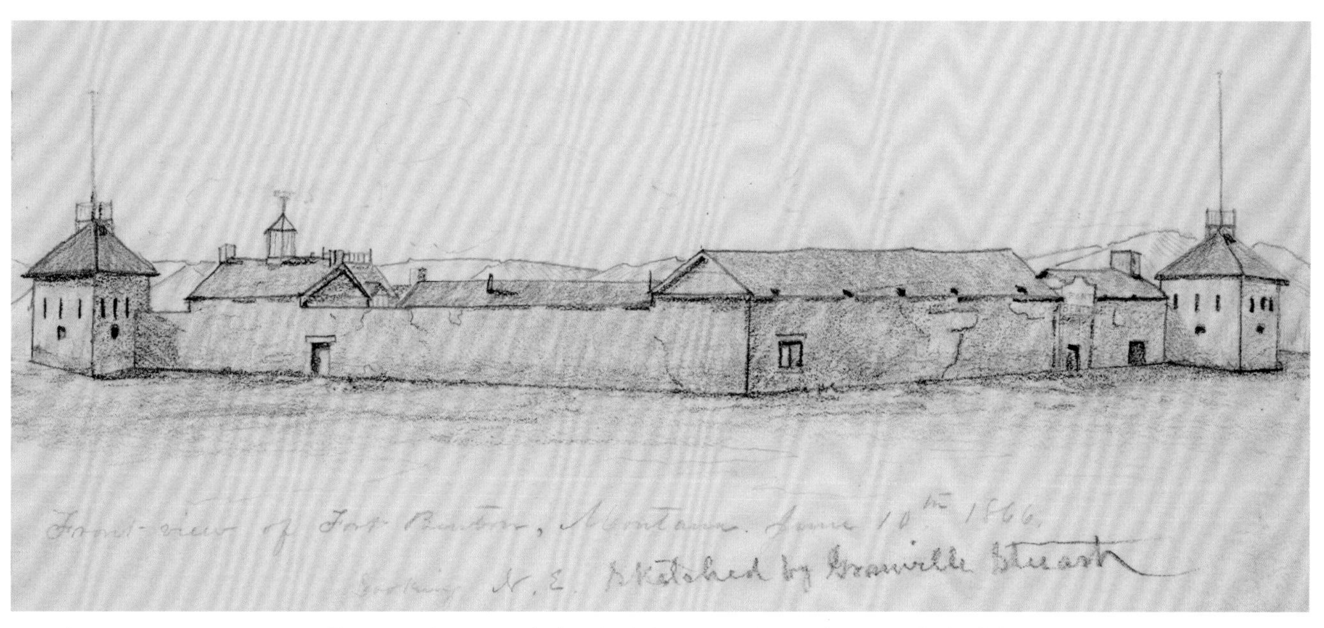

Noted Montana pioneer Granville Stuart (1834–1918) sketched the scenes he saw from the deck of the *W. B. Dance* as he traveled upriver from St. Louis to Montana in 1866. In this pencil drawing of Fort Benton, the bison-shaped weathervane can be seen atop the kitchen, adjacent to the blockhouse on the left. 10" × 7", X1968.43.01 k

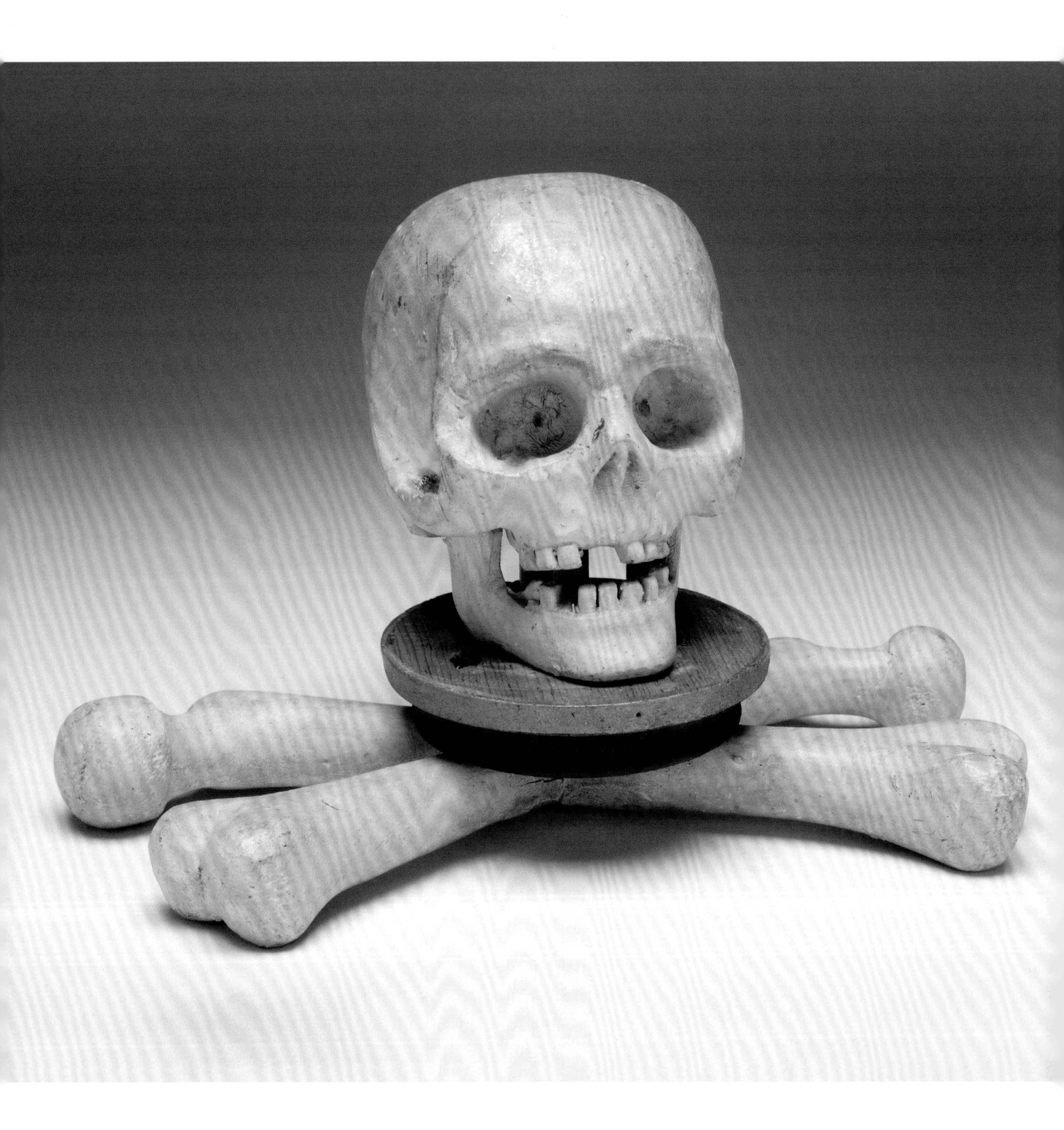

11. Skull and Crossbones

ca. 1865, 10½" × 6", by Father Anthony Ravalli (1812–1884). Gift of St. Ignatius Mission, x1904.01.02

◈

THIS wooden sculpture of a human skull and crossed femur bones was carved by Father Anthony Ravalli, a beloved priest who ministered to both Native Americans and non-Indians from the time of his 1845 arrival in the Bitterroot Valley until his death in 1884. An accomplished sculptor, Father Ravalli created this carving as a *memento mori*—an artistic convention dating from the Middle Ages that reminded viewers that death was inevitable, but adherence to Christian principles in this life ensured paradise in the next.

Father Ravalli was born in Ferrara, Italy, in 1812, and schooled in his native country in theology, medicine, mathematics, chemistry, philosophy, mechanics, architecture, and art. He arrived at St. Mary's Mission in summer 1845 and, except for a sixteen-year period when the mission was closed, devoted the remainder of his life to serving the Salish Indians, the area's original inhabitants. According to one of Ravalli's admirers, Louis W. Reilly, "The gentle, refined and cultured Blackrobe adopted their life. He learned their language. He ate their food."

Father Ravalli's primary concern was the spiritual welfare of those to whom he ministered, but he also gained a reputation as a skilled physician and pharmacist. As historian Dave Walter noted, "Father Ravalli became a fabled figure, riding his Indian pony through the countryside to assist the sick, the wounded, the injured, and the dying. His compassion for natives and white settlers alike made him welcome wherever he traveled in Montana Territory."

Additionally, Father Ravalli was celebrated as an artist and craftsman. He designed the Sacred Heart Mission chapel in Cataldo, Idaho, and the second church building at St. Mary's. He filled these structures with ecclesiastical furnishings, carvings of saints, and ornamental detail. "He understood that beauty is something we all yearn for," explained photographer Harold Allen. "He never made the mistake, as most of us do, of putting it in second place—and so [he] piled up treasures in heaven and left treasures on earth, too."

In the early 1900s, mindful of Father Ravalli's contributions to Montana history, MHS librarian Laura Howey contacted St. Ignatius Mission on the Flathead Reservation asking for help securing "what relics may still be had of the writings and handy work of Fr. Ravalli." In response, Fathers Lawrence Benedict Palladino and Leopold Van Gorp arranged the donation of this carving, along with a chair, a crucifix, and an ornamental wall bracket, all made by Father Ravalli, as well as a set of French buhrstones (see page 130)—the first millstones of their kind in Montana—that Father Ravalli brought with him from Europe. *–KL*

In addition to his other contributions to St. Mary's Mission, Father Ravalli helped design this chapel, which was completed in 1879. Robert Swanberg, photographer, August 1940, PAc 2001–39.52

12. Sketch of the Montana Territorial Seal

1865, 3¾" × 6¼", by Francis Thompson (1833–1916). Gift of Francis M. Thompson, Francis M. Thompson Papers, SC 839

◈

EACH state in the United States has a seal composed of iconic images meant to capture the essence of the people and geography within its boundaries. Montana's seal—found on official government documents, our state flag, and on state buildings—signifies the authority of state government and is intended to represent the people who call Montana home.

The Montana seal has roots in the state's territorial beginnings. Francis Thompson, the seal's designer, was a native of Massachusetts who arrived in the goldfields of Idaho Territory in 1862. He then served as one of seven members of the Montana Territorial Council during the first legislative assembly in 1864–1865. On January 17, 1865, Dr. Erasmus D. Leavitt, a fellow council member, sponsored a resolution to create a committee charged with designing an official seal for Montana Territory. Thompson, as committee chair, headed the effort, which resulted in this sketch. After Thompson submitted his report, and following five days of debate among council members, both houses approved. On February 9, 1865, Governor Sidney Edgerton signed Council Resolution No. 13 and Montana Territory had its official seal.

Thompson's design stood the test of time right up through Montana's transition to statehood in 1889. In 1893, however, Governor John E. Rickards called for the creation of a new version, insisting that continuing to use the territorial seal was "unbecoming the dignity of our State." Three members from the state's House of Representatives—A. F. Bray, J. B. Losee, and J. H. Murphy—and two members from the Senate—C. H. Eggleston and Paris Gibson—took up the task of creating a "proper design" for the state seal. On March 2, 1893, Rickards signed a bill into law that officially adopted the result of their efforts. The revised seal, however, looked much like the original territorial seal in design and description, only the word "territory" had been replaced with "state."

On July 4, 1899, Governor Joseph K. Toole raised another concern regarding the state seal during a speech dedicating the capitol cornerstone. Noting the ongoing Spanish-American War, Toole observed that the motto "*Oro y Plata*" ("Gold and Silver") was written in the language of a hostile power, that "unhappy land which has brought desolation and death to hundreds of thousands of its own people and filled its trenches with the rich blood of so many American soldiers." At Montana's capitol dedication four years later, former U.S. Senator Wilbur Fisk Sanders also expressed his dissatisfaction with the seal and its motto. He suggested that a state seal and motto should express the "dominant idea of its people and should signalize their devotion to high ideals." For Sanders, the imagery and motto evoked a people more concerned with material wealth—or, as he put it, the "jingle of the guinea"—than the lofty ideals of justice, liberty, and moral law.

Despite these reservations, Montana's seal and motto remain true to Thompson's original sketch. With the plow underscoring the state's agricultural roots, the rugged mountains and the Missouri River celebrating Montana's beauty, and the pick, ax, and motto "*Oro y Plata*" symbolizing the siren call that attracted fortune seekers, the seal captures much that was and remains alluring about the Treasure State. *–JF*

Original sketch of
proposed Seal for the
Territory of Montana.
made by
Francis M. Thompson.
member of Committee
on Seal.
In first Legislative Asembly.

BRITISH POSSESSIONS
MONTANA
IDAHO
DAKOTA
Map of the
Territory of Montana
with portions of the adjoining Territories.
Showing the Gulch or Placer diggings actually worked, and Districts where Quartz (Gold & Silver) Lodes have been discovered up to January 1865.
Quartz Lodes
Drawn by W. W. de Lacy
For the First Legislative Assembly.
Scale of Miles
Little Rocky Mountains
Belt Mountains
Big Horn Mountains
Black Hills
Yellowstone River
Big Horn River
Powder River
Snake River
North Fork of Platte River
Milk River
Missouri River
Fort Laramie

13. Map of Montana Territory

1865, 30" × 23", by Walter W. DeLacy (1819–1892). Map B-1

◈

Bannack's 1862 gold strike and Virginia City's in 1863 attracted thousands of fortune-seekers to present-day southwestern Montana, then part of Idaho Territory. This population surge spurred Congress in 1864 to carve out the Montana Territory from Idaho Territory. Eager to promote settlement and investment, the first Montana Territorial Legislature on December 17, 1864, passed a resolution to hire "a competent person to draft a map of the Territory at as early a day as practicable." The task of finding a mapmaker fell to Charles Bagg of Madison County, who served on the Committee on Mines & Minerals, which sought to promote gold mining in Montana. Bagg acted with dispatch, and four days later he hired Captain Walter W. DeLacy to produce a map within fifteen days for a sum of $625.

At the age of forty-six, Walter DeLacy had already experienced a distinguished career, first as a civil engineer building railroads in Illinois and Missouri during the 1840s, followed by service in the Mexican War, during which he surveyed a road from San Antonio, Texas, to Chihuahua, Mexico. In May 1858, DeLacy had arrived in the Pacific Northwest as a member of the team headed by Captain John Mullan and charged with surveying a military road between Fort Walla Walla in Washington Territory, near the Columbia River, and Fort Benton, on the Missouri River in what would become Montana. In the early 1860s, he tried his hand at gold mining, but he returned to cartography in 1864–1865, platting the towns of LaBarge City (Deer Lodge) and Fort Benton. Between 1867 and 1871, DeLacy worked with the office of surveyor-general creating maps for the Northern Pacific Railroad. In 1883, he became the city engineer of Helena and later served as chief clerk to the U.S. surveyor-general until his death in 1892.

It is difficult to overestimate the significance of DeLacy's map to the infant territory of Montana. The document provided a much-needed guide for the newcomers flooding into the region, depicting the nine original territorial counties, mountain ranges, waterways, and the location of both placer diggings and quartz lodes. A version of DeLacy's manuscript map appeared in Granville Stuart's *Montana As It Is; A General Description of its Resources, Both Mineral and Agricultural,* published by C. S. Westcott & Co., New York, in 1865. Three other lithographers—Hutawa in St. Louis, Friedenwald in Baltimore, and Rae Smith in New York—subsequently printed the DeLacy map, and C. B. Colton revised the map for new editions in 1870 and 1874. In this way, DeLacy's work served as a resource for miners, ranchers, farmers, and land speculators for two decades. Carl Wheat, in his monumental six-volume work, *Mapping the Trans-Mississippi West,* praised DeLacy's skill, writing, "He wrought a memorable map of a new Territory, and had he never done anything else, he would have given us sufficient reason to honor his memory."

The DeLacy map stands alone as the first map of Montana Territory, but it is only one of more than eleven thousand maps that make up the Research Center's map collection at MHS. These documents illustrate every aspect of Montana's past, and over the years they have been used by a wide range of researchers, from genealogists and historians to city and county planners, novelists, and filmmakers.

–BS

14. Charley Thomas's Boot

1866, 8¼" × 3" × 12". Gift of Charles Lienesch, 1977.10.01

◈

THIS boot, worn by seven-year-old Montana immigrant Charley Thomas, was among the few items discovered at the site where Charley, his father, Rev. William K. "Bill" Thomas, and their hired hand, Joseph Schultz, were killed en route to the Virginia City goldfields. The group began their travels in Illinois, lured westward by correspondence with Bill's brother, George D. Thomas, who had recently settled in the Gallatin Valley and established a farm and flour mill near present-day Manhattan. With aspirations of achieving new wealth and opportunity, Bill, Charley, and Schultz set out from their home state with a pair of mules on May 15, 1866. That August, they were found dead along the Bozeman Trail.

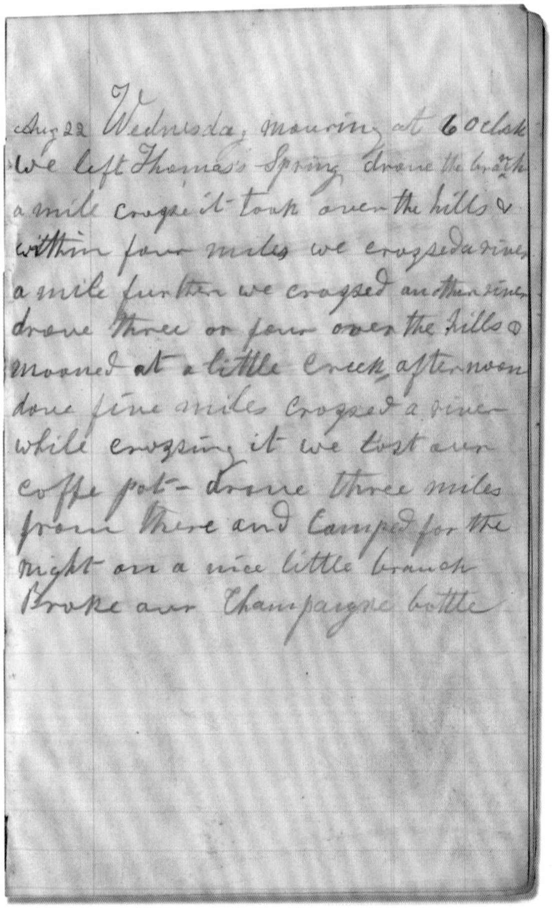
71
Aug 22 Wednesday morning at 6 oclock
we left Thomas's Spring drove the branch
a mile crossed it took over the hills &
within four miles we crossed a river
a mile further we crossed another river
drove three or four over the hills &
nooned at a little Creek afternoon
done fine miles crossed a river
while crossing it we lost our
coffee pot - drove three miles
from there and Camped for the
night on a nice little branch
Broke our Champagne bottle

Bill Thomas documented his travels with Charley in a diary. The last entry on the Bozeman Trail is dated August 22, 1866.
4" × 6½". Gift of Charles Lienesch, SC1303

Among early emigrants' journals along the Bozeman Trail, Bill Thomas's diary stands out as a poignant reminder of the risks early travelers faced while traversing Montana Territory. His descriptions are simultaneously breathtaking and eerily prophetic. Once, remarking on the sight of distant mountains, he wrote, "[C]old chills run through my blood."

Thomas was impatient with the slow pace and decided to leave the safety of the train. For a week, the trio traveled unmolested, and Thomas's final journal entry notes that they made camp upslope from the Yellowstone River near present-day Greycliff.

Thirteen arrows pierced Bill's body; Charley's carried three. Both had been scalped. Schultz's body, found in the river, contained a dozen arrows. He had been fishing, it appeared, and two trout lay on the bank nearby. The attackers, presumed to be Indians, had stolen some belongings and scattered the rest. The remaining items included one of Charley's boots, Bill's diary, and a hunting knife.

More than one hundred years later, the three bodies were buried in a common grave near the frontage road between Greycliff and Reedpoint. Relatives gave the party's few salvaged belongings to the Montana Historical Society. Today, Charley's single boot and the group's lonely grave symbolize the hope, conflict, and uncertainty many experienced during their efforts to settle in Montana. –*EB*

SACRED
to the
memory
of
LANGFORD PEEL,
BORN IN
LIVERPOOL.
JULY 23RD 1867
aged
36 YEARS.
IN LIFE BELOVED BY HIS FRIENDS
AND RESPECTED BY HIS ENEMIES
VENGENCE IS MINE
SAYETH THE LORD.
I KNOW THAT MY REDEEMER LIVETH
ERECTED BY A FRIEND

15. Wooden Grave Marker

1867, 16" × 2" × 60⅓". Gift of Wilbur Fisk Sanders, x1928.27.01

◈

Some who came to Montana stayed whether they intended to or not. One such man was Irish-born immigrant Langford Peel (1831–1867). A gambler and gunslinger, Peel was known equally for his generosity toward those who had fallen on hard times and for his hair-trigger temper. Before being murdered by his business partner in 1867, Peel was reportedly responsible for the death of more than eight men. This weathered plank of oak marked Peel's grave in Helena before his body was moved to the Benton Avenue Cemetery in 1875.

Peel—who was born in Belfast, not Liverpool as incorrectly recorded on his grave marker—arrived in the United States as a young child. As soon as he was able, he followed his stepfather into the First U.S. Dragoons in the Mexican-American War, ultimately becoming a first sergeant. Discharged in 1856 at the age of twenty-five, Peel became a peripatetic gambler and abandoned his wife, Jacobine Lay, and their young son. After spending time in the mining camps of California, Utah, and Nevada, Peel followed his friend and business partner, John Bull, to Helena in 1867.

In July of that year, Peel slapped Bull across the face for reasons unknown. Some said his ire resulted from a card dispute, while others attributed it to money wasted on a worthless mine. Bull retaliated by ambushing and fatally wounding Peel outside a Helena saloon. He was buried in the city cemetery, established just two years earlier. In 1875, when the city began building its first graded school (Central School) on that site, Peel's body, along with many others, was relocated to the Benton Avenue Cemetery, founded in 1870. His marker, however, did not travel with him.

Wilber Fisk Sanders, then serving as a member of the Territorial House of Representatives, was passionately committed to preserving the territory's history, and he retrieved the large wooden grave marker, taking it home for safekeeping. It was placed in his attic and forgotten until the family moved out in 1928. The marker was later transferred to the Montana Historical Society, where it remains as a rare, well-preserved relic of Helena's early and tumultuous history. *–RH*

Wilbur Fisk Sanders (1834–1905)—who preserved Peel's grave marker for posterity—was a Bannack, Virginia City, and Helena attorney, vigilante, and Republican politician. Perhaps more significantly for lovers of Montana history, he was also founder and early champion of the Montana Historical Society.
R. A. Lewis, photographer, ca. 1865. 944–847

16. Teddy Blue Abbott's Chaps

ca. 1890–1900. 2016.57.01

◈

If a holy scripture of cowboys existed, certainly it would be found in the writing of Edward C. "Teddy Blue" Abbott (1860–1939). Abbott's 1939 book, *We Pointed Them North: Recollections of a Cowpuncher*, is an eyewitness account of Montana Territory's short-lived but long-celebrated era of the open range, from 1850 to 1887.

Born in Cranwich, England, Abbott immigrated with his parents to Lincoln, Nebraska, where his father invested in Texas cattle and had them driven north. A sickly ten-year-old, Teddy was allowed to ride with the men moving the herd so as to improve his strength. He later wrote, "If I hadn't been a cowpuncher I never would have growed up."

When they had this photograph taken in Miles City in April 1919, Montana's two most famous cowboys—Teddy Blue Abbott (L) and Charlie Russell (R)—had been friends for almost thirty-five years. 940-046

His writing recalls the hardscrabble life of working on a cattle drive and details the countless dangers, the harsh weather, and the rare days off. Abbott arrived in Montana Territory in 1883, finding it an unfenced paradise for cattlemen until the devastating winter of 1886–1887 wiped out whole herds and snapped wranglers back to the reality of the West's unforgiving climate. Despite the hardships, Abbott admitted, "Old-timers have told all about stampedes and swimming rivers and what a terrible time we had, but they never put in any of the fun, and fun was at least half of it."

Indeed, Abbott's account is full of fun. *We Pointed Them North* includes songs, anecdotes, and recollections of his encounters with colorful characters along the trail, like legendary artist Charles M. Russell, showman "Buffalo Bill" Cody, and Connie the Cowboy Queen, who frequented the saloons of Miles City and wore a striking dress adorned with every cattle brand "from the Yellowstone down the Platte and over in the Dakotas."

After his cowpunching days, Abbott worked for Granville Stuart, the stockman, pioneer, and historian widely known as "Mr. Montana," who owned one of the largest ranches in the state. Teddy married Stuart's daughter, Mary, and together they established the 3 Deuces Ranch near Lewistown. Toward the end of his life, Abbott had the satisfaction of seeing his memoir in print, thanks to Helena Huntington Smith, who recorded his story. Reflecting on the bygone days of the men who rode the open range, Abbott told Smith, "Only a few of us are left now, and they are scattered from Texas to Canada. The rest have left the wagon and gone ahead across the big divide, looking for a new range. I hope they find good water and plenty of grass. But wherever they are is where I want to go."

Abbott was widely mourned when he passed away, as his friends and neighbors recognized he was among the last of his kind. During his funeral, his favorite hat rested on his coffin, and, in keeping with cowboy tradition, he was buried with his boots on. His leather chaps, however, made their way into the Montana Historical Society's collection, where they are proudly displayed as a reminder of the authentic cowboy spirit Teddy Blue left behind. *–SAT*

17. Chinese Embroidered Pouch

ca. 1880, 3⅞" × 5¼". Gift of John M. Mitchell, x1968.15.01

◈

Ah Hei, the owner of this exquisitely embroidered pouch, was one of thousands of Chinese laborers who came to Montana and contributed to the construction of the Northern Pacific Railroad in the late nineteenth century. The pouch has three pockets and is adorned with intricately stitched silk lotus blossoms. When acquired by the Society in 1968, it had several items inside: two good luck coins, a comb, a flint case, and a letter from home written by Ah Hei's brother, Hao Hsing.

In the 1880s, Northern Pacific president Henry Villard recruited workers from Canada, the United States, and China to clear land, blast through mountains, and lay tracks across Montana, Idaho, and Washington. The work was grueling and extremely dangerous. In 1884, officials estimated at least one thousand Chinese workers lay buried along the Northern Pacific line. "Verily," reported Helena's *Independent Record*, "it was a railroad paved with Chinaman's bones."

Chinese immigrant Ah Hei carried this ornate case—designed to hold flint and tinder for starting fires—inside the pouch. The stylized brass bats on the corners of the flap and the central Fu character symbolize happiness. 3¼" × 2½". Gift of John M. Mitchell, x1968.15.06

Chinese laborers performed more than two-thirds of the overall labor involved in laying the tracks, and archaeological evidence from line camps along the Thompson River indicates they endured poor living conditions. The Chinese were segregated from non-Chinese workers, and their camps were located in the most inhospitable, mosquito-infested areas. Common artifacts found in such sites include opium paraphernalia, suggesting that workers used the drug to ease the severe physical pains of hard labor. Despite their significant contribution, Chinese laborers earned about a dollar per day, only half the amount paid to their Canadian and American counterparts.

Far from his native country, Ah Hei likely cherished this pouch as a reminder of his family. The letter from his brother pleads movingly for him to come back to China, asking that he "just make enough to buy a ticket home so our mother won't have to worry about you." Indeed, most of the Chinese immigrants who worked on the railroad did not intend to stay, but many did not make it back home due to the dangerous conditions in which they labored. That the pouch and its contents remained in Montana implies that Ah Hei, like so many of his fellow countrymen, probably never saw his native China again. *–EB*

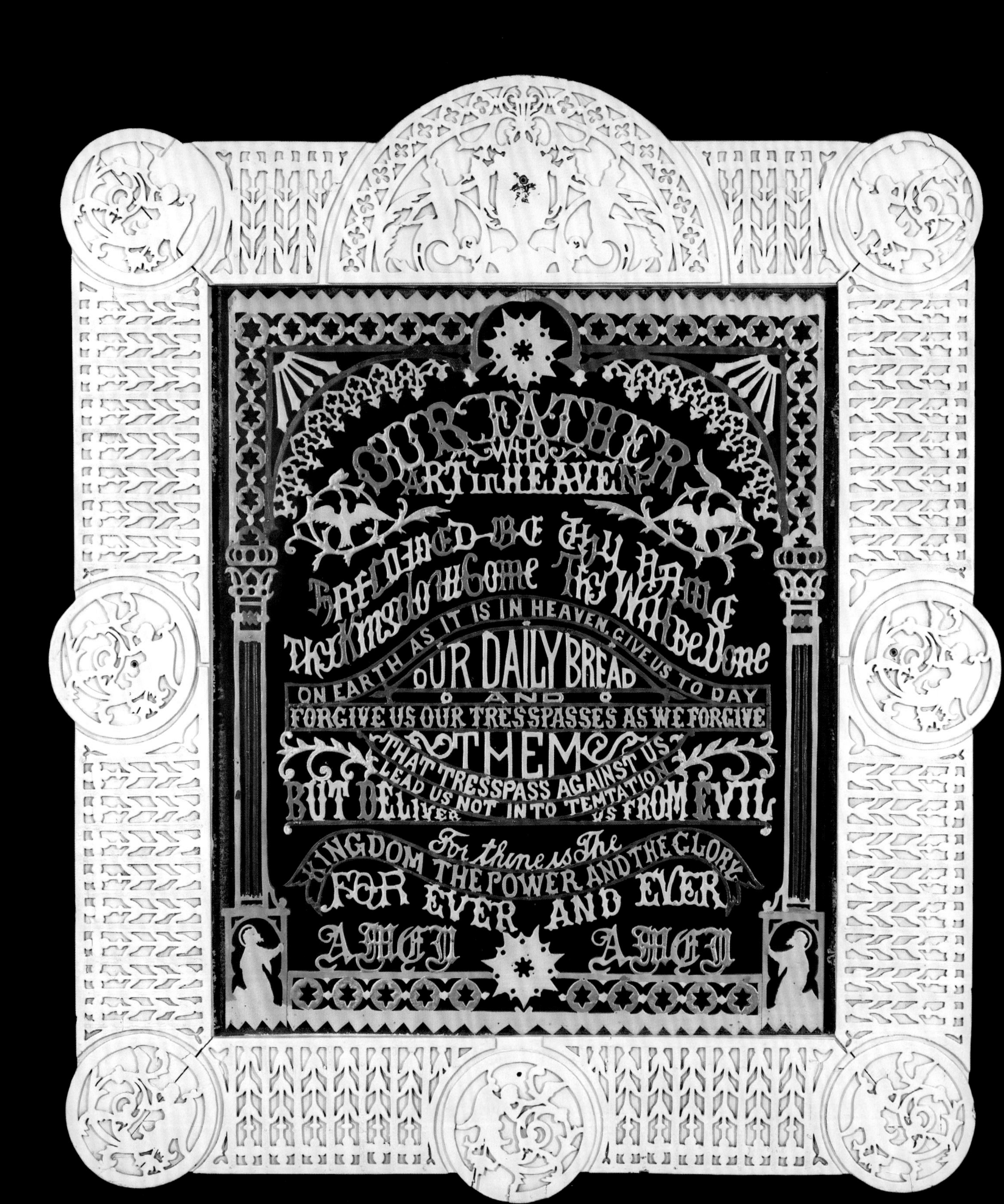
OUR FATHER WHO ART IN HEAVEN
HALLOWED BE THY NAME
Thy Kingdom Come Thy Will Be Done
ON EARTH AS IT IS IN HEAVEN, GIVE US TO DAY
OUR DAILY BREAD
AND
FORGIVE US OUR TRESSPASSES AS WE FORGIVE
THEM
THAT TRESSPASS AGAINST US
LEAD US NOT INTO TEMTATION
BUT DELIVER US FROM EVIL
For thine is The
KINGDOM THE POWER AND THE GLORY
FOR EVER AND EVER
AMEN AMEN

Building Montana

◈

As immigrants settled in Montana, they sought to build community by re-creating the institutions and organizations that had previously defined their lives "back home," whether that was the eastern United States or elsewhere in the world.

For many newcomers, establishing religious institutions was of the utmost importance. The majority of immigrants coming to Montana were Christians of all denominations, while other religious traditions—including Judaism, Taoism, Buddhism, and Confucianism—accounted for a much smaller percentage of the growing population. Religious groups erected houses of worship, conducted services, and established cemeteries, as well as founded the first schools, hospitals, and orphanages in the young territory.

Newspapers were essential to any community hoping to achieve permanence. Serving many functions, they connected individuals on the remote frontier with the outside world. They also kept people informed of local and territorial politics, business developments, and social happenings. As was common at the time, most of Montana's earliest newspapers expressed explicit partisan and ideological leanings. In addition to Democratic and Republican papers, various others represented the interests of groups ranging from Communist farmers to Butte's famed Copper Kings. Some newspapers served specific ethnic communities, including African Americans and foreign-language immigrants.

Education also constituted a high priority for Montana's settlers. Rural dwellers built one- and two-room schoolhouses as soon as they had a handful of students. Teachers, themselves often not much older than the students, lived in simple on-site accommodations or roomed with a nearby family. Larger towns constructed imposing school buildings, stately structures that spoke to the community's belief in its future.

Carving of the Lord's Prayer, ca. 1905, 31" × 35½", by Carl K. Alstad (1860–1950). Gift of Alan and Mary Bowers, 2011.18.01

Fireman's hat from Choteau (note that the town's name is misspelled "Chateau").
ca. 1890–1910, 2002.48.01

Over time, new systems of healthcare also took shape in Montana. Traditionally, the sick and injured were cared for at home, primarily by wives and mothers. Where there were large populations of single men, women operated "rooming" or "boarding" hospitals in their homes. Individual physicians sometimes opened private hospitals to care for their patients, while community hospital associations eventually joined these other entities in providing medical care.

Tragically, while immigrants to Montana established familiar institutions and replicated faraway cultures, tribal communities fought to retain their customs and traditions as they were pushed onto reservations to make room for the newcomers. Subjected to cultural repression, Indigenous peoples were pressured to abandon their spiritual practices, languages, and beliefs, in addition to other aspects of tribal life. In an effort to assimilate them, federal authorities forcibly removed Indian youth from their families, often at very young ages, and placed them in distant boarding schools where they were forbidden to speak their native languages or engage in traditional cultural practices.

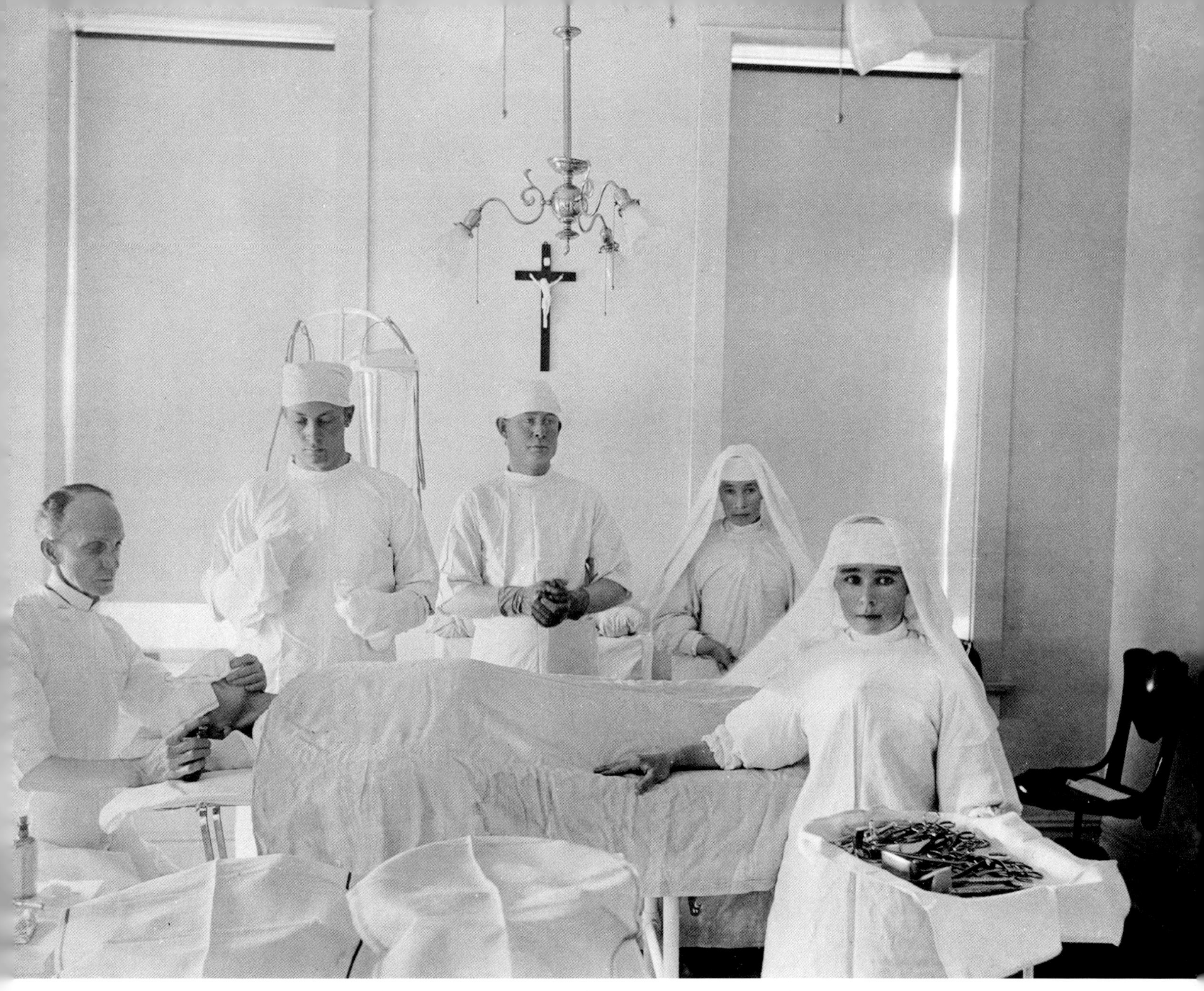

Doctors and nurses pose with an anesthetized patient prior to performing surgery at St. Joseph's Hospital in Lewistown, Nov. 8, 1909. W. H. Culver, photographer. 949-002

Into the twentieth century, ideas of what constituted "community"—and the organizations necessary to achieve it—continued to evolve. As federal, tribal, state, and local governments developed and reorganized, they assumed greater responsibility for caring for their citizens. At the same time, individuals banded together to form labor unions and service clubs to improve their own circumstances as well as their communities, while private businesses, like insurance companies, developed to meet other needs not addressed by government.

18. Lowe Printing Press No. 2

ca. 1860, 51" × 25½" × 17". Gift of W. Cheely, x1898.01.01

◈

As new towns sprang up across Montana Territory, local newspapers became an essential part of community life. The *Montana Post*, published weekly between August 27, 1864, and June 11, 1869, was the first of its kind issued as a regular edition in Montana Territory. The *Post* measured twenty-one by thirty-one inches and six columns wide and was printed on this Lowe Press No. 2. Initially, the paper was produced in Virginia City and then, after March 1868, in Helena.

Although the *Post* was only published for a few years, it established a vital record of information regarding frontier vigilantism, territorial politics, business, and the social whirl of one of the territory's major gold rushes. From 1864 to 1869, its publishers included John Buchanan, Daniel Webster Tilton & Co., Benjamin R. Dittes, and the Montana Post Publishing Company. After the first four issues, Buchanan sold the *Post* to Tilton, who immediately hired as editor Thomas J. Dimsdale, a sickly English-born

The Lowe Press No. 2 was used in Virginia City to print Montana's first newspaper, the *Montana Post*. In addition to this September 17, 1864, edition of the *Post* (opposite), the Montana Historical Society holds newspapers in microfilm, print, and digital formats from 243 communities across all fifty-six Montana counties, dating from 1864 to the present day.

schoolteacher. Dimsdale became known for his 1866 book, *The Vigilantes of Montana*, which first appeared in a serialized format on the pages of the *Post* in 1865. He regularly editorialized from the vigilantes' perspective, defending the need for citizens to respond to lawlessness. Storied though it was, Dimsdale's career at the *Montana Post* was brief: he resigned his position shortly before succumbing to tuberculosis on September 22, 1866, at the age of thirty-five.

Captain James H. Mills, a decorated Union officer, served as the *Post*'s third editor. To keep up with the demands of publishing a newspaper with long columns, small headlines, and no graphics, Mills relied on gold-prospecting reports to attract readers, many of whom were miners, merchants, and farmers from the area. Post–Civil War politics also accounted for many popular stories. The *Post*'s Republican editors fanned the flames surrounding the issue of racial equality, which angered territorial Democrats, many of whom were Confederate sympathizers.

After an April 1869 fire devastated much of Helena, the *Post* was sold, and within the month Mills moved to Deer Lodge, where he founded the *New North-West*. Virginia City did not have another paper until 1873, when the *Madisonian* began publication.

In addition to the *Montana Post*, dozens of foreign-language and ethnically affiliated papers—including German, Swedish, Serbian, Croatian, Irish American, and African American publications—flourished during the early part of the twentieth century. Woolgrowers, stockgrowers, miners, farmers, socialists, and labor unions all published special-interest newspapers as well. Today, the Montana Historical Society holds 95 percent of all the newspapers ever published in the Treasure State, providing researchers with a remarkable record of daily life, culture, and politics from 1864 to the present. *–BS*

19. Chinese Altar

ca. 1885, 47⅜" × 15⅜" × 62". Gift of Walter and Doris Marshall, 1973.17.01

◈

GOLD rushes in the American West coincided with famine, overpopulation, and civil war in southern China, resulting in push-pull forces that commonly drive immigration. Many emigrants from Guangdong (Canton) Province set out for the United States following the earliest discoveries of the rare metal in 1848 in California, and they were certainly among the waves of miners that flocked to Grasshopper Creek during the 1862 gold rush. By 1870, Chinese immigrants comprised 10 percent of Montana's territorial population. Despite facing fierce discrimination and cultural isolation, they played important roles in Montana's development during this period.

Chinese "Masonic" building, Helena, Montana, no date. L. H. Jorud, photographer. 953-317

As placer mining dwindled, the construction of the Northern Pacific Railroad provided a surplus of work. On the cusp of the federal Chinese Exclusion Act, passed in 1882, the Northern Pacific hired thousands of Chinese laborers to build tracks across Montana and the Northwest. In urban areas, Chinese residents provided services to this growing population of workers, owned property, and paid taxes.

Most Chinese immigrants never intended to stay in the United States, and by the 1920s many had long since returned to China or, more tragically, died far from home. Montana's once-vibrant Chinatowns began to decay, and time erased their architectural and cultural footprints, leaving few physical remains standing as testament to these important pioneers. Some sites survive, however, such as the Mai Wah/Wah Chong Tai building (now a museum) in Butte; "China Row," a Chinese burial ground at Forestvale Cemetery in Helena; and the Yee Wau cabin in Helena.

Urban temples were a place of refuge and relief for Chinese workers far from home, and most communities that supported Chinatowns had at least one. This altar from Helena's Chinese temple is of unknown origin, but a penciled address on the bottom—206 Clore Street—identifies a log dwelling in Helena labeled as "Chinese" on the 1888 Sanborn-Perris Fire Insurance map. The altar's intricate carvings include flowers, birds, silkworm moths, and bats with outstretched wings (a potent symbol of good fortune). The top center words, *Xie Tian Gong*, refer to the name of an ancient military hero, Guan Yu, to whom the temple was dedicated. The two vertical lines of characters flanking the altar's central portion translate: "Throughout the ages, his firmness and loyalty shine bright as the moon and sun / For eons, his bravery and sincerity with the hills and rivers is one."

Helena's Chinese temple was torn down in the 1930s. Afterward, Doris Marshall, a local high school drama teacher and founder of the Brewery Theater, acquired the altar and used it as a theatrical prop. In 1973, she gave the altar to the Montana Historical Society. Now impeccably restored to its original appearance, it is the only Chinese community temple altar known to have survived in Montana. *–EB*

協天宮
萬古精忠貫日月
千秋義勇壯山河

20. *The Trading Post*

1892, 16⅜" × 12½", by Emma Wells (ca. 1878–1939). Gift of James A. Frank, 1993.11.15

◈

The Trading Post, a sketch by Emma Wells, was donated to the Montana Historical Society in 1993 by James A. Frank, her great-nephew. Emma drew the picture a century earlier while attending St. Peter's Mission boarding school northwest of Cascade. St. Peter's, one of the first religious and educational institutions in Montana, was established in 1856 by the Jesuits and later became an Ursuline academy to educate both white and Indian children.

Emma entered St. Peter's in 1885, following the death of her father, James Wells, an Irish immigrant who had moved to Montana Territory twenty

years earlier. From 1874 to 1884, Wells managed Fort Claggett, a trading post located at the mouth of the Judith River near the former site of Camp Cooke. The post served several tribes, including the A'aninin (Gros Ventre), Blackfeet, Assiniboine, River Crow, and Cree, as well as the Métis traders, bone-pickers, and woodcutters who moved to central Montana from North Dakota and Minnesota in the mid-1860s and 1870s. Wells married Morning Star Horse Capture, an A'aninin woman who had converted to Catholicism and been baptized Margaret Walsh.

In 1885, James Wells succumbed to a chronic illness and the three Wells children were placed under the guardianship of Fort Claggett's owner, Thomas C. Power, and his brother John, even though their mother was still alive. The practice of assigning white male guardians to the children of Indigenous women and white men was not uncommon at the time, particularly when the father was a military man or had left a substantial inheritance. Wells bequeathed ample money for the care of his children, and almost immediately the Powers sent young Emma and her siblings to St. Peter's Mission, where Emma drew *The Trading Post* in 1892 when she was twelve years old.

This hand-colored tintype, six inches in diameter, depicts young artist Emma Wells (left) with her older sister Mary Ursula, about 1894. Gift of James A. Frank, C993-002

From 1885 until 1895, mission schools received a small federal stipend to board, convert, and educate Indian children. Indian and Métis students, like the Wells children, were educated alongside white students, but boarded in a separate facility. In the early 1890s, the establishment of compulsory, federally funded off-reservation Indian boarding schools meant a loss of subsidies for the parochial schools. Over the next few years, most of St. Peter's white students moved to a new school in Great Falls, while some of the Indian students transferred to Fort Shaw, a government-run school that opened in 1892.

Margaret Horse Capture Wells died in 1895, likely while Emma and her siblings were still in school. St. Peter's Mission school closed permanently around 1918. Emma died in 1939, leaving little trace of her life and experiences as the daughter of a white trader and a A'aninin mother, neither of whom she had a chance to know particularly well.

The Trading Post demonstrates the artistic training Emma and her peers received at St. Peter's, which complemented their instruction in music, religion, literature, sewing, mathematics, and science. The sketch recalls a period of Montana's past that only lasted for a few decades, when the influx of traders, prospectors, and the U.S. military set in motion the dispossession and displacement of the region's Indigenous peoples. Whether its scene was derived from memories of her father's trading post or solely from Emma's imagination will never be known. In the sketch, a small cluster of log buildings are framed by a backdrop of snowy hills. Two armed men stand guard near the post, while a third man—perhaps the trader himself—approaches a woman in a long dress bearing a load of wood on her back, evoking an impression of the first meeting between Emma Wells's white father and Indigenous mother.

–LF

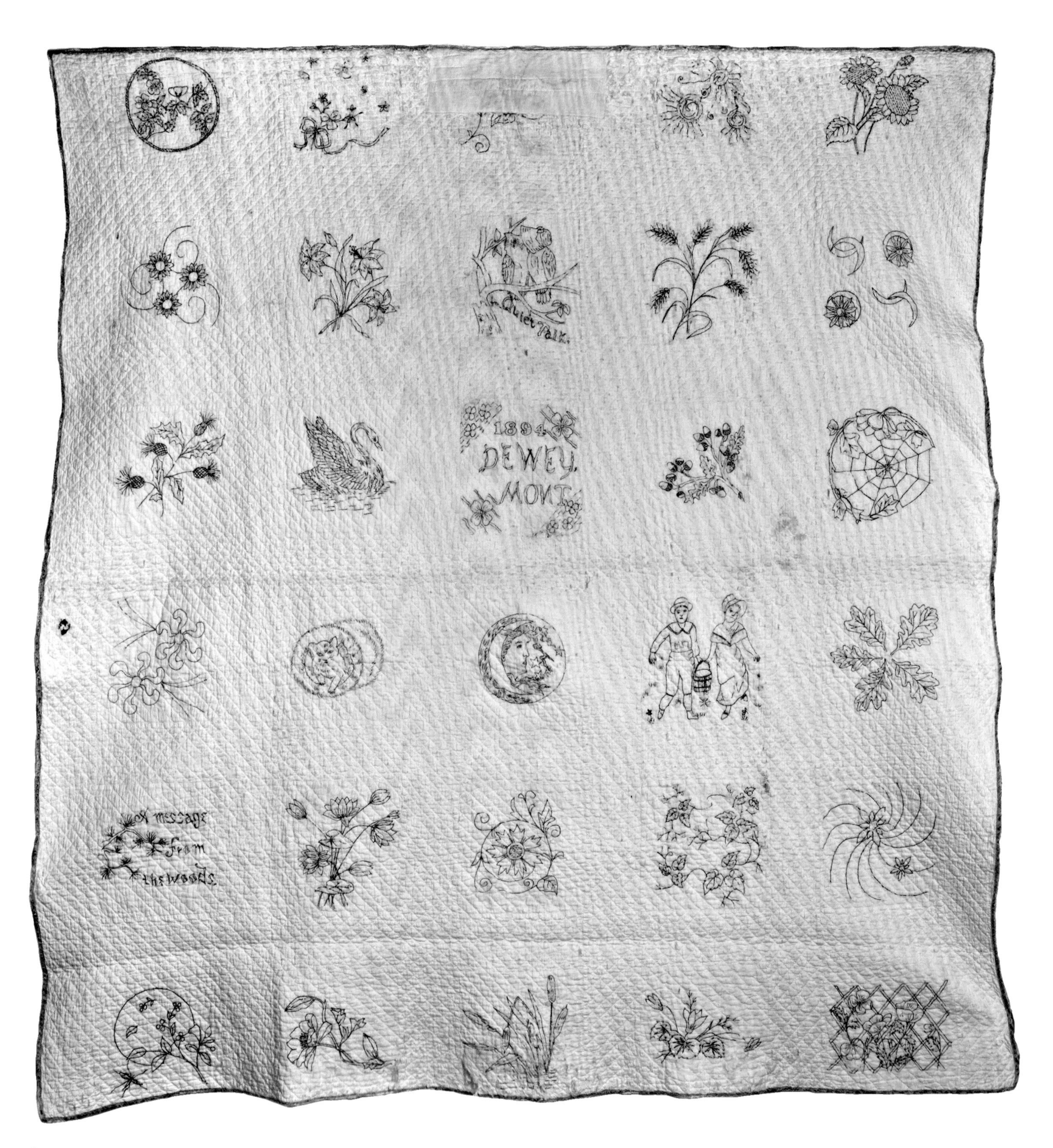
Quiet Talk.
1894
DEWEY.
MONT
A message
from
the woods.

21. Embroidered Quilt

ca. 1894, 67" × 72", by Maggie Halbert Hand (1869–1948).

John Reddy, photographer. Gift of Susan Hand, x1964.12.03

Arriving in Montana in the early 1890s, Maggie Halbert (ca. 1869–1935) taught at a one-room schoolhouse in Beaverhead County near Dewey. At the turn of the twentieth century, rural teachers ran the day-to-day operations of schools, from teaching classes to chopping firewood for the woodstove. They had to be resourceful, as school districts did not have large budgets for materials and supplies. In addition, students often left school for large portions of the year to work on family farms, so teachers had to adjust the curriculum to fit their students' truncated schedules.

Despite its difficulties, teaching was an empowering act for many rural women. Although they worked just as hard, female teachers were typically paid 20 percent less than their male colleagues and were forced to resign if they married. The profession afforded women a place in the economic sphere and provided opportunities to shape and contribute to their community outside of the household. Rural schools often hosted events like dances, holiday programs, and church services outside school hours, making them a hub of social and cultural life.

Maggie Halbert, who came to Montana at the age of twenty-one and taught at Dewey, used this quilt, which she stitched with her mother, to keep her students warm when they became ill at school. Decorated with thirty nature-themed vignettes, the quilt is embroidered in a whimsical style that reflects popular children's art during this period. Halbert retired from teaching after 1894 when she married Horace Hand, a Canadian farmer, and moved to a ranch near Lavon Station in Madison County. She continued to use the quilt while raising her own children. In 1964 her daughter, Susan Hand—also a teacher—donated it to the Society's collections. Today, the quilt's worn condition testifies to its frequent use and many washings, a reminder of the sacrifices made by rural schoolteachers and the care they showed their students. *–AK*

22. American Federation of Labor Charter

1908, 13¼" × 22½". Gift of Al Ekblad, Executive Secretary, Montana AFL-CIO, Montana State AFL-CIO Records, 1895–2000, MC 341

◈

BUTTE has long been referred to as the Gibraltar of organized labor. The 1893 industrial depression made it clear that only well-organized labor unions with large treasuries could survive troubling economic conditions, and this realization motivated Montana's two central labor bodies—the Butte Industrial Conference and the State Trades and Labor Assembly in Helena—to meet in 1895 and merge into one organization, the State Trades and Labor Council of Montana. In 1903, the federation officially changed its name to the Montana Federation of Labor (MFL).

Initially, the state federation rejected the conservative policies of the craft-oriented American Federation of Labor (AFL), allying instead with the Western Federation of Miners in the creation of the American Labor Union, whose mission stated a commitment to "organizing all workers regardless of craft, skill, race, gender, or ethnic origin." By 1902, the MFL openly endorsed the Socialist Party of Montana, but a growing number of federation members disagreed with this affiliation and local unions increasingly began to endorse Democratic and Republican candidates who pushed for labor legislation.

A fight over union chartering weakened the MFL in 1906, and a year later its president, Alex Fairgrieve, attended the national AFL convention in an attempt to shore up the state federation. While there, he assured the delegates that his own organization differed little in policy and procedure from the national body. Fairgrieve admitted that while historically the MFL had "been controlled by those who rebelled against the other States and against the American Federation of Labor," a more collaborative relationship was in store. Upon his return to Montana, Fairgrieve completed the necessary paperwork for AFL affiliation, and the state federation received this AFL charter on January 2, 1908.

Charters signify much more than the establishment of legal entities. They celebrate the organization, announce its goals and values, and declare its role in the larger society. Such documents identify major figures by name and represent many members in spirit. This 1908 Montana Federation of Labor charter embodies a moment in time when the organization rejected its more radical past to join the nationally powerful, politically conservative American Federation of Labor. Along with other union charters donated to the Montana Historical Society, it represents the battle for the soul of Montana's labor. *–RA*

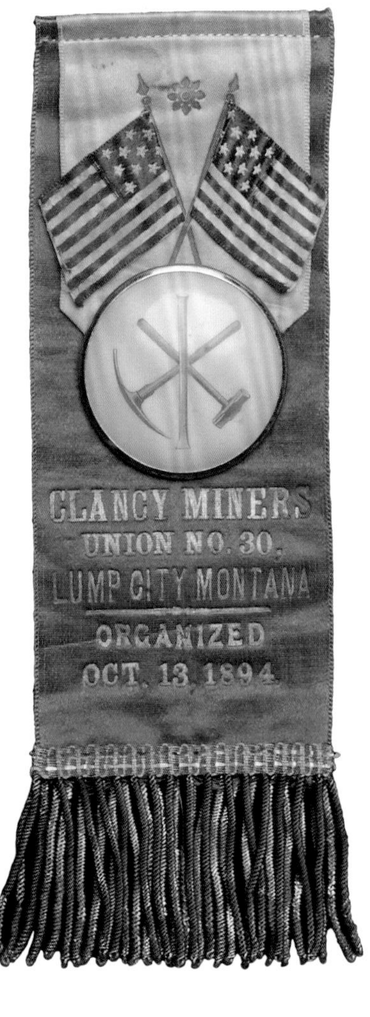

Miners throughout the state proudly wore silk ribbons like this one from Clancy for parades and Union Day celebrations. The reverse side of this ribbon is black with silver lettering for wear at funerals or on other solemn occasions. 2¼" x 7⅝".
Gift of Jess Wilkinson, X1940.02.01

AMERICAN

FEDERATION of LABOR

DOTH GRANT THIS

Certificate of Affiliation

To Alexander Fairgrieve M. M. Donoghue Howard O. Smith,
Thomas J. Chope A. D. Pengh Hugh McDonald W. G. Jarrett
Frank C. Ives A. Brown John Egan
F. A. Bigelow S. D. Anderson J. A. Weodahl

and to their successors legally qualified, to constitute the Union herein named and known under the title of

Montana State Federation of Labor,

for the purpose of a thorough organization of the trade, and a more perfect Federation of all **TRADES** *and* **LABOR UNIONS.** *And the Union being duly formed, is empowered and authorized to initiate into its membership any person or persons in accordance with its own laws. And to conduct the business affairs of said Union in compliance with the best interests of the trade and labor in general. The autonomy of the Union is hereby ordained and secured.*

Provided, *That the said Union do conform to the Constitution, Laws, Rules and Regulations of the* **AMERICAN FEDERATION OF LABOR,** *and in default thereof, or any part, this Certificate of Affiliation may be suspended or revoked according to the laws of this* **FEDERATION.** *And should the said* Montana State Federation of Labor *be dissolved, suspended or forfeit this Certificate of Affiliation, then the persons to whom this Certificate of Affiliation is granted, or their successors, bind themselves to surrender the same with such other property as shall properly belong to this* **FEDERATION.** *And further, in consideration of the due performance of the above, the*

AMERICAN FEDERATION OF LABOR

does hereby bind itself to support the said Montana State Federation of Labor *in the exercise of all its rights, privileges and autonomy as an affiliated Union.*

In Witness Whereof, *We have subscribed our Names and affixed the* **SEAL** *of the American Federation of Labor, this* Second *day of* January *A. D. One Thousand Nine Hundred and Eight.*

	Sam Gompers	President.
	James Duncan	1st Vice-President.
	John Mitchell	2d " "
	Jas. O'Connell	3rd " "
	Max Morris	4th " "
EXECUTIVE COUNCIL.	Denis A. Hayes	5th " "
	Danl. J. Keefe	6th " "
	Wm. D. Huber	7th " "
	Jos. F. Valentine	8th " "
	John B. Lennon	Treasurer.
	Frank Morrison	Secretary.

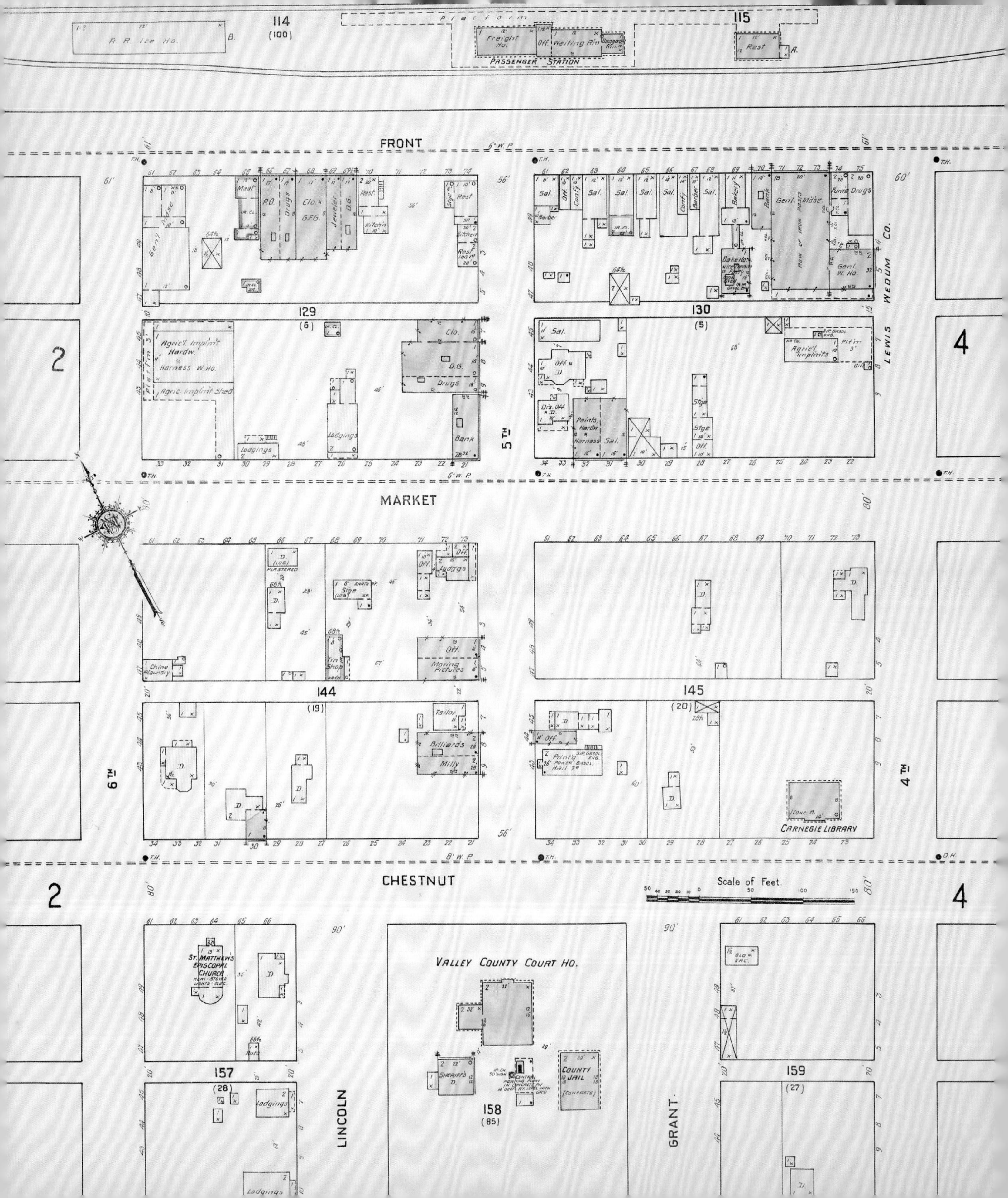

114
(100)
115
R. R. Ice Ho.
Platform
Freight Ho.
Off.
Waiting Rm
Baggage Rm.
PASSENGER STATION
Rest
FRONT
MARKET
CHESTNUT
5TH
6TH
4TH
LINCOLN
GRANT
LEWIS
WEDUM CO.
2
4
129
(6)
130
(5)
144
(19)
145
(20)
157
(28)
158
(85)
159
(27)
Genl. Mdse
Meat
P.O.
Drugs
Clo. & G.F.G.
Jeweler
D.G.
Rest
Kitchn
Stge
Sal.
Barber
Conf'y
Bakery
Bank
Furn.
Bake Ho.
Genl. W. Ho.
Row of Iron Posts
Agric'l. Implmt Hardw. & Harness W. Ho.
Platform
Agric'l. Implmt Shed
Lodgings
Clo.
D.G.
Drugs
Bank
Off. & D.
Drs. Off.
Paints, Hardw & Harness
Agric'l. Implmts
Chine Laundry
Tin Shop
Off.
Moving Pictures
Lodgs
Tailor
Billiards
Milly
Print'g
Hall 2d
CARNEGIE LIBRARY
Scale of Feet.
ST. MATTHEW'S EPISCOPAL CHURCH
VALLEY COUNTY COURT HO.
SHERIFF'S D.
COUNTY JAIL (CONCRETE)
Auto

23. Sanborn Map of Glasgow

1910, 21½" × 25½". Sanborn Map #3

◈

THE Sanborn Map Collection constitutes the largest and one of the most important collections among the eleven thousand maps archived at the Montana Historical Society Library. Created to help insurance companies determine fire risk, these maps document the growth of Montana's towns and cities, large and small, from 1884 to 1967.

Sanborn maps take their name from Massachusetts civil engineer and surveyor Daniel Alfred Sanborn. In 1866, the Aetna Insurance Company asked Sanborn for fire insurance maps of several Tennessee cities, which he created, coding his work in such a way that provided a detailed overview of the width and names of streets; house and block numbers; water main locations; construction materials; the sizes and heights of each building; the locations of windows, doors, and additions; and the uses and occupants of each structure. Following his initial project, Sanborn began mapping other towns and selling his information. By the time of Sanborn's death in 1883, the Sanborn Map Company employed a battalion of surveyors and cartographers who mapped communities throughout the nation.

Initially, the maps were bound in large volumes by city and town. The Library of Congress served as the primary repository (twelve thousand municipalities were included) for these resources, but in 1955 it donated duplicates to archives and libraries across the country, including the Montana Historical Society.

While the needs of fire insurance companies shaped the information included on the Sanborn maps, today they provide invaluable information to city planners, historic preservationists, urban geographers, social historians, and genealogists. They are of particular value for studying the development of cities and towns in the West, many of which were established not long before the Sanborn surveys in the 1880s.

Because the Sanborn Company periodically resurveyed communities, the maps are a valuable source for tracking change over time. Butte's maps, for example, span the years between 1884 and 1959.

The illustrated maps contain information unavailable in any other documentary source, and the Montana Historical Society's collection includes maps of Montana's major cities and small towns, from Absarokee to Worden. Through their detailed drawings, they reflect the story of Montana's development: the growth and decline of mining camps and homesteading communities, the impact of the railroad and the automobile, where people lived, and the type of work they performed.

Like all other Sanborn fire insurance maps, this detail of a 1910 lithograph of Glasgow is coded with color: pink for masonry construction, yellow for wood-frame, and blue for stone. Drawn at a scale of fifty feet to one inch, the map measures just over twenty-one inches tall by twenty-five inches wide. *–BS*

24. Rural Letter Carriers' Banner

ca. 1923, 27½" × 41½". Gift of Montana Rural Letter Carriers Association, 1995.48.01

◈

This banner was displayed at annual conventions of the Montana Rural Letter Carriers Association (MRLCA). The forty-one-inch-high standard is made of silk, trimmed with gold braid and fringe, and boasts a hand-painted scene of a distant homestead nestled against a backdrop of massive mountains. Clusters of bitterroots—Montana's state flower—complete the decorative motif.

Montana had over six hundred post offices by the time it achieved statehood in 1889, yet rural residents did not have adequate access to mail service. Consequently, Montanans joined the fight for Rural Free Delivery, and in 1896 Congress appropriated forty thousand dollars for rural mail service across the nation. Country dwellers could now petition for mail delivery directly to their homes. Montana's first successful petition came from farmers near Billings in 1901, and many others followed suit. By the late 1930s, nearly 180 rural letter carriers across the state covered a total of six thousand miles each day to deliver mail.

Rural Free Delivery had a tremendous impact on life in rural Montana. It encouraged county and municipal governments to invest in infrastructure, as roads had to pass a U.S. Postal Service inspection to be included on routes. Mail carriers came to be known as the "eyes and the ears of rural communities," ensuring the welfare of infirm or elderly customers and guaranteeing the arrival of goods or medicine to those in need. In addition, by providing more reliable communication, Rural Free Delivery alleviated the isolation felt by many rural Montanans.

Despite all they did for their communities, rural letter carriers received little pay, sometimes barely enough to cover the costs of delivering the mail. They were not reimbursed for upkeep of the horses or automobiles that they used to carry out their job, and the routes they worked were often over thirty miles long, which on a good day could take ten hours to complete. During the winter, a route could become a two-day job, with carriers sleeping at families' homes along the way.

Montana's rural mailmen organized the MRLCA in 1923, twenty years after the formation of the National Rural Letter Carriers Association (NRLCA). The NRLCA and MRLCA advocated for increased compensation and better working conditions. The groups had limited success in the first half of the twentieth century, with Montana carriers winning some reimbursement for mileage they accrued on routes, but the fight for adequate pay proved more difficult. Public service employees, including the postal service's mail carriers, did not gain the formal right to bargain collectively until 1962. Once they did, rural letter carriers selected the NRLCA as their collective bargaining representative, making it one of the first formally recognized public-sector trade unions. Through these accomplishments, rural carriers and unions affected the course of national politics.

Montanans brought rural mail delivery to their communities by organizing and petitioning for their right to access information. Rural letter carriers went—and still go—above and beyond, delivering more to their communities than just letters and packages. The MRLCA's banner represents the ties of interdependence that bind our state's rural communities together. *–AK*

R.L.C.A.
MONTANA.

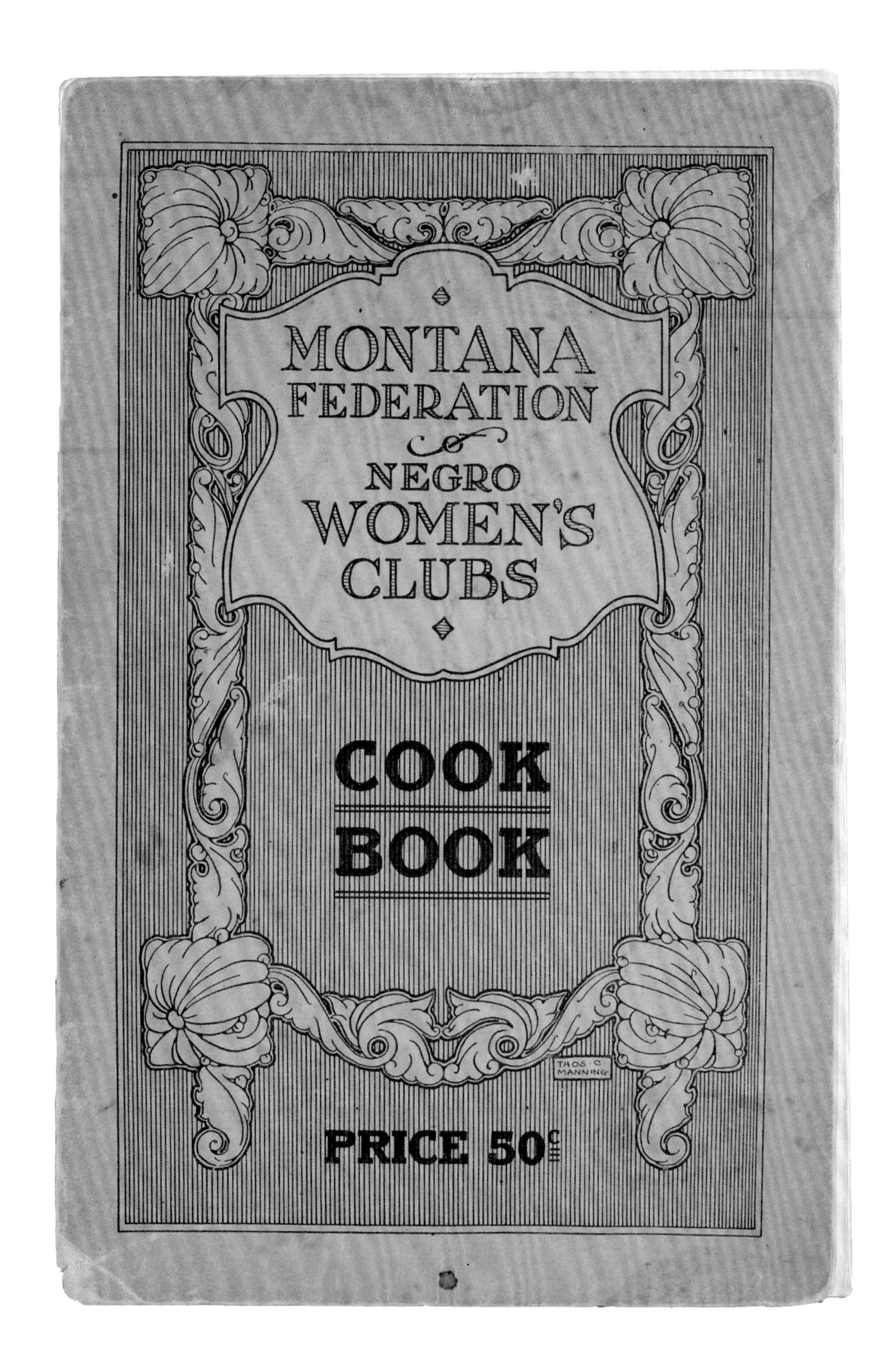
MONTANA
FEDERATION
of
NEGRO
WOMEN'S
CLUBS
COOK
BOOK
THOS. C. MANNING
PRICE 50cts

25. Montana Federation of Negro Women's Clubs Cookbook

ca. 1926, 6" × 9¼". Gift of Montana Federation of Negro Women's Clubs, Locker CKB 641.5 N312

◈

PROMISING "choice recipes of cateresses and the best cooks in the state," this cookbook is a culinary time capsule, offering recipes for such diverse preparations as "creamed ludiefisk," "sauerkraut salad," and "mashed potato doughnuts." Sold for fifty cents, it fits neatly into the history of fund-raising cookbooks, just as the Montana Federation of Negro Women's Clubs—from 1947 on known as the Montana Federation of Colored Women's Clubs (MFCWC)—fits into the larger story of the women's club movement. Both the book and organization are exceptional in many ways, as they help tell the story of African Americans in Montana.

Affiliated with the National Association of Colored Women's Clubs, the MFCWC was formed "to encourage true womanhood . . . [and] promote interest in social uplift." It represented ninety individual members and fifteen clubs across the state, including the Kalispell Mutual Improvement Club (est. 1913), the Helena Pleasant Hour Club (1916), the Butte Pearl Club (1918), and the Billings Phyllis Wheatley Club (1920). These clubs undertook many of the traditional tasks of socially organized women, such as providing educational scholarships, ministering to the sick, and hosting get-togethers.

At the same time, the MFCWC and its affiliated clubs helped build community for African American women living in a state that had fewer than 1,700 black residents in 1920. They also provided a platform for asserting their community's respectability and defying negative stereotypes while advocating for civil rights. Among other causes, MFCWC supported the work of the National Association for the Advancement of Colored People, sought enforcement of anti-lynching laws, and worked to abolish the poll tax. Through its legislative committee, the MFCWC fought for civil rights protections in Montana, where in the 1940s establishments in cities like Great Falls still refused to serve African Americans, including servicemen stationed at the nearby airbase. In 1955, it successfully lobbied for the passage of H.B. 52, which guaranteed "the full and equal enjoyment of all places of public accommodation and amusement." The bill as passed did not include any mechanism for enforcement, but it was nonetheless a symbolic victory.

In 1971, the MFCWC affiliated with the General Federation of Women's Clubs, and club president Marie Lacey suggested that "integration has limited the need for an all-black club." The next year, MFCWC voted to disband. It left behind a fifty-year history of working for equality for all Montanans while providing a welcoming community for its members. Throughout the MFCWC's existence, members proudly embraced the federation's values, expressed in the song "Lifting as We Climb," composed for the organization by Billings member Emma Harris, who also compiled the cookbook:

> "On to Victory" is our cry,
> Lifting others as we climb high;
> Trusting God to lead the way—
> Onward march into the fray:
> Work in faith and harmony
> Preserve in Unity.
> We're for the right we will win our fight
> And shall gain the victory.

–*SAT*

26. Glazed Earthenware Block from St. Peter's Hospital

1930, 17" × 4" × 18¼". 1991.43.01

◈

A SERIES of ornamental, hand-pressed, glazed-earthenware blocks such as this one once adorned the entry of the Conrad Kohrs Memorial wing of the old St. Peter's Hospital at the corner of 11th Avenue and Logan Street in Helena. Founded by Episcopalians in the 1880s, St. Peter's was Montana's first Protestant hospital. The wing, financed in 1932 by Augusta Kohrs in memory of her late husband, was part of a large hospital complex designed by renowned architect Cass Gilbert.

While frontier doctors battled gunshot wounds, mine accidents, tuberculosis, and epidemics, women helped establish hospitals and developed nurses' training courses. Women's efforts played vital roles in refining Montana's healthcare.

Only haphazard medical services existed in the Helena area when five Sisters of Charity of Leavenworth, Kansas, arrived in 1869. Theirs was a threefold mission: to teach youth, care for orphans, and tend the sick. Within a year, these trained nurses founded St. John's Hospital, the first of Montana's many Catholic teaching hospitals. Other sisters soon came from Kansas to found more hospitals: St. Joseph's at Deer Lodge (est. 1873), St. Mary's at Virginia City (1875), St. James at Butte (1881), and St. Ann's at Anaconda (1889).

In 1883, Montana's Episcopal bishop, Leigh Brewer, and his board of trustees sought to establish a Protestant alternative to the growing number of Catholic institutions. Although men made up the board of trustees, Helena women took the lead in running St. Peter's Hospital. Women hired staff, oversaw patient care, managed the books, cooked, cleaned, and organized the hospital's finances. Dr. Maria Dean, one of Montana's first licensed female physicians, was long associated with St. Peter's.

While St. Peter's operated a Protestant nursing school, Catholic sisters remained at the forefront of nurse training in Montana. The first class at Butte's St. James School of Nursing graduated in 1909. By 1967, more than one thousand nurses had graduated from St. James, and 60 percent of all nurses in southwestern Montana had trained there.

The Deaconess movement, which rose from within Methodist and other Protestant denominations, also greatly impacted Montana's medical care. The Chicago Training School sent many of its graduate Deaconess nurses to Montana. Augusta Ariss, among the first, arrived in 1902 to take charge of the fledgling Montana Deaconess Hospital in Great Falls. As its longtime superintendent, Ariss helped establish the Montana State Board of Nursing in 1913. Because of her influence, nurses—not doctors—administered the board. Later, Deaconess-run hospitals opened in Butte, Sidney, Havre, and Billings, with teaching hospitals in Glasgow and Bozeman.

The historical record shows that dedicated women were the driving force behind the hospitals that today serve Montanans across the state. They set a precedent for expanding medical services to meet the state's growing population and, in so doing, left a profound legacy that lives on in Montana's modern healthcare. *–EB*

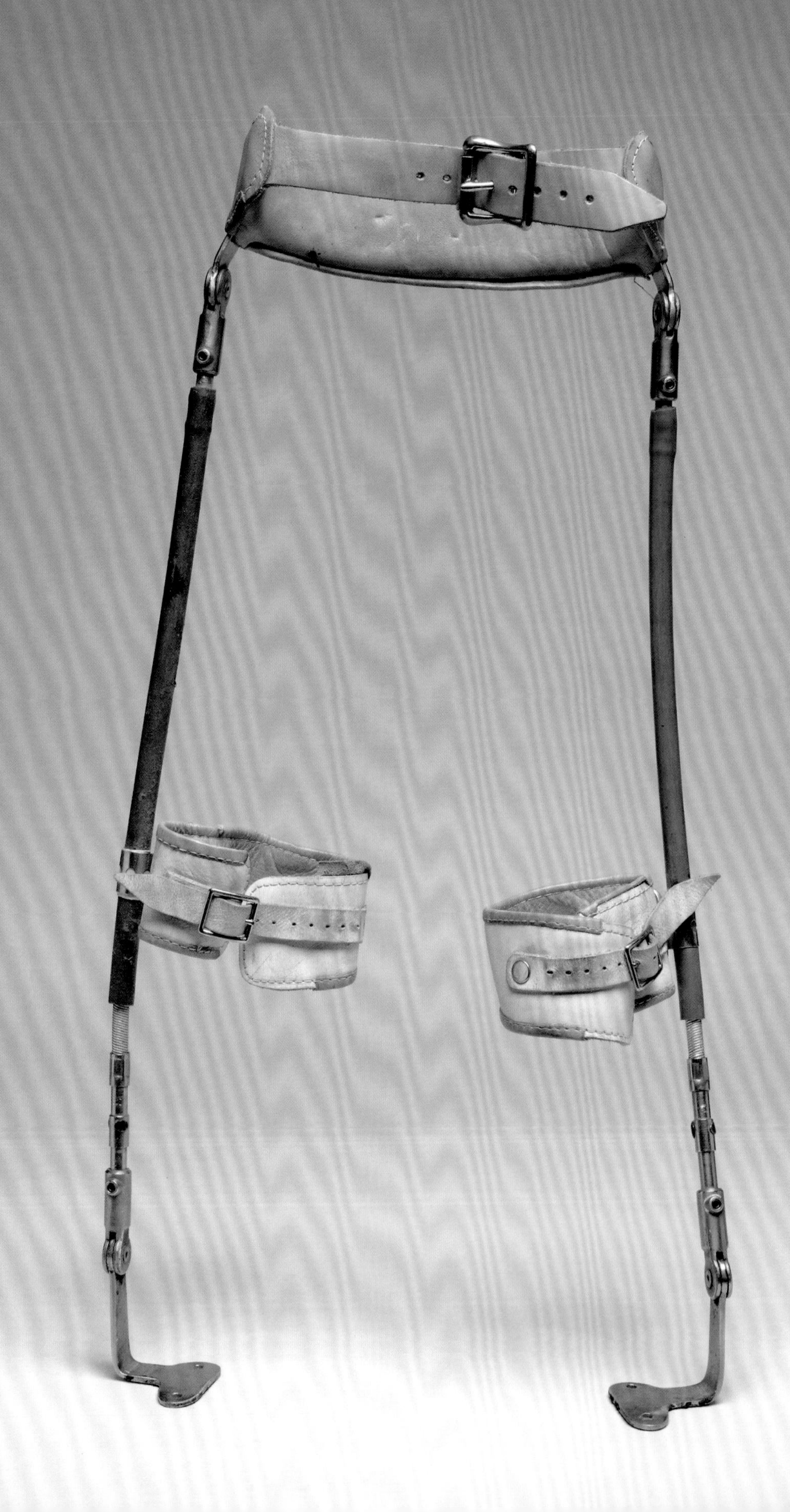

27. Child's Polio Braces

ca. 1950, 8¾" × 4⅝" × 22⅜". Gift of Steve Nistler, 2015.59.02

◈

Nearly every summer throughout the early twentieth century, the poliomyelitis virus swept through the United States. Attacking the nervous system, the virus causes severe respiratory difficulty and muscle atrophy, and can lead to permanent paralysis and even death. In 1916 alone, a nationwide polio epidemic killed six thousand American children and crippled twenty-seven thousand more. That year, Montana's public health officials documented more than one hundred cases of polio in the state and twenty-four deaths. Sounding the alarm, the *Helena Independent* ran a sensational headline: "Awful Scourge Creeping West, Baby Paralysis Yet Unchecked."

Remarkably, throughout the 1910s, polio received no more than a sentence in the Biennial Reports from the Montana State Board of Health. At the time, the board expressed greater concern regarding the more common diseases of tuberculosis, scarlet fever, measles, and smallpox. It was polio, however, that many parents feared most. The disease often caused paralysis, leading to segregation and stigmatization. Since most of the work in Montana's farming, ranching, mining, and logging communities required physical strength and agility, paralysis often prevented the afflicted from earning a living or contributing to a family enterprise. It also meant isolation, as discrimination against those with disabilities would not be prohibited by law (and public accommodations to serve them required) until the 1990 Americans with Disabilities Act.

In 1916, St. Vincent's Hospital in Billings became an early center for treating children crippled by polio. Later, families across Montana brought their children to Shodair Children's Hospital in Helena for treatment. The hospital had grown out of the Montana Children's Home, founded as a Protestant orphanage in 1897. Since many of the children living at the orphanage required medical attention, the institution constructed a children's hospital in 1930. In 1938, grocer and successful real estate developer Louis Shodair donated two hundred thousand dollars to finance the construction of a new wing, where an "up-to-date physical therapy department made it one of the region's best hospitals for pediatric polio care." The hospital was renamed in his honor.

Polio continued to menace children throughout the 1940s and 1950s. In 1954, children in four Montana counties took part in clinical trials for a "killed virus" polio vaccine, the largest of their kind in U.S. history. The following year, after the vaccine had been proven safe and effective, nationwide immunization programs began in earnest. By 1960, polio cases fell to one hundred per year nationally—a grand victory considering that the state of Montana alone suffered over one hundred cases per year between 1950 and 1954. The disease was successfully eradicated from Montana by the early 1970s.

Recalling the experience of wearing polio braces, commonly used by those afflicted with the disease, one survivor said, "It was stand stiff-legged or don't stand." A leather belt helped secure the rigid metal braces around the waist, while shorter straps, or "sleeves," attached the irons farther down each leg. Hinged below the knee, the braces allowed some flexibility of movement but not much. The mid-twentieth-century braces shown here are child-sized, measuring just twenty-two inches from shoe plate to waist. They were found stuffed in a crawl space during 2015 renovations to the building that housed Shodair Hospital from 1938 to 1997. *–MK*

Liberty

Montana Mosaic

◈

The history of the Treasure State is a colorful mosaic pieced together by many different cultures. As the first residents of this region, Indigenous peoples—Plains and Plateau tribes, each with its own unique history and culture—jointly laid the foundation from which the rest of Montana's story evolved. The fur trade brought in the first significant upsurge of non-Indians, followed by the discovery of gold, which lured (mostly) men from around the world. Thereafter, successive waves brought not only men, but women and children, seeking economic opportunity and a better life.

Initially, immigration was largely unregulated, but in the early 1880s federal rules began restricting entry into the United States. Efforts to prohibit or curtail immigration were focused on those perceived to be incompatible with the dominant Anglo culture. Consequently, people from Canada and western Europe comprised the majority of Montana's immigrant population throughout the early twentieth century, while Asians, Latinos, and eastern Europeans encountered new and consequential barriers. In Montana, minority populations—like the Chinese and Japanese, as well as Indigenous peoples—faced increasing legal and social discrimination.

From the beginning, foreign-born individuals like Irish general Thomas F. Meagher made their mark on Montana. Later, broader developments, including the advent of industrial mining in Butte and Red Lodge and the homesteading boom in eastern Montana, brought multitudes of newcomers in numbers far surpassing those who had come before. Many of these immigrants came directly from distant countries, while others had temporarily stayed in other parts of the United States and Canada but nonetheless maintained strong ethnic identities to their country of origin. Once here, these groups often maintained close ties and held on

Mounted Crazy Quilt, ca. 1889, 25" × 39½", made by Minnie Fligelman (1867–1891). John Reddy, photographer. Gift of Frieda Fligelman and Belle F. Winestine, X1949.04.01

Railroads employed large numbers of Asian laborers, generally assigning them more menial and dangerous jobs at lower pay than their white counterparts. These four Japanese men—identified only as Charlie, Jim, Flag, and Tom—worked for the Northern Pacific Railway at Hell Gate, near Missoula, May 19, 1909. PAc 75–78.26

Born enslaved, Mary Fields came to Montana in 1885 at the behest of the Ursuline Sisters who operated St. Peter's Mission. Known for both her tough persona and kind heart, she later secured a U.S. post office contract to deliver the mission's mail by wagon from Cascade, fifteen miles away. The job earned her the moniker "Stagecoach Mary."
Mary Fields, by Amy Brakeman Livezey (b. 1964), oil on board, 2018, 25½" × 25½". 2018.17.01

to cherished aspects of their heritage; at the same time, they embraced life in their new home.

As the twentieth century progressed, the mosaic continued to change. African American, Chinese, and Japanese populations shrank, while other groups increased in number. Following World War II, Mexican Americans and Hutterites—members of a communal, Anabaptist ethnoreligious group—expanded their presence in the state's agricultural sector. In addition, new groups, like the Laotian Hmong, escaped from war-torn homelands to find refuge in Montana. Today, the contributions of some ethnic groups—such as the Irish, Métis, and Germans from Russia—are relatively well-known. The stories of others remain largely untold, but they nonetheless belong to the diverse patchwork of Montana's history.

28. *Thomas Francis Meagher*

1905, 72" × 36" × 108", by Charles J. Mulligan (1866–1916).

Gift of the Meagher Memorial Association, x1905.16.01

◈

In the summer of 1867, Irish revolutionary and Montana's acting territorial governor Thomas Francis Meagher disappeared along the banks of the Missouri River at Fort Benton, his ineffectual term cut short at age forty-four. Despite his lackluster career in the territory, Meagher's successful early life made him a symbol of Irish Catholic pride in Montana. His statue stands today not in honor of his specific accomplishments in the Treasure State, but as a monument to its Irish Catholic heritage.

The son of a wealthy merchant, Meagher emerged as a fiery revolutionary for Irish independence in 1847, earning the nickname "Meagher of the Sword." By 1848, his rhetoric against the British secured him lifetime banishment to a penal colony in Tasmania. In 1852, Meagher escaped the island and made his way to New York City. Once established in the United States, Meagher founded the *Irish News*, lectured across the country on Irish independence, opened a law office, and dabbled in various business ventures. With the outbreak of the Civil War, he organized and led the Sixty-Ninth New York Regiment as part of the Union Army's "Irish Brigade." Meagher rose to the rank of brigadier general, fighting and surviving unscathed through some of the war's bloodiest battles.

Following the war, President Andrew Johnson offered Meagher a sinecure: the post of secretary of Montana Territory. Barely a week after arriving in Montana in September 1865, Meagher became acting governor when Governor Sidney Edgerton left the state. Facing bigotry and bitter partisan politics, Meagher held a fruitless legislative session in which all of the bills passed were nullified by Congress a year later. He also convened a statehood convention, but the constitution was never put to a vote. His opponents called his administration opportunistic and corrupt. When he died, Meagher had nothing to show for his efforts.

When statehood did finally come for Montana in 1889, copper magnates William Clark and Marcus Daly differed on the question of where to site the new capital. The state's Protestant Irish, or "Orangemen," rallied around Clark in support of Helena, while Irish Catholics led by Daly favored Anaconda. Though Helena won out in 1894, Anaconda's supporters still sought to make their mark on the capital. In 1904, the Meagher Memorial Association, with Daly at the helm, raised twenty thousand dollars by public subscription to fund a statue of Thomas Francis Meagher to be placed in Helena.

Thirty-eight years after he met a mysterious fate along the Missouri River, Meagher reappeared on the state capitol lawn, cast in bronze, sitting atop his horse in full military regalia, and wielding his favorite sword. Designed by artist Charles J. Mulligan and cast by the American Bronze Foundry in Chicago, the statue drew thousands to a dedication ceremony on July 4, 1905. Enthusiasm for it and for Montana's Irish Catholic heritage has never waned. A three-year fundraising effort saw the statue restored in 1964. In 2004, the Helena members of the Irish civic organization, the Ancient Order of Hibernians, and the Montana Historical Society raised funds to restore the statue again, just in time to celebrate its centennial and rededicate the statue on July 4, 2005.

–*CB*

M
1899
MONTANA

29. Gabriel Dumont's Saddle

ca. 1870, 35¼" × 44" (including stirrups). Gift of Luke D. Sweetman, x1964.16.01

◈

This Plains Cree–style saddle was owned by Métis rights advocate Gabriel Dumont. The saddle was made with deer hide and wool cloth, stuffed with buffalo wool, and decorated with glass seed beads. Rawhide straps hold metal stirrups that have been modified to prevent the toe from slipping. It can be distinguished as a pad saddle—common among the Métis, Blackfeet, Assiniboine, Cree, Dakota, and Sarcee peoples—in that it has no pommel, which enables its rider to lean forward to shoot or to avoid being hit by enemy fire.

Its elaborate beadwork and asymmetrical floral designs are typical of the Métis style and reflect the longstanding cultural exchange between Indigenous peoples and the French, who were the first Europeans to introduce beads as a trade item in North America. Intermarriage between French fur traders and Cree, Chippewa, and Dakota women in the 1600s produced a new ethnic group: the Métis, whose language, religious practices, and customs reflected the syncretic merging of cultures from both continents. Métis men and women worked in the fur trade and moved with it across the continent. By the early 1800s, large Métis populations occupied both sides of the U.S.-Canadian border in what are now Alberta, Saskatchewan, Manitoba, Montana, North Dakota, and Minnesota.

Gabriel Dumont, 1885 942–021

Although the Métis population dominated the Red River region, the newly formed Canadian federation—created by the British parliament in 1867—did not recognize their claims to the territory. Without a voice in government when Canada annexed the region in 1869, French-speaking Métis representatives led by Louis Riel were frustrated in their attempts to secure the full rights of citizenship, a shared government, and land tenure. Fearing that their Francophone, Catholic culture would be marginalized by Anglophone settlers, they eventually established their own provisional government in what became known as the Red River Rebellion. The Manitoba Act of 1870 established the region as a Canadian province and ostensibly acknowledged Métis land claims and cultural rights, but Riel was soon forced into exile by the Canadian government following the execution of a British Canadian official.

In subsequent years, Gabriel Dumont, a prominent political and military leader, continued to champion autonomy and land rights for the Métis. Born in 1837 in St. Boniface, Assiniboia (now Winnipeg, Manitoba), Dumont was the son of French voyageur

Isidore Duncan and his Cree or Chippewa wife, Louise Laframboise. Early in life he earned a reputation as a skilled bison hunter and marksman, and in the 1870s he established Gabriel's Crossing, a ferry and store on the lower Saskatchewan River near Batoche.

In 1884, Dumont traveled to Montana Territory to bring Riel, who had been teaching at St. Peter's Mission on the Sun River, to lead an armed resistance against the Canadian government. Known as the adjutant general of his people, Dumont acted as Riel's war chief in the 1885 North-West Rebellion. Although the Métis won some impressive victories against the more numerous and better-armed Canadian military, ultimately the Anglo-Canadians prevailed.

Riel was hanged for treason, but Dumont fled across the "Medicine Line" into Montana Territory, where he would remain until the Canadian government promised amnesty to the resistance fighters. He traveled briefly with Buffalo Bill's Wild West Show, which billed him as the "Exiled Chieftain of the Riel Rebellion." After returning to Canada in about 1893, Dumont lived peaceably as a farmer and hunter until his death in 1906.

For a century, the Métis people continued the struggle to assert their political and civil rights while maintaining their cultural heritage. In the 1980s, Métis groups in Canada established the Gabriel Dumont Institute and the Louis Riel Institute to promote Métis history, language, and culture. Today, both men are regarded as cultural heroes—Louis Riel as the "Father of Manitoba" and Gabriel Dumont as a freedom fighter who defended Métis and First Nations existence against Anglo-Canadian imperialism. Now in the possession of the Montana Historical Society, Dumont's saddle stands as testament to his legacy and to the unique cultural traditions of the Métis.

–LF

30. Railroad Press Pass

1893, 5" × 3¼". Gift of Geraldine Austin, Mattie Cramer Papers, MC 255, box 1

◈

Mattie Cramer, a newspaper editor from Iowa and New York, moved with her young son to Malta in 1908 to file papers on a homestead claim. As was true for many homesteaders in the early twentieth century, she had little experience working the land and had to rely on other skills to support her family while proving up. Cramer's railroad press pass, dated 1893, speaks to the different ways in which individuals could make a life for themselves in the West, as well as the boosterism that drew many homesteaders to Montana in the late nineteenth and early twentieth centuries.

Cramer's newspaper background landed her work as the managing editor of the *Malta Enterprise*, and

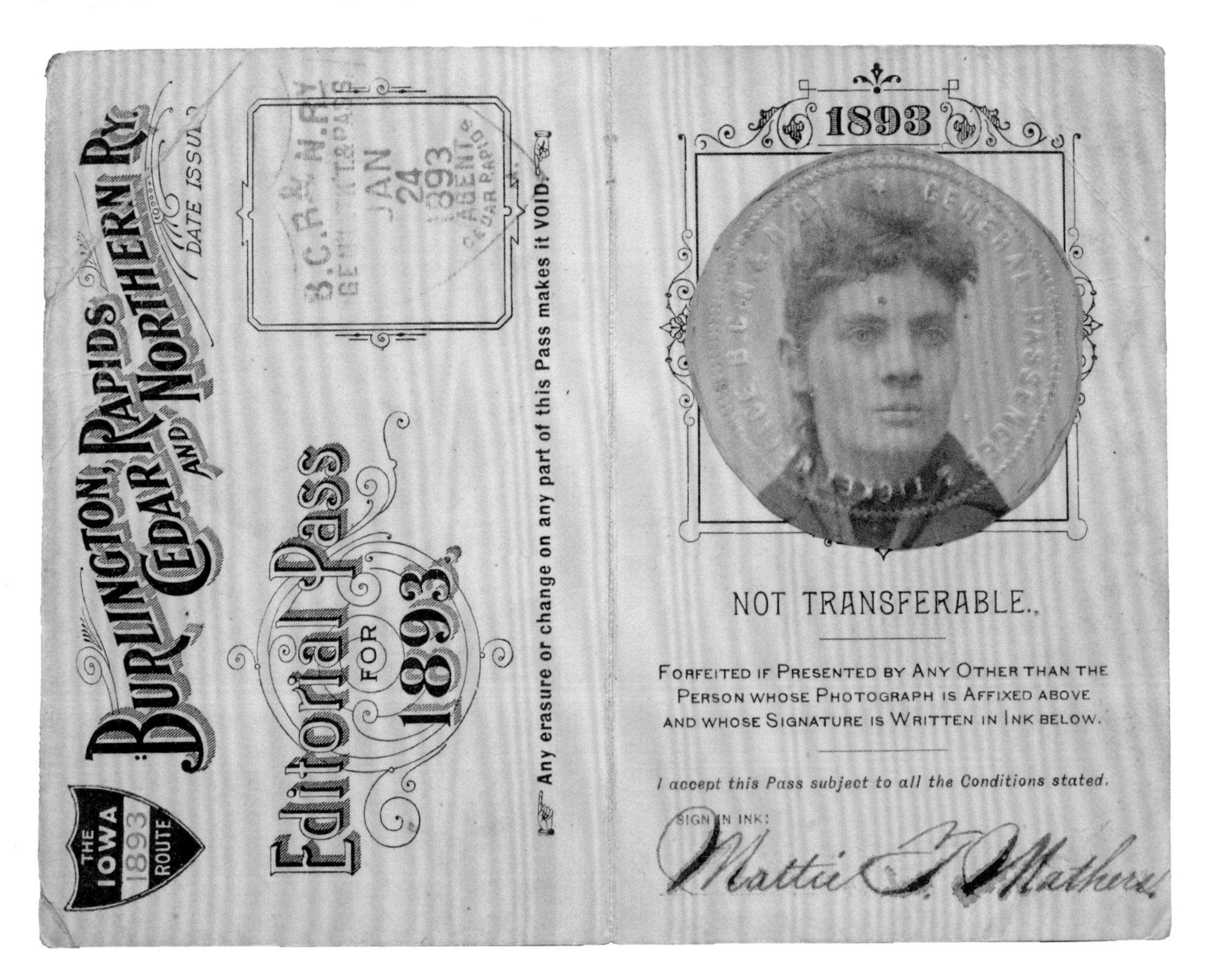

her writing skills garnered a request from Great Northern Railway authorities to submit a testimonial letter regarding her homesteading perspective. Aggressive railway campaigns promising tillable land and wealth for the enterprising homesteader lured thousands westward, many of whom, like Mattie, had no background in agriculture. Mattie's letter was specifically aimed at promoting homesteading among single women, who, according to historian Sarah Carter, made up approximately 18 percent of Montana homesteaders. Cramer wrote skillfully of the challenges and the potential rewards, using humor and offering practical advice.

Between 1913 and 1915, Cramer received correspondence from hundreds of women and men from across the United States requesting information about how to file a claim, what supplies to bring, and what to expect when homesteading in Montana. She responded with personal advice and encouragement:

> Some of my relatives back in Iowa City, Iowa, thought I was mentally deranged when I announced to them in 1908 that I was going to take my little boy, and move to Montana . . . having less than $100.00 . . . I have built a two story frame house on my claim . . . a barn, a chicken house, dug a well, fenced all the land and 21 acres is under cultivation. I consider this a land of unlimited opportunities.

Initially her optimism rang true. The unusually wet years of the early 1900s produced bumper crops of wheat. However, a cycle of drought beginning in 1917 forced many homesteaders to abandon their claims.

Although Cramer enjoyed success on the land and in her profession, by 1914 she had resigned her newspaper job to care for her ailing mother, who had joined her on the homestead. When her mother died in 1919, Mattie leased her homestead and moved to the Puget Sound area. There, she wrote for *The Oracle* in Orting, Washington, and was a secretary at the local chamber of commerce. Cramer returned to her Montana homestead in 1926, where she remained through the 1940s. In the early 1950s, she moved to Great Falls, where she continued writing.

Mattie Cramer's papers, including this press pass, provide invaluable insight into the lives of those who faced the challenge of homesteading, many of whom were not farmers by trade. Her collection complements the many other records of homesteaders found throughout the Society's archives. Together these diaries, writings, letters, and reminiscences provide a colorful glimpse of Montana's homesteading heritage.

–*JF*

1003 Whitney St.
Belvidere Ills. 2/11/14.
Mattie T. Cramer.
Malta Montana.
Dear Madam.
I take this liberty to write to you, after reading your letter in "The Great Northern Land Book."
Desiring to find out more about the great state of Montana, after reading your letter of experience, I chose you to write to, thinking I would get a willing & intelligent reply.
If a "lone woman" can go out there, and do what you have, then surely, one with a strong husband ought to do as much.
The west has been calling us for a long time, but we are not brave, or wise, (I know not just the word to use) to get up & go. we are quite tired of living on a salary, & trying to lay a little by, that little amounts up so slow, with this high cost of living. we feel we must go where land is cheap.
Would it be asking too much of you to answer the following questions: How cold is it in winter, and how warm in summer? how does it compare with Iowa? Have you rain fall enough?

Illinois resident Mrs. A. J. Cassidy, author of this letter, was one of many Americans who sought Cramer's advice after *The Great Northern Land Book* published Cramer's own letter encouraging women to homestead in Montana.
Feb. 11, 1914, 8" × 10". Gift of Geraldine Austin in 1993, MC 255

31. Ruff-Krenzler Wedding Photograph

1912, by Evelyn Cameron. Gift of the estate of Janet Williams. Evelyn J. Cameron Photograph Collection, PAC 90-87.G065-002

On February 22, 1912, British-born photographer and rancher Evelyn Cameron rode to the home of neighboring homesteaders to photograph the wedding party of John Krenzler and Christina Ruff. Recalling the event, Cameron wrote, "About 30 or 40 people. Many fair German girls. Bride & groom, 3 brides maids & ushers sat facing dining room door. I had dinner at small table with a Dakota German who didn't speak English, but never been to Vaterland." In her daily diary, she also noted that in attendance were only five native English speakers, besides herself, and that the rest of the guests were German.

Although they identified themselves as German, both Krenzler and Ruff were born in Besserabia, Russia (present-day Moldova). Like many of the other homesteaders settling in Cabin Creek and Fallon Flats near the now-defunct town of Marsh, in Dawson County, they were descendants of Germans who had settled in Russia in the 1760s at the invitation of Russia's ruler, Catherine the Great. To attract these able farmers, Catherine had offered free transportation to Russia, religious and political autonomy, and exemption from most taxes and military service.

The Germans who came to Russia formed tight-knit communities organized by religious denomination (most commonly Catholic, Lutheran, or Mennonite) and maintained their distinct language, culture, and religious practices. Thus, when Alexander II instituted a "Russification program" in the 1870s, requiring them to serve in the military and to send their children to Russian-speaking schools, whole villages immigrated en masse to the United States, Canada, and South America. Lured by the promise of free land and an escape from compulsory military service, new arrivals—like John Krenzler, who immigrated in 1905, and his bride Christina, who arrived at Ellis Island in 1911—renewed the Russian German community's language and cultural connections.

Of course, their traditions were reflected in their wedding celebrations. The bride's headdress and the groom's and groomsmen's ribbons in this photo follow longstanding customs, as did the home-cooked wedding feast and the liberal consumption of home-brewed beer and "German whiskey."

The community's strong connection to its Russian German heritage even survived World War I, when the state banned the teaching of German in schools and its use in church. After the war ended, German services resumed at both the aptly named American Lutheran Church and the rival Jehovah Lutheran Church, where they continued until the 1950s. Long before that time, however, drought and economic depression had pushed many dryland farmers in the area, including John and Christina Krenzler, off their land. The Krenzlers moved to California in 1938.

–MK

32. Croatian Masonry Tools

ca. 1900–1950, chisels, hammers (including a toothed crandall or finishing hammer), and wooden mallet. Gift of Anton "Tony" and Anna Tuss, 1987.52

◈

Montana's remarkable landscape is famous not only for its natural beauty, abundant grasslands, and precious metals, but also for its many types of stone: granite, phyllite, quartzite, limestone, volcanic rock, and sandstone. Using these quarried materials and simple, yet highly specialized tools, skilled stonemasons laid the foundation for the state's built environment.

Among the most revered craftsmen were Italian and Croatian masters who immigrated to Montana at the turn of the twentieth century. The long traditions of expert masonry in the rocky hills of their homelands translated well to the Montana landscape. Settling in communities like Columbus and Lewistown, these artisans instilled many of Montana's main streets with a sense of beauty and permanence.

Columbus sandstone—abundant in Montana and highly regarded for its quality—graces the exteriors of the state capitol building, county courthouses, bridges, monuments, commercial buildings, and residences across the Treasure State. Italian stone carvers Michael Jacobs (formerly Jacobucci) and Pasqual "Pete" Petosa applied their skills to sculpting monuments. Using a variety of chisels, hammers, and other implements, they plied the hard stone into affecting memorials. The Mountain View Cemetery in Columbus, for example, features a poignant display of their talents.

Pete Tuss, another successful mason and builder, grew up in Bribir, Croatia, and learned the ancient traditions of stonework from his father and grandfather. After working throughout eastern Europe, South America, Canada, and the eastern United States, he arrived in Great Falls in 1897. Soon thereafter, he settled in Lewistown with fellow Croatians. While trees were scarce in central Montana, building stone was abundant, and Tuss found plenty of work there as a mason. He encouraged other countrymen to follow, and by 1915 Lewistown's Croatian population neared one hundred.

Tuss and his fellow masters relied on quality tools, often those they carried with them from the old country. With skill and patience, using hand drills and black powder, they removed six-foot slabs of rock from the sandstone formations at Big Springs Quarry. Two-man teams worked in synchronicity—one swung the hammer, while the other held the drill against the rock, turning the tool gradually between each strike. The quarrymen cleaned and then filled the holes with blasting powder and lit a rope fuse. When the slabs were free, stonecutters used wedges to rough-cut the rock for transportation. Once on the building site, Tuss recalled, "free masons would shape the stone with precision. . . . Using a comb-like axe and different types of chisels, a mason could pitch, carve, or decorate the face of each stone block."

In 1987, Anton and Anna Tuss donated most of a stonemason tool set to the Montana Historical Society. The set includes hand drills and hammers as well as several specialized chisels and smaller mallets used for carving. Made of iron, a stonemason's tools were prized possessions, often handed down through generations. Montana artisans like Tuss, Jacobs, and Petosa used tools such as these to build lasting structures, and Montana towns continue to enjoy the rewards of their hard work and fine craftsmanship.

–KH

33. Finnish-Style Loom

ca. 1916, 71" × 73" × 69", by John "Jack" Veeda. Gift of Marv Hoffer, 1992.26.01

◈

Amanda Perälä Kraftenberg (1882–1952) came to Montana from Lapua, Finland, in 1899. After marrying Fred Kraftenberg two years later, she homesteaded near Little Belt Creek in the Korpivaara (or "Wilderness Hill") community in Cascade County. From 1916 until her death in 1952, Amanda produced a variety of items on this four-harness, counterbalance loom made from pine and willow harvested in the nearby Highwood Mountains. Kraftenberg's textile work was exceptional not only because of her skill as a weaver, but also because she used yarn she had washed, carded, and spun from wool gathered from sheep raised on her family's ranch. Consequently, the rag rugs she wove exemplified both Finnish traditions and Montanans' penchant for making the most out of available resources.

The loom's builder, John "Jack" Veeda, lived near Geyser and crafted many others like it for ranch families in the Highwood area. This loom is typical of those built and used by Finns and embodies the quality associated with Finnish craftsmanship. Wilderness Hill is well-known for its finely crafted log homes with their innovative combination of traditional Finnish construction and modern design, but Amanda's loom offers a strong reminder of the incredible work performed and cultural practices sustained within those homes. The loom was described by Montana weaver Milly Dover, who grew up in Belt, as "Wonderful! Workable!"

Through her textile crafts, Kraftenberg expressed her identity as a Finnish American, integrating her ethnic heritage with patriotism for her adopted country. During the First World War, the *Belt Valley Times* featured a front-page article on Kraftenberg's needlework:

> The yarn is heavier, softer, and warmer than any which can be purchased. . . . The socks are sure to outlast several pairs of socks knitted from manufactured yarn. Mrs. Krafenteberg [*sic*] is to be especially complimented upon the true American spirit which prompted her to go to all the labor which makes it possible for her to do her 'bit' for the boys at the front.

In 2017, members of the Helena Weavers' and Spinners' Guild set up Kraftenberg's loom—using hand-tied heddles like those she had used—to weave a green, brown, and white checked blanket, based on the design of a blanket Kraftenberg had woven for her daughter, Tekla. By doing so, these contemporary artisans paid tribute to Montana's rich traditions of textile work and cultural expression. *–MO*

34. Taylor Gordon Steel Record

1929, 7¼" × 7¼". Gift of Emmanuel Taylor Gordon Estate, Emmanuel Taylor Gordon Papers, MC 150

TAYLOR Gordon (1893–1971), an African American native of White Sulphur Springs, first achieved fame as a singer of spirituals in New York City during the Harlem Renaissance. As a young man, Gordon had worked for circus impresario John Ringling on his private railroad car, which traveled regularly from Montana to New York. It was in the corridors of the train that Taylor's soaring tenor drew the attention of passengers, who encouraged him to pursue a career in music. This steel record, produced in 1929 as an audible letter to his family, is one of the few recordings made of Gordon and includes him singing the spiritual "By and By."

This photograph of nineteen-year-old Gordon was taken by Apeda Studio in New York City. 951–707

Taylor's father, John Gordon, was a classically trained chef, and his mother, Mary Goodall, a former slave. John came to Montana to work as a cook for a Fort Benton mining company in 1881. Mary followed in 1882, and the family eventually settled in White Sulphur Springs. During the depression of 1893, John left his family to find work and was killed in a train wreck. Mary supported the family thereafter by working as a cook and laundress for the cowboys, miners, and prostitutes that dominated the young mining town.

The youngest of five children, Taylor attended school and hustled work wherever he could find it. Upon leaving his hometown, he supported himself as a chauffeur, mechanic, and eventually as a chef and porter on Ringling's private railroad car. During a layover in New York, he joined a traveling vaudeville group that crisscrossed the nation and even performed in England and France. When he was not on the road, Gordon was a favorite in the Harlem nightlife scene. His natural talent as a musician and knack for self-promotion won him many influential admirers, including heiress A'Lelia Walker, who supplied him with free room and board in her Harlem townhouse known as the Dark Tower.

Today, Gordon is best remembered for his 1929 memoir, *Born to Be*, which chronicles his rise from servant to high society and from mining camp to New York City. The publication of his memoir, however, marked the pinnacle of his success. Gordon dissolved his partnership with the vaudeville troupe in the early 1930s. Although he completed another manuscript, titled *Daonda*, and tried to revive his musical career, both efforts failed.

In 1947, Gordon suffered a mental breakdown and was hospitalized in New York for twelve years. He grappled with severe depression, which was exacerbated by the belief that his second manuscript had been plagiarized by John Steinbeck in *The Grapes of Wrath*. Feeling cheated out of a return to wealth and fame, Gordon fell into further mental decline.

In February 1959, Gordon was released to the care of his sister, Rose, and he returned to White Sulphur Springs, where he survived on rental incomes, an antiques business, occasional concerts, and sales of his later writings, *Born to Be Sequel* and *The Man Who Built the Stone Castle*. He remained in White Sulphur Springs until his death in 1971.

The clear and powerful tenor voice on this rare recording captures a talented musician at the height of his talents. It provides a unique window into the experiences of African Americans in the West and how they intersected with larger cultural movements like the Harlem Renaissance. –*JF*

35. Flora Wong Letter to Charles Wong

1948, 7" × 8¼". Gift of Flora L. Wong, Wong Family Papers, SC 2523

◈

THIS letter tells the story of a match made in China that came to fruition in Helena, Montana's capital city. In 1936, at the age of seven, Flora Wong moved from the United States to China with her native-born parents. Less than a year later, Japan invaded China, embroiling the two nations in a violent war. Flora's father died in 1939, leaving his wife to raise eight children under the brutal Japanese occupation. The family worked hard in their rice fields, cultivated a garden, fished, and trapped to survive. All the while, Flora's mother worked tirelessly to transport her children, one by one, out of China, relying on the services of a matchmaker to locate suitable husbands for her daughters.

When Flora's turn came, the matchmaker found Charles Wong. Born in Canton Province near Flora's parents' village, he had immigrated in 1923 to Helena, where he worked as a waiter at the Yat Son Noodle Parlor. Wong saved his money and in 1939 purchased Wing Sheng and Company Grocery. Charles and Flora met in Hong Kong on January 14, 1947, and they were married the next day. The couple spent several months in Hong Kong before Charles returned to Montana. Unfortunately for Flora, she had lost her paperwork and, despite her U.S. birth and citizenship, was not allowed to leave China for many months.

The Society's collection of Wong Family papers includes these correspondences between Flora and Charles, which document the newlyweds' travails, their growing love for each other, and their dream of starting married life in Helena. In a translation of this September 11, 1948, letter, Flora describes her thoughts as she watches her husband, Charles, sail away:

> Thinking back to the time when you left, I have the memory of seeing your boat leave. You were on the boat but I couldn't see you. It was hard to see the boat sail away. I stayed until the boat moved and disappeared. It took my breath away.

After Flora's exit papers were granted in late 1948, the couple was finally reunited. By then, Flora was six months pregnant. In the months that followed, Flora's remaining siblings left China as well. Her mother, however, remained behind, where she was murdered in her home village during a Communist attack on rural landowners. Flora and Charles raised five children in Helena, where they ran the Wing Sheng and Company Grocery store until Charles's death in 1968.

As this document shows, immigration to Montana was not just a part of its earliest history, but continued through the twentieth century and into the present. The Wongs' letters, including this one, reflect the hopes and dreams of a young, married couple and illustrate the diversity of ethnic groups from Europe, Asia, and Africa who chose to make Montana their home. *—JF*

延年我的親愛貢夫如見，吾今看你来之信，甚是
令吾傷心，知你我愛情難捨，但兄之愛我、吾亦
明白，我之愛兄想兄，你亦可知，惟有靜坐，我早
日行程復遲長，於共同快樂对枕言談方
能盡訴回思往日同床共枕之時，更動你我
愛情之緣，吾曾知離別之痛苦，但未免一刻
想得共同快樂，吾亦得知你姊角偉難回家
謹你自處自食，獨坐獨眠之緣，惟望我們早
日相逢，於慰你我之寂寞，如他未有消息，請
吾兄千祈不可與他出戰，如有失手，如何是可
对于愛员之婚事，吾母親云他还年細未能許
他婚事，請汝姊見諒可也。
今日天時寒冷，請吾兄保重五体為要
今信内有港币紙吾亦得收，但吾懷孕
以未身体安康，見字勿念，紙短情長，筆
難盡述，下次再告，望吾兄保重身体精神
暢快，此囑

1948 十月廿三号

你的親愛 重娣手草

36. *Getting the Bacon*

1950, 24" × 18", by William Standing (1904–1951).

Gift of the Greater Montana Foundation, Ed Craney Collection, 2006.38.30

UNLIKE the ethnic groups who immigrated into the region, Native Americans have resided in what is now Montana since time immemorial. Despite this fact, by the close of the nineteenth century, American Indians found themselves living as minorities in a society dominated by Euro-American culture. Life had changed for them in many dramatic ways, oftentimes against their will, but other times by choice. By drawing on European—rather than Indigenous—artistic conventions, Assiniboine artist William Standing (1904–1951) exemplified one way in which Native Americans adopted aspects of a foreign culture and reinterpreted them as their own.

Born on the Fort Peck Reservation, Standing was educated in day and boarding schools in Montana and later at the Haskell Institute in Kansas, but he received no art instruction. He noted later in life, "I was always painting and drawing, but the only training the teachers gave me in this line was jobs of painting the outside of buildings." Standing credited his mother's family for his talent and interest in art and cited "nature" as his only instructor.

Getting the Bacon shows the whimsical side of Standing's work. A sow grizzly holds one of her twin cubs up to nab a slab of bacon while keeping a wary eye on the rightful owner's cabin door. In addition to such humorous scenes—many of which depicted the foibles of contemporary reservation life—Standing, according to ethnographer John Ewers, was also "uniquely versatile as an interpreter of the little-known aspects of the history and traditional culture of his own tribe in buffalo days." In 1938, Standing reminisced, "I invariably take my subjects from familiar scenes, episodes from the stories of my people dealing with epic and heroic feats in Indian history and tradition." Adding that he also relied on his "aged father and many other aged friends," Standing said, "I know what I draw and paint."

As a student at Haskell Institute in Kansas, Standing lettered in football. A handwritten note on the back of this self-portrait reads, "Papa looks like he understanding football!"
Bill Standing with His Father, undated watercolor, 10⅝" × 8⅝". Gift of the Greater Montana Foundation, Ed Craney Collection, 2006.38.35

Standing was able to support himself through the sale of his artwork, both original paintings and humorous ink sketches reproduced as postcards. His first exhibit in Great Falls attracted considerable attention, and he went on to show his work in Paris, Washington, D.C., and across the United States. During the Great Depression, he taught art classes for the Works Progress Administration (WPA) and provided one hundred pen-and-ink illustrations for *Land of Nakoda: The Story of the Assiniboine Indians*, which was published by the WPA Writers Project in 1942. Many consider these images to be among the finest of his life's work. Tragically, Standing died in an automobile accident at the age of forty-six, yet he left behind a unique legacy of images depicting Plains Indian life and other Montana scenes, both serious and amusing. *–KL*

37. Hmong Story Cloth

ca. 1999, 31⅛" × 30", by Nou Yang (Chia Lia Moua). John Reddy, photographer. Gift of Mary Yang, 2001.89.01

◈

In this colorfully embroidered scene of Hmong village life, a border of blue and gray triangles represents the mountains of Laos and symbolizes protection from outside danger. Men and women grind corn, pound and winnow rice, feed animals, harvest sugarcane and bananas, tend crops, and transport goods along a winding mountain trail. Nou Yang, a refugee displaced by the Vietnam War, embroidered the story cloth in Missoula, far from the mountains where she was born.

Hmong refugees came to western Montana in the 1980s due to the efforts of former Missoula smokejumper Jerry Daniels. Daniels had served with the CIA during the Vietnam War, recruiting members of the Hmong ethnic group to fight against the North Vietnamese Army as part of what became known as the Secret War in Laos. Thirty thousand Hmong soldiers died fighting for the United States, and many more died after the communist organization Pathet Lao and North Vietnamese took over Laos in 1975 and persecuted its people for collaborating with the Americans.

In 1975, at great risk, Daniels organized an air evacuation of 2,500 Hmong from Long Cheng airbase to Thailand. Fearing for their lives, tens of thousands more made the harrowing journey by foot, crossing the Mekong River into Thailand between 1975 and 1986. There, the Hmong lived in refugee camps, waiting for a regime change in Laos so they could return home or for permission to resettle in the United States, France, Australia, or elsewhere.

The average stay in the refugee camp was seven years. Unable to practice their traditional means of subsistence (slash-and-burn agriculture), the Hmong looked to capitalize on other skills. Hmong women were fine needle workers who produced beautiful clothing and elaborate ceremonial outfits. Many of their geometric and ornamental designs had been handed down for generations. *Paj ntaub* (pronounced pa dnau)—or flowery cloth—incorporated reverse appliqué, direct appliqué, counted cross-stitch, batik, and embroidery.

In the refugee camps, the Hmong—a preliterate culture—were exposed to picture books, and a new type of *Paj ntaub* emerged: story cloths. These embroidered pieces featured pictorial representations of Hmong myths, traditional village scenes, personal family histories, and stories from the Vietnam War. These pieces served multiple purposes: to preserve and pass down Hmong history to the next generation, to solicit support for the Hmong by sharing their plight with the Western world, and to provide income through their sale.

Story cloths came to Montana in the late 1970s, when Daniels, who dedicated himself after the war to helping resettle Hmong refugees, arranged for the legendary Hmong leader General Vang Pao and others to move to his hometown of Missoula. In 1979–1980, 366 Hmong arrived in Missoula, and by the mid-1980s, between 700 and 1,000 Hmong lived in western Montana. These new Montanans included Nou Yang, the creator of this story cloth, who journeyed here with her husband in 1985.

In 1999, Mary Yang, a Hmong refugee herself, donated this story cloth to "the people of Montana" when, under the auspices of the Bitterroot Development Corporation, she applied to the State of Montana's Cultural and Aesthetic Trust for funding for the Montana Asian Cultural Project. The Montana Arts Council Folk Life Project transferred the story cloth to the Montana Historical Society in 2001.

–MK

MONTANANS AT HOME

◈

While thoughts of home have always evoked strong emotions from Montanans, the specifics of what exactly home looked like varied greatly by time, place, and economic status.

For some Plains Indians, it most often meant a buffalo hide tipi, situated according to the tribe's territory and the season of the year. Since households had to be easily transported on dog- or horse-drawn travois, possessions were minimal. Even after Indians adopted permanent structures, tipis remained important as dwellings and as symbols of traditional lifeways.

Well into the twentieth century, the first home for newcomers to the Treasure State was most often a one-room cabin, dugout, or tarpaper shack; a spartan barracks or bunkhouse; or even a bedroll on the ground. In western Montana, where timber was plentiful, miners—mostly single men—hastily constructed crude log cabins to provide shelter from the elements. Furnishings were basic and often made on-site from materials already on hand. As greater numbers of family units arrived, most notably during Montana's homestead boom beginning in the 1910s, women worked hard to add elements of both comfort and beauty to otherwise rudimentary structures.

As industrial mining replaced placer mining and cities grew, boarding and apartment houses helped meet the needs of denser urban populations. With the completion of the first transcontinental railroad, which crossed the state in 1882, wealthy Montanans had access to the same architects and building materials as well-to-do Americans living elsewhere. The Treasure State's mansions soon rivaled those found in more populous parts of the country. Likewise, furnishings manufactured in the East or overseas could easily be brought in by train. The ability to pay for luxuries, ranging from fine furniture and oriental carpets to new inventions like electric bathrobes, became the only limiting factor to their acquisition.

Yellow Buffalo Tipi of Cecil and James White Calf, 1946, 12" × 15", by Jessie Wilber (1912–1989). Gift of Museum of the Rockies, 1997.04.06

As evidenced by the dining room in Helena's Original Governor's Mansion (see page 116), the arrival of the railroad meant that, for those with sufficient funds, people living on Montana's formerly remote frontier could now have greater access to the same luxuries as Americans living in more developed parts of the country. Tom Ferris, photographer. BD2013-09-12

As depicted in Olga Ross Hannon's (1890–1947) 1941 watercolor, *Life in the Open—Crow Fair*, home for American Indian peoples often combines elements of both traditional lifeways and Euro-American adaptations. 26½" × 23". Gift of Mrs. Isabel Haynes, Haynes Foundation Collection, 1977.39.236

Homes changed over time not only in their appearances and physical contents, but in their functions as well. For earlier generations of Montanans, the home encompassed far more than day-to-day life: babies were born at home, the sick were cared for at home, and bodies were laid out or waked at home. Today, we rely on relatively modern institutions like hospitals and funeral parlors for such major events, services, and rites.

Regardless of their differing characteristics throughout the past, Montana's homes have served many of the same purposes over time: providing their occupants with a refuge from the elements, a space to maintain traditions and family customs, and a sense of belonging to a particular place and other people.

38. Niimíipuu Cornhusk Bag

ca. 1890, 15" × 19". Gift of William A. Clark, x1900.03.14

◈

The numerous tribes of the Columbia Plateau specialized in producing a diverse array of baskets and bags for everyday use. The bag or basket's shape and style reflected its purpose, and many were used for storing or carrying foods. Typical materials included bear grass, cedar root, cedar bark, Indian hemp, and dogbane—most of which could be harvested locally—and others, like cornhusk, which were obtained through trade. Over time, designs and styles changed to accommodate new purposes and to incorporate new raw materials.

Flat twined bags such as this Niimíipuu (Nez Perce) bag typically featured differing geometric designs in symmetrical patterns on the front and back, with a plain band at the top and bottom of the bag. A drawstring of twined dogbane or hemp allowed the top to be pulled shut. Botanically dyed cornhusk, or the darker cedar or bear grass, provided variation in color, and weavers used a technique called false embroidery to incorporate vibrant patterns into their work. By 1890, when this bag was made, weavers had adopted commercially dyed wool for their designs.

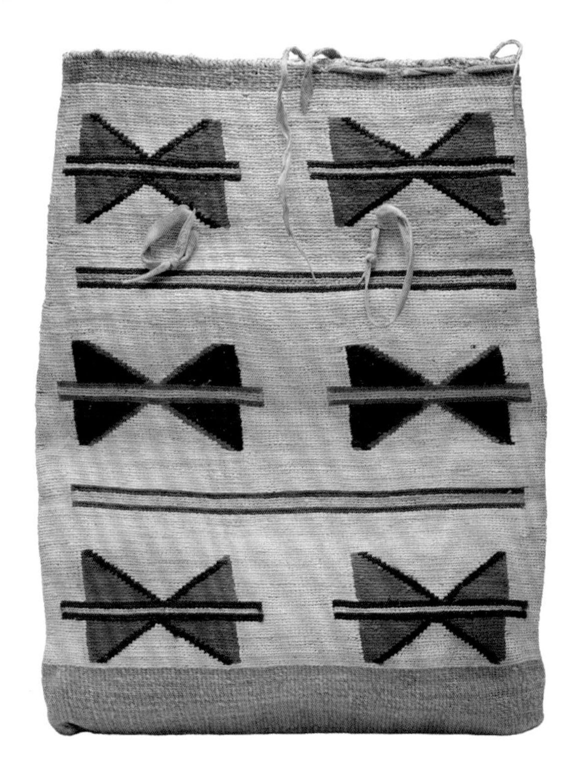

Often as large as twenty by thirty-six inches, highly durable cornhusk bags were excellent containers for storing dried roots, bulbs, and tubers, making them indispensable to the household economy. Traditionally, bags and baskets of all types were popular wedding gifts as well as prized trade items. An adept weaver could earn a living for herself by producing them. Montana's Salish and Crow peoples frequently traded with Nez Perce and other Plateau tribes to obtain these utilitarian bags. According to oral histories, Lewis and Clark attempted unsuccessfully to secure a quantity of durable cornhusk bags from the Salish, who refused to part with any significant number—so necessary were such bags in day-to-day life.

By the early twentieth century, changes in the daily life of tribal communities compelled weavers to modify their crafts. Confined to reservations and unable to follow traditional seasonal rounds to gather raw materials and customary foods, they adapted by substituting new materials, like wool, cotton, and jute, and innovated by making smaller bags suitable for holding personal belongings. At the same time, a growing market for Native bags inspired new design motifs featuring animals, plants, and people and included purse-style leather handles. Weavers could earn much-needed cash by selling their handiwork to non-Natives. Today, very few artisans continue the basket-making traditions that once produced this staple domestic and trade item. *–LF*

39. *My Cabin in Montana*

1865, 10½" × 8½", by Peter Tofft (1825–1901). 1996.89.01

◈

Due to the scarcity of cameras as well as the technical difficulties faced by photographers in dark spaces, there exist very few photographs of domestic interiors in mid-nineteenth-century Montana. Even artists in the region at that time had little interest in depicting these spaces. This detailed self-portrait by Danish artist Peter Tofft (1825–1901), therefore, provides an extremely rare glimpse inside an early miner's cabin.

Tofft poses himself reading by a cozy fire in what appears to be a typical cabin on Montana's mining frontier. Sunlight filters through a small window. A stone fireplace provides heat, a place to cook, and a "dryer" for wet socks. Bagged provisions hang from the log rafters and walls. The simple wooden furniture and water bucket were likely made on-site, while the cast-iron coffee grinder, pot, and skillet were manufactured elsewhere and arduously transported to this remote mountain location. A miner's pan resting in the corner hints at the resident's occupation, while the book in his hands represents an article of pioneer life that, while highly prized, was more commonly available on the frontier than traditional stereotypes would indicate.

Tofft depicted many aspects of daily life on Montana's mining frontier. In this painting, *Prickly Pear Canyon, King and Gillette Toll Road #1*, he captured two ox-drawn, covered freight wagons traveling between Helena and Fort Benton.
Watercolor and gouache on paperboard, ca. 1866, 16½" × 22½". Bequest of Laura B. King, x1940.03.01

What is decidedly atypical in this image, however, is the artwork that adorns the cabin walls. Unlike Tofft, most miners were not in the position to create paintings worthy of formal display, nor would they have traveled with the requisite art supplies. Few would have had the available resources, or inclination, to purchase one of Tofft's watercolors, which sold for five dollars each—in gold!

As a teenager, Peter Petersen Tofft left his native Denmark on a whaling ship. He traveled widely before signing aboard the U.S. gunboat *Ohio* during the Mexican-American War. In 1849, he landed in San Francisco and, like so many others, unsuccessfully sought his fortune in California's goldfields. Always adventurous, Tofft remained on the West Coast, eventually traveling around Oregon, Washington, and British Columbia before settling in Montana Territory in 1865. There, in the Elk Creek Mining District in what is now Deer Lodge County, recuperation from a riding accident forced Tofft to abandon his transient lifestyle. A painter since childhood, he resolved to assume the profession of an artist.

After leaving Montana in 1867, Tofft continued to travel but resided primarily in London, where his accommodations were quite different from the rustic Elk Creek cabin he once called home. Although he never achieved the degree of artistic success that he hoped for, his portrayals of life in Montana now serve as valuable windows into this region's history. –*KL*

My Cabin.
Montana 1866.

40. Chuck Wagon Photograph

1880, "Mex John Making Pies," L. A. Huffman, photographer. 981-254

It would be difficult to find a more iconic Western image than the cattle-camp cook and his chuck wagon. Cooks played an integral role in Montana's food history and were mainstays on cattle drives and open-range roundups across the West. Folklore has given us romantic notions of the chuck wagon as an oasis of camaraderie and of the cook as a curmudgeonly yet endearing character turning out a steady supply of sourdough biscuits, bacon, beans, and, of course, coffee. The job's reality, however, was much more complex.

A camp cook's responsibilities demanded constant readiness and planning. The day began long before sunrise to allow time for breakfast's preparation and its consumption by the crew. While the cowhands joined the herd before dawn, the cook extinguished fires, cleaned dishes, loaded the wagon, and prepared to move to the next site. Cooks relocated their wagons at least once a day and often twice or more, coordinating with trail bosses to identify locations with access to the necessary fresh water and fuel. All the while they also maintained a running inventory of supplies.

Charles Goodnight, a Texas freighter and rancher, produced the first wagon specifically for "chuck" transportation. By the 1880s, the portable kitchen had evolved from crude, drawered boxes to sophisticated devices for storage and food preparation. Chuck boxes offered accessible compartments for items in constant use, such as spices, utensils, and coffee grinders. When dropped open, the hinged end of the box created a worktable. The remainder of the wagon was organized into storage for bulk foods, water, kindling, skillets, pots, ropes, portable wood cookstoves, and more. Larger drives often included "bed wagons" to carry additional gear, including bedrolls, tack, and tents.

While there were certainly chuck-wagon cooks of unremarkable skill, the accounts of legendary Montanans such as Teddy Blue Abbott and L. A. Huffman do not mention them. Rather, their tales describe dedicated men gifted with strong work ethics and no small amount of culinary ingenuity. In the words of one cowboy from the Powder River, a good roundup meal "leaves nothing to be desired." This coffee pot, ca. 1900–1930, represents one of the most important instruments employed by camp cooks throughout Montana. Made of enameled steel and worn from use, the vessel serves as a reminder of the efforts required to sustain Montana's early ranchers while out on the range. *–ZAS*

Cowboys were willing to tolerate many hardships on the trail—from sleeping on the ground and long hours in the saddle to relentless exposure to extreme weather—but not poor food or bad coffee. Enamelware coffee pot, ca. 1915, 8½" × 6¼" × 9½". X1980.19.13

41. A'aninin Tipi liner

ca. 1900, 175" × 103". Bequest of Julia Ereaux Schultz, 1981.67.09

◈

Staying warm in a region where temperatures fell well below zero and remained there for extended periods required great adaptability and resourcefulness. Plains Indian peoples nestled their winter camps among trees that provided both a windbreak and fuel for the fires they used to heat their lodges and cook their food. Tipi liners—originally made of tanned bison hide—were secured to the inside of the tipi poles to produce a second wall that offered insulation. The liner also helped circulate fresh air into the tipi by causing an updraft of air behind the liner. This gentle flow of air improved the draw of smoke up through the hole at the top of the tipi.

Illustrated tipi liners also sometimes served a second, cultural function: to memorialize and tell the stories of warrior deeds. For countless years, Plains Indians have chronicled their histories in magnificent graphic pictorial styles. Powerful images painted on buffalo robes, hides, and tipis chronicled men's personal exploits and feats. Joe D. Horse Capture (A'aninin/White Clay), a noted Plains Indian scholar, wrote of warrior culture: "Tribes had developed rules of engagement among themselves and specific ways to attain honor. The highest form of honor was not to kill enemies but to touch them while they were defending themselves. This was called 'counting coup.' It was done with a special object, such as the butt of a gun or a riding quirt, or with the hand." This painted muslin liner, created by several unidentified A'aninin warriors, features drawings that document their exploits—including counting coup on the enemy, gunfights, battles, scalping, horse capture, escape, and hand-to-hand combat.

The tipi liner provided lively decoration for the interior of a lodge and a continual reminder of the brave achievements of the warrior artists. The home would be a welcoming, safe place for a family to spend the winter and cool and comfortable in the summer. Occupants could cast their gaze on the images and perhaps sleep more soundly comforted by the stories of their tribesmen's amazing achievements.

In 1959, A'aninin elder Julia Ereaux Schultz bequeathed this exceptional tipi liner to the Montana Historical Society, saying, "I am proud of the Indian heritage in Montana, and I want future generations of Montana people to see some of the wonderful things left to us." *–JBO*

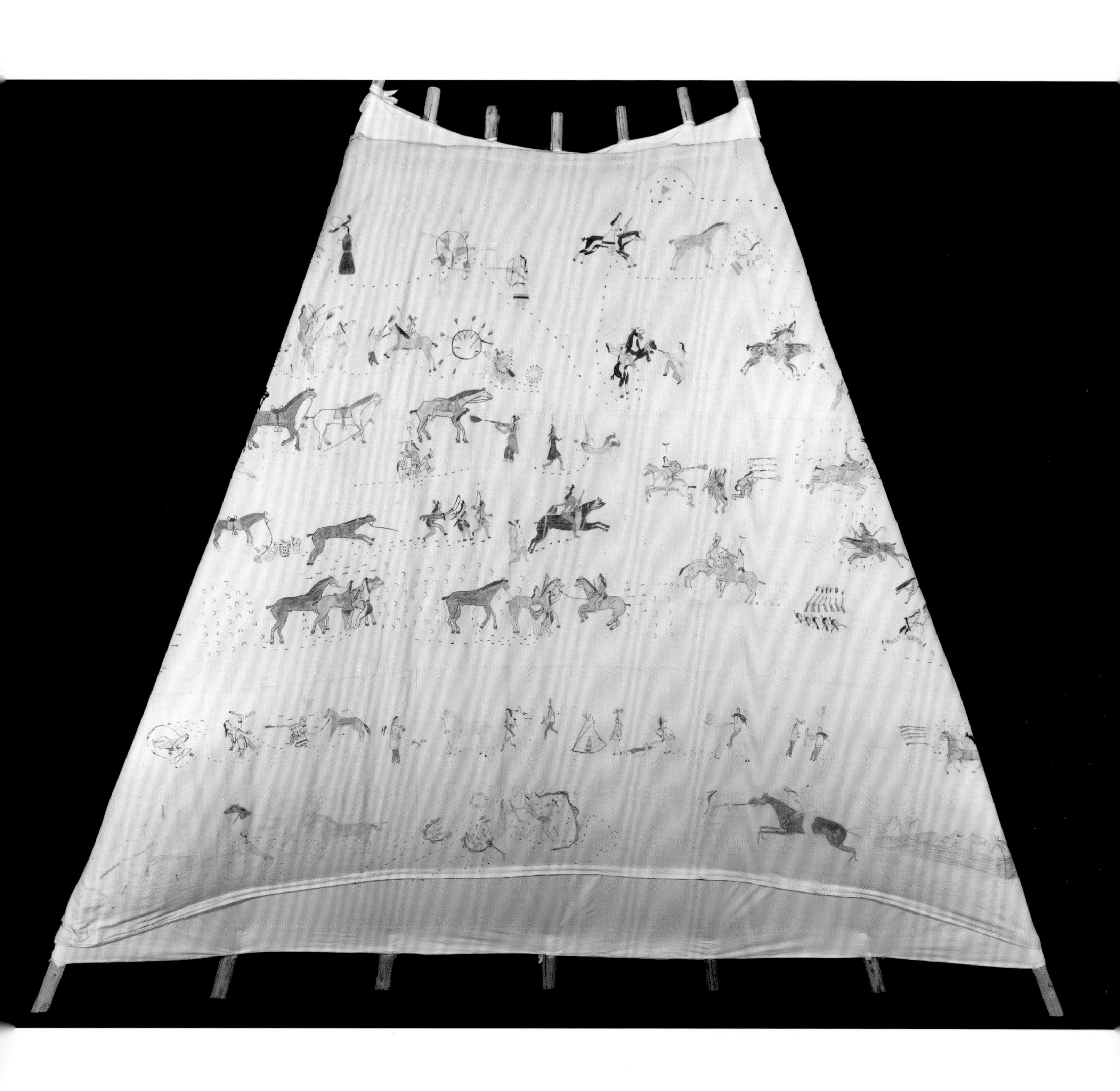

42. Bison Horn Chair

ca. 1886, 25¼" × 25" × 43½", by David Hilger (1858–1937). Gift of David Hilger, x1927.01.01

◈

DONATED in 1927 to the Montana Historical Society by David Hilger (1858–1937), this buffalo horn chair stands as a Montanan variation on a national trend. At the 1876 Chicago Industrial Exposition, the Tobey Furniture Company displayed an upholstered sofa and chair with horn arms, sparking nationwide demand for similarly styled furniture. Other manufacturers were soon producing similar horn chairs, tables, and nightstands. The meatpacking industry provided the main supply of steer horns for these pieces, but by the 1890s buffalo horns were considered far more desirable.

While the exact date of this chair's manufacture is uncertain, we know its horns came from bison that David Hilger hunted in the Judith Basin. Hilger's family came to Montana from Henderson, Minnesota, and settled in Helena in 1868. In 1881, David expanded his sheep-ranching venture in Lewis and Clark County to Fergus County at Salt Creek, thirty-five miles north of Lewistown. In his first winter there, he saw "buffalo roam[ing] all over the northern part of the county . . . by hundreds and thousands."

Hilger was an avid hunter, and he estimated that he killed around three hundred bison in the Judith Basin, sometimes as many as eighteen in a single "stand." Hilger ate the meat of the animals he killed and sold their hides for five dollars apiece. He would be one of the last to hunt bison in the Judith Basin.

By the time Hilger took his first bison, commercial hunting was a thriving industry, particularly after 1871 when tanners began treating bison hides for leather. Individual hide-hunters came to Montana and wiped out whole herds, taking the meat from the humps of their kills, along with their hides and tongues, but often leaving the rest of the carcasses to rot. By 1883 there were fewer than two hundred bison remaining on the Great Plains, whereas only two decades prior there had been thirteen million.

The near extermination of the bison changed Montana forever. Hilger himself commented that "the passing of the buffalo did more to subdue the Indians than all the troops employed by the government." Bison had been a central food source for Indigenous peoples across the Great Plains, and their disappearance led to mass starvation among Montana's tribes.

The numerous carcasses left behind by hide-hunters created a market for bison bones—and horns. Across the nation, Americans embraced horn furniture as a way to add frontier flair to their homes. Although Hilger's chair conveys a certain enthusiasm for the romanticized West, he later expressed great regret for his role in the decline of the bison: "I plead guilty to ruthless slaughtering of these noble animals, and little did I think at the time how soon the end of these monarchs of the plain would come."

–AK

43. Original Governor's Mansion

1888, 304 North Ewing, Helena, designed by architects Hodgson, Stem, and Welter.

Owned by the State of Montana since 1913. Tom Ferris, photographer. BD2015-26-004

◈

THIS stately Queen Anne–style residence holds a myriad of stories. Many, but not all, are associated with the nine first families who called the Original Governor's Mansion home between 1913 and 1959. Today, the historic house is a museum curated by the Montana Historical Society and offers visitors a window into the life of affluent Montanans in the first decades of the twentieth century.

Entrepreneur William Chessman built the mansion in 1888 for his wife, Penelope, and their children. Located a mile west of the state capitol on Ewing Street in Helena, the three-story, twenty-room house is made of pressed brick, terra-cotta, and granite. The pressed brick and terra-cotta were sourced from Zanesville, Ohio, and the hardwoods from the eastern United States and South America, while the basement's granite blocks were cut from Helena quarries.

The view from the library into the dining room in the Original Governor's Mansion. 2013, Tom Ferris, photographer. BD2013-09-009

It features seven elaborately decorated fireplaces and also boasts a second-floor bathroom—only the third in Helena at the time.

In 1900, railroad contractor Peter Larson and his wife, Margaret, purchased the home and lavishly refurnished it, selling it the following year to Harfield and Kathryn Conrad, who lived there until 1913. That year, the State of Montana acquired the mansion to serve as the first official governor's residence for Governor Samuel V. Stewart and his family. The first families of governors Joseph M. Dixon, John E. Erickson, Frank H. Cooney, W. Elmer Holt, Roy E. Ayers, Samuel C. Ford, John W. Bonner, and J Hugo Aronson lived there in the following years. In 1959, after Governor Aronson moved into a newly constructed executive residence, the mansion sat largely unused. Ten years later, a dedicated group of private citizens began the building's complete restoration. In 1980, the Montana Historical Society assumed the administration of this historic house museum.

The Original Governor's Mansion provides a wonderful place to explore the stories of its past residents and household staff as well as the wider world in which they lived. As noted by author Larry Gill,

> Within these walls have been enacted all the protocol required of dinners and receptions of state, many of the inter-party councils of war and of peace through which the wheels of government are greased. Here also have been played all the little dramas and tragedies, the heartaches and happiness of private family life. . . . The house was built to be a home.

–MO

OPEN

44. Copper Grotesque

1890, 47½" × 33" × 17½". Gift of Glen Wilson, x1975.17.01

LONGTIME Helena resident, musician, alderman, and real estate broker Homer Hewins built his namesake Homer Block (at the corner of Park and Clarke) for twenty-five thousand dollars in 1890. The building's construction began at a time when Helena—as one of several communities vying to become the permanent state capital—aspired to establish a more cosmopolitan reputation and shed its rustic gold camp image. One of a matched pair, this four-foot-long copper grotesque is emblematic of the grand, high-style architecture Helena and other Montana cities embraced in their attempts to "civilize" the formerly "wild" West.

The Homer Block, which consisted primarily of apartments with ground-floor retail space, was known for its striking architectural elements. Varied wall surfaces of brick and stone, arched windows, and heavy ornamentation showcased Helena's grand ambitions to be known as the Queen City of the Rockies. Like Helena's celebrated Novelty Block, which stood at 13 South Main Street, the Homer Block's stunning contrast of light and shadow produced a rare textural quality when viewed from the street. The architect of the Homer Block is unknown, but its remarkable similarity to the Novelty Block, designed by John C. Paulsen, suggests a possible connection. Neither building survived the urban renewal movement, and the Homer Block was torn down in 1971.

When the Homer Block was demolished, donor Glen Wilson purchased the two grotesques for $250. He had a soft spot for the creatures, apparently, because his aunt had once managed a shop in the Homer Block's commercial space. Wilson recalled fondly that each year his aunt had re-painted the creatures' eyes and details. After purchasing them he stripped the paint from one of the sculptures and discovered its radiant copper hue. Once perched on pedestals on either side of the apartment building's entryway, the Homer Block's twin grotesques recalled ancient mythical creatures, or chimeras, that once guarded temples and other buildings. These types of architectural features are often mistakenly referred to as "gargoyles." Technically, gargoyles function as waterspouts as well as decorative motifs, while grotesques like these are strictly ornamental.

Although Homer Hewins left Montana in the mid-1890s to homestead in Canada, the block that bore his name—and the mythical figures that guarded it—became longtime community landmarks. Later known as the Central View Apartments, for more than eighty years the Homer Block's numerous flats were home to hundreds of Helenans. *–EB*

This copper grotesque is one of a matched pair that once guarded the entrance to the Homer Block, which stood at the corner of Park Avenue and Clarke Street in Helena. The grotesques were removed prior to the building's demolition during urban renewal and later donated to the Historical Society. L. H. Jorud, photographer, ca. 1965. 953-196

45. Maternity Dress

1905. Gift of Rachel Fisher, 2014.20.01

◈

Regina Parker Davis (1878–1910), the wife of Wibaux sheep rancher Al Davis, wore this maternity dress (seamstress unknown) made of copper-colored sateen, velvet, and lace, in 1905. A treasured item lovingly preserved, the dress has an elegance that belies the difficulties of childbirth in Montana's rural areas during the homestead era.

From 1911 to 1919, nearly nine thousand Montana women and infants died during childbirth, creating one of the highest maternal death rates in the nation. Trained medical assistance was seldom available at the time of delivery, and when physicians were at hand, they often did more harm than good, resorting to the dangerous use of opium and forceps to expedite the process. More often, women relied on each other, their husbands, or—when available—an experienced midwife. Some women attempted to educate themselves by reading books and magazines on childbirth, but nevertheless, many rural Montana mothers received worse healthcare than women living in urban poverty.

A mother in eastern Montana shows off her newborn, ca. 1910–1930. Until the 1950s, most Montana women gave birth at home, with or without medical assistance.
L. A. Huffman, photographer. 981-963

Recalling her self-taught skills as a midwife in and around Milltown, Catherine Hayes Murphy, a mother of ten, explained:

> You study and you learn as you go along. You feel the pulse in the cord and when it quits pulsating you tie it. . . . You did the best you could when you were in a place where you had coal or woodstoves and the water had to be brought in. You tried to make it so there wouldn't be infection. . . . You'd take a piece of cloth and iron it until it was scorched, sterile as you could make it, then put it around the navel.

Montana midwives like Murphy received little, if any, pay for their services and frequently confronted harsh conditions while traveling to assist mothers in labor. The introduction of "lying-in" rooms and maternity homes in the 1920s and 1930s greatly improved the resources available to pregnant women, and by 1950 the majority of births took place in hospitals, where safe and sanitary obstetric practices had begun to take hold.

The impressive condition of this maternity dress—a garment that was typically repurposed for children's clothes or passed down to another expectant mother—implies the fondness Davis had for it as a keepsake from the time she spent carrying her daughter Esther. Today, it speaks to the uncertainties faced by Montana women in the early 1900s, when safe childbirth and reproductive health depended on the industrious, caring networks sustained by Montana's rural women. *–SAT*

46. Electric Bathrobe

1908. Gift of Lee C. Sweeney, 1978.28.01 a-c

◈

ONCE the height of technology and luxury, this electrified bath coat was manufactured by General Electric in 1908 and belonged to wealthy businessman and Helena resident Thomas Cruse (1834–1914). Known as the Standard Electro Thermo Coat, the gadget symbolizes the opulence and eccentricity of one of Montana's most prominent figures.

Thomas Cruse's real-life tale of drama and wealth rivals a Shakespearian tragedy. In 1856, Cruse immigrated to the United States from the small parish of Drum Lummon in County Cavan, Ireland. In his quest for fortune, Cruse first tried his luck—unsuccessfully—in the goldfields of California, Nevada, and Idaho. In 1867, he made his way to Montana, staking a mining claim near present-day Marysville. Eight years later, he became one of the rare few who struck it rich, discovering a vast source of gold in a mine he named Drumlummon, which he sold in 1882 to the London Company Associated in England for nearly $1.5 million. Cruse subsequently expanded his business interests to include cattle ranching and finance, establishing the Thomas Cruse Savings Bank of Helena, the territory's first savings bank.

In 1886, Cruse married Margaret Carter in an event heralded by the *New York Times* as "the most brilliant of its kind ever held in Montana." The nuptial ceremony in Helena was overseen by Bishop Brondel on a beautiful wintery day in March, when "snow clad summits of the mountains on all sides [were] glistening like silver in the flood of sunshine." Amid praise for the elaborate reception at Helena's Cosmopolitan Hotel, the *Helena Herald* characterized "the winning of such an admirable wife as another link" in Cruse's "chain of good fortune."

But happiness would not last long for the storied couple. A mere ten months after the wedding, Cruse's beloved Margaret died at the age of twenty-five after giving birth to their only child, a daughter named Mary.

Mamie, as she was called, grew up in protective isolation in Cruse's palatial twenty-two-room home and was only allowed to play with a few selected friends, as her domineering father feared she would be a target for kidnappers. At the age of seventeen, Mamie ran away with her sweetheart, only to be stopped at Elliston and returned home. Despite Cruse's best efforts to protect his daughter from the outside world, she finally managed to leave his household, and after a string of marriages and estrangements she was found by police in a roadhouse outside Butte in 1913, quite ill and apparently addicted to alcohol. She was returned to Helena, where it was hoped she would recover, but soon thereafter died at the age of twenty-seven.

Heartbroken, Cruse turned to religious devotion. He sank money into the development of St. Helena Cathedral, paying for its fifteen bells in memory of his daughter. Cruse's own health began to fade shortly after Mamie's death, and he passed away on December 20, 1914. On December 26 that year, "Mamie's Bells" rang out for Thomas Cruse's funeral, the first funeral mass held in the cathedral.

Many landmarks in and around Helena now bear Cruse's name, and this robe is a small reminder of the ambitious Irishman who found both great fortune and great tragedy in Montana. An instruction label sewn inside the robe reads:

> The garment must be turned off every ten minutes for one minute. Continue this as long as you care to stay in the Garment. Ordinarily forty minutes is sufficient time. The Garment must be turned off for one minute, every ten minutes, no longer and no less.

–JBO

47. Florence Story's Diary

1935, 4⅜" × 6⅜". Gift of Joel Story, Alma Togstad Papers, SC 2339

◈

THIS small diary, written by Florence "Honey" Story of Minot, North Dakota, was found next to a garbage can in Billings and sent to the Montana Historical Society in 2002. Its entries, written between January 1 and April 27, 1935, provide an extraordinary record of a young girl's life before it was cut short by a mysterious illness.

Reading these diary entries, one learns that Florence was often home from school because of an unidentified ailment. However, despite the fact she was homebound, she was rarely alone. Schoolmates brought homework and visited daily:

> January 8: Bing came & helped me with geometry. Linda told me about Caesar, biology & literature.

Friends also joined Florence around the radio, cheering on the school basketball team during the 1935 season:

> March 22: Gladys Roland, Helen Jessen, & Marie Steinmetz were here. . . . We listened to the tournament between Minot and Wahpeton. Wahpeton won. Heck.

Others visited regularly, bringing food and small gifts, including items difficult to find in the West during the Depression:

> March 12: Mrs. Haginsen & Mrs. Vangen brought me silk stockings!

Like most young people, Florence was especially fond of chocolate and other sweets, and she described these gifts with particular relish:

> January 8: Today I had part of a Snickers, two chocolate covered cherries & Lindy brought me a chocolate bar.

> January 24: Mrs. Purdy came over and brought me candy and caramel rolls. Then she made some potato chips.

Popular culture was also on Florence's mind. For example, she describes reading the "funnies," looking through popular magazines, attending movies, listening to radio shows, and cutting out fashion paper dolls:

> January 6: I read just oodles of funnies today which kept me busy for quite a while. Dad brought me a magazine . . . & I laid and read alotta [*sic*] swell stories.

> January 28: I listened to . . . Fish Face & sure did laugh.

Florence's condition often left her with high fevers, overall weakness, and painful backaches. Despite these hardships, local newspapers indicate that she was active in the Girl Reserves, a YWCA service organization for high school girls that began during World War I. She was also confirmed in the Lutheran Church, and many of the visitors she mentioned in her diary were volunteers from these organizations.

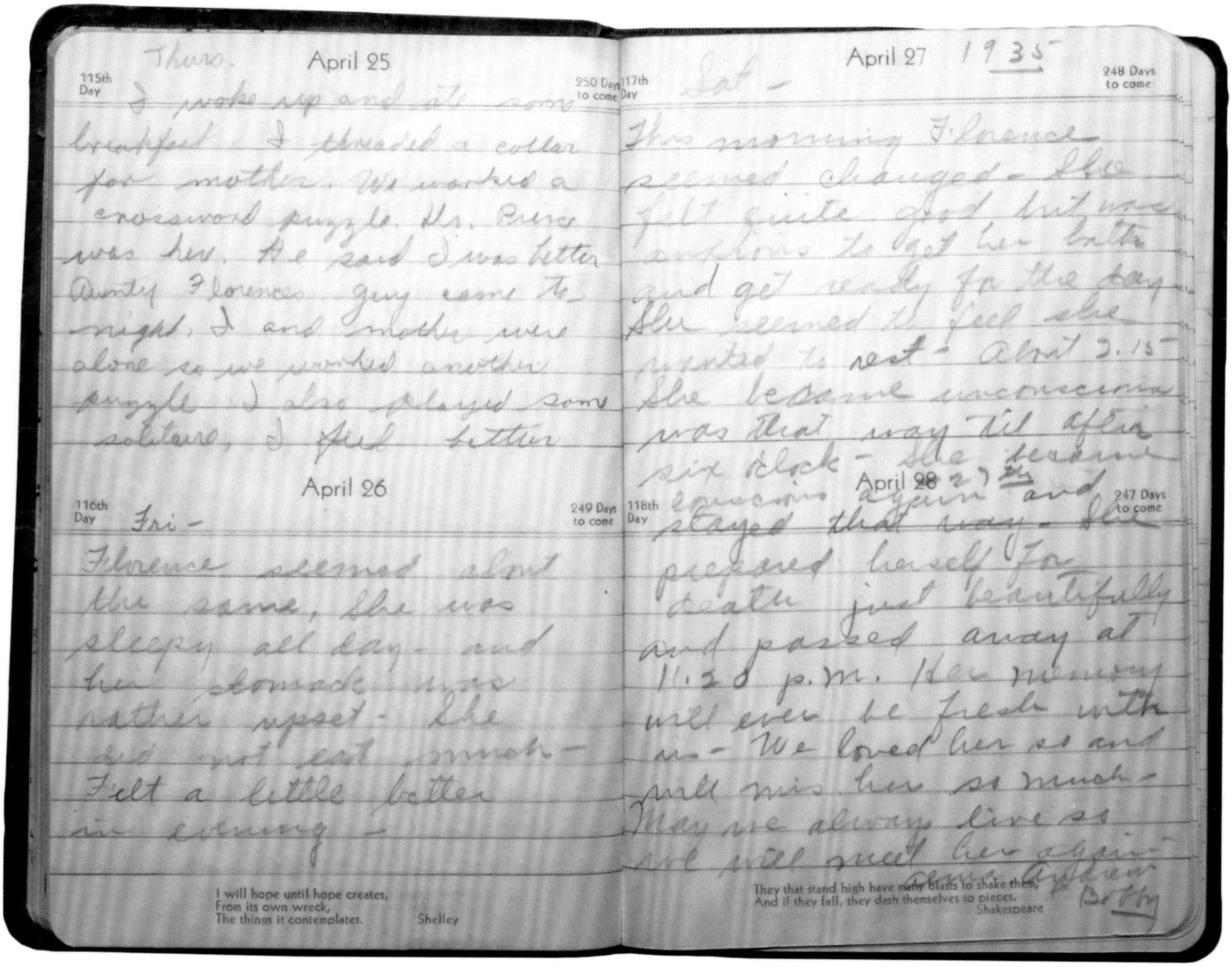

As the diary entries proceed toward the spring of 1935, it becomes apparent that Florence's health was failing. She talks more about doctor's visits and less about friends and school. The final entry is not written in Florence's hand at all, but in her mother's. Dated April 27, 1935, the entry reports that Florence died in her home, surrounded by family, just a few days shy of her seventeenth birthday.

Florence's mother, Alma, moved to Bozeman in 1947, and kept this diary and four others in a trunk as treasured possessions. After Alma died, however, her son Joel, who lived in Billings at the time, inherited the trunk and its contents, which were put away in storage. In 2002, when Joel was downsizing to move into a smaller home, the diaries were accidentally thrown out. A passerby rescued the diaries from the garbage and donated them to the Montana Historical Society. MHS staff were able to locate Mr. Story and he officially donated Florence's diary, as well as three others kept by his mother, on behalf of his family.

The diary provides rare insight into the life of an average teenager during the Depression, as well as an equally rare account of how a community came together to support the young girl and her family during her illness.

–*JF*

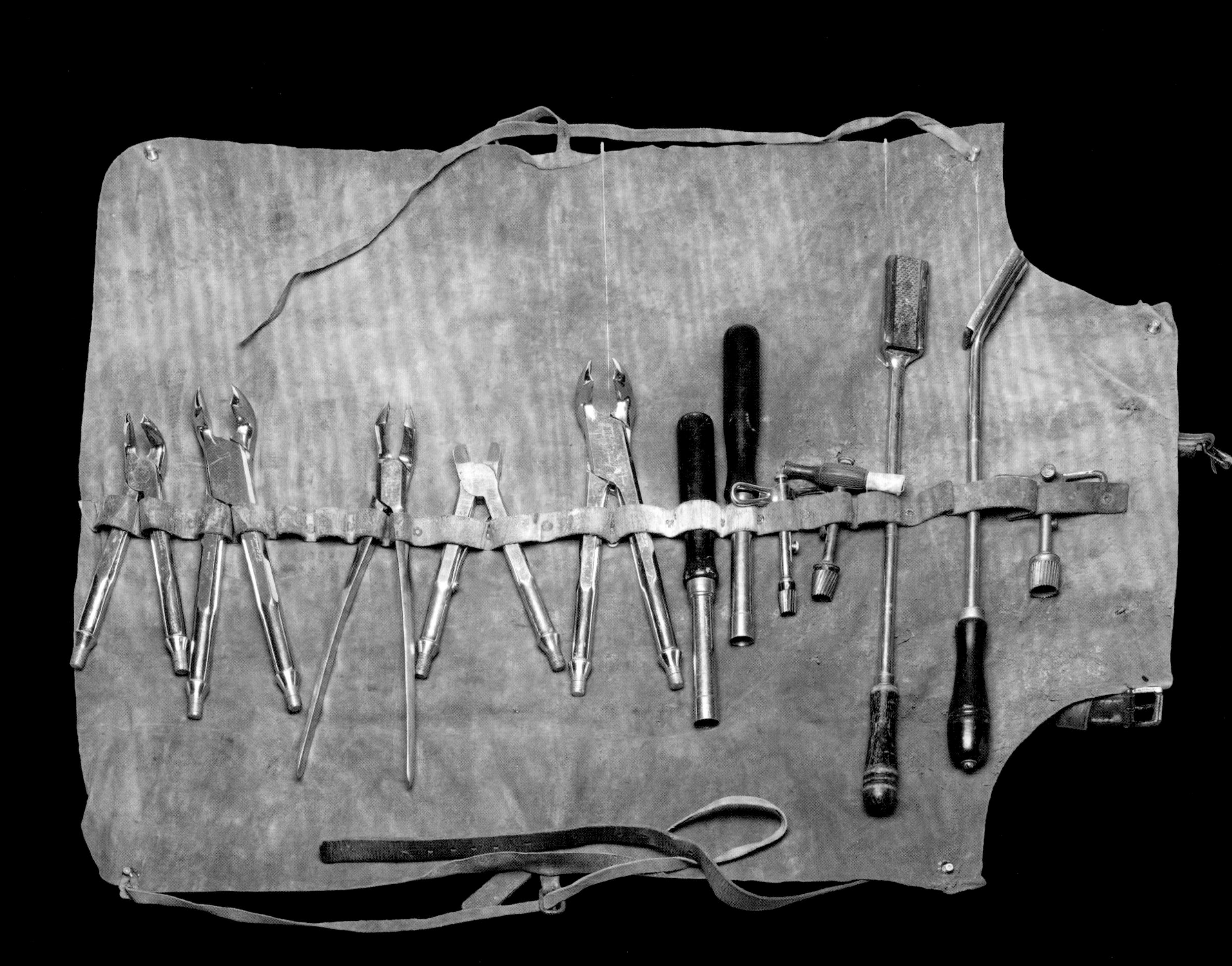

Montanans at Work

◈

Montana's history has been profoundly shaped by the ways in which its inhabitants have provided for themselves and their communities. Before the arrival of Euro-Americans, Native peoples lived off the land. Men hunted, traded with neighboring tribes, crafted tools, and served in military societies. Women gathered edible and medicinal plants, fed their families, and processed hides from which they crafted clothing, moccasins, and tipis; they also engaged in trade and dismantled, moved, and set up camps. Beginning in the 1840s, missionaries attempted to introduce European farming practices, but only after the bison were nearly extinct and the federal government had forced tribes onto reservations did this region's Indigenous peoples abandon their traditional ways of making a living. Some Indians prospered as ranchers, farmers, and wage laborers, despite the obstacles placed in their way; for many more, poverty defined reservation life.

The first Europeans who worked in Montana also utilized the state's natural resources to earn a living. Just as beaver attracted trappers, gold lured miners, and timber enticed lumberjacks, Montana's rich grasslands led to the development of a thriving cattle industry. Livestock was initially brought in to supply trading posts in the 1830s, and the first trail drive from Texas reached the territory in 1866. By the heyday of the open-range era in the mid-1880s, five hundred thousand head of cattle grazed Montana's plains. After the devastating winter of 1886–1887 decimated the free-roaming herds, ranching practices transformed to include barbed-wire fencing and the production of hay and other crops for winter feeding. Throughout the twentieth century—with continuing advances in technology and medical science—veterinary medicine played an ever-greater role in ensuring the health of livestock.

Veterinary dental tools in elk hide apron, ca. 1920, 36" × 35". Gift of Dr. Jack Ward, 1984.100.101

In this 1926 oil painting, *Drifting in a Blizzard, Montana*, Western artist Robert Lindneux (1871–1970) captures the fierceness of a northern Plains snowstorm and its toll on both man and beast. 38½" × 24¼". Gift of W. B. Davis, x1960.06.01

While farming arrived in western Montana with trading posts and missions, it was the homesteading boom of the early twentieth century that drew farm families to the Treasure State in large numbers. Free land, atypical rainfall, irrigation infrastructure, and railroad advertising led eighty-two thousand homesteaders to file claims on 25 million acres between 1909 and 1919. "Proving up" required arduous labor of both men and women, but homesteading women had the additional duties of caring for their families. Women's employment opportunities outside the home were generally limited, but many enterprising women, including photographer Evelyn Cameron, managed both to run a household and to find ways to bring in needed income.

Alongside agriculture, mining has long remained an important industry in Montana. Like placer operations, underground mining required backbreaking labor in harsh conditions, while also being exponentially more dangerous. During the 1890s, accidents in Butte's copper mines killed between three and four men every week, and mine workers suffered high rates of miner's consumption and

When the state commissioned Billings artist Robert C. Morrison (1924–2013) to create a mural for its new Labor and Industry Building (now the Walt Sullivan Building) in 1960, he chose to honor *Montana Workers—Mining, Ranching, Building*. The mural is made of hand-blown glass tiles—called tesserae—imported from Italy. 60" x 82". Capitol Art Collection, x1960.18.01

related lung diseases as a result of their work. Union strikes and tragedies like the 1917 Speculator Mine explosion, which killed 168 men and remains the deadliest disaster in Montana's hard-rock-mining history, gradually led to improved working conditions. Even so, danger remained a constant for the industry, as exemplified by the Smith coal mine disaster near Bearcreek in 1943.

Today, Montanans continue to take pride in their work. The iconic figures of the miner, the cowhand, and the homesteader symbolize the effort required to make a living under the Big Sky.

48. Father Ravalli's Buhrstones

ca. 1845, 42½" × 36¼". Gift of St. Ignatius Mission, x1904.01.05

◈

FATHER Anthony Ravalli brought this set of French buhrstones to St. Mary's Mission in the Bitterroot Valley and constructed the area's first gristmill in 1845. Used for grinding grain into fine flour, buhrstones were crucial tools in the milling industry and enabled the mission's residents to process their harvest with improved efficiency.

Father Pierre-Jean De Smet, a Jesuit, had founded St. Mary's Mission in 1841. Using seeds he obtained at Fort Colville, Washington Territory, De Smet and other Jesuits planted wheat, potatoes, and oats in the valley, harvesting their first crops in 1842. Italian-born Father Anthony Ravalli, S.J., arrived at the mission in 1845 by way of Fort Vancouver, Washington, bringing with him—among other supplies—these cumbersome buhrstones.

A man of many talents, Father Ravalli immediately set about using his mechanical skills to construct a water-powered mill at St. Mary's. With the help of lay brothers Claessens and Specht, and a French Canadian builder named Biledot (who may have been a millwright), Father Ravalli completed the small milling plant. The team built an overshot waterwheel—that is, a vertical wheel with a horizontal axis—and installed the buhrstones. The buhrstones are approximately sixteen inches and twenty inches in diameter, and their iron hardware, still attached, offers clues to how they functioned. The smaller stone, set in an iron casing, sits at one end, and an iron axle runs through both stones and a thick wooden disc. Powered by the overshot waterwheel, the stones' inside surfaces would have ground the grain as they rubbed against one another. The mill could grind a dozen bushels of grain into flour each day.

Following his purchase of the St. Mary's Mission properties in 1850, John Owen continued to use Father Ravalli's buhrstones until building larger mill works. In 1866, Danish artist Peter Tofft (1825–1901) painted this watercolor of the replacement mill that Owen had constructed on the site about 1865.
Flour and Sawmill Attached to FT. Owen, Bitterroot, MT, 9¼" × 6".
Gift of Matilda Ackely Donaho, x1930.01.01

St. Mary's Mission and its mill flourished, but conflict between the Salish and the Blackfeet put the Jesuits in danger, forcing the mission to close in 1850. The Jesuits found a ready buyer in John Owen, a former sutler who carried goods and supplies for the military. Owen purchased the mill, mission buildings, and fields for $250. He put Father Ravalli's buhrstones to use grinding wheat. The mill continued to function at Fort Owen until 1857, when it was replaced by a larger apparatus, and Jesuits took the buhrstones to a mill in St. Ignatius.

Although the Jesuits reestablished St. Mary's Mission near Stevensville in 1866, the buhrstones remained at St. Ignatius until 1904, when they were donated to the Montana Historical Society. Today, the buhrstones remain on display at the Society's museum, representing one of the earliest industries during Montana's colonial settlement. *–EB*

49. Buffalo Robe Sale Flier

1877, 8¼" × 10¼". Gift of Garner Lane, Benning & Barsalou Auctioneers Records, sc2366

◈

With its enormous, shaggy head, deep grunt, powerful gait, and surprising agility, the American bison inspires awe and respect. For Plains Indians, the animal's physical presence was surpassed only by its role as sustenance for both body and soul. Historian Dan Flores noted that the bison and Native peoples were entwined for centuries in a "dynamic equilibrium" that sustained all and inspired creation stories, sacred ceremonies, and rituals. Tragically, for both the bison and the Plains Indians, the hide and bones of the majestic beast also meant big business for nineteenth-century trappers and traders. As beaver fur declined in popularity in the late 1830s, bison robes assumed preeminence. By 1883, the rampant slaughter of bison—at an estimated rate of 1.5 million head per year in the 1870s—brought the once vast herds and Native peoples' traditional ways of life to the brink of extinction.

The hide trade that devastated Indigenous economies played a critical role in Montana's economic development. This 1877 broadside, with a stylized sketch of a charging bison, illustrates one reason for the extent of the hide trade's impact on Montana. The flier announces the auction of twelve thousand "specially selected" bison robes by Fort Benton merchants T. C. Power & Brothers and I. G. Baker & Company through a Montreal auction house located nearly 1,800 miles away from their home base in Montana Territory. Trade in bison robes formed the bedrock of the financial success of these two companies, ultimately allowing them to diversify into banking, steamboats, overland transportation, and livestock operations.

The remains of the mass slaughter of bison by recreational and commercial hunters, buffalo skulls and bones are piled along the tracks of the Northern Pacific Railroad in eastern Montana, n.d. 945-968

The unregulated slaughter by commercial and sport hunters—compounded by the construction of the railroad, cattle-borne diseases, drought, interrupted migration patterns, and competition for grazing land—all but wiped out Montana's bison herds, bringing an abrupt end to the hide trade. For I. G. Baker and T. C. Power, declining bison populations simply required a shift in business strategy, but for Montana's Native peoples, the animal's disappearance was catastrophic, leaving tribal nations starving and dependent on the federal government. Plenty Coups, an Apsáalooke chief, described the loss poignantly: "When the buffalo went away the hearts of my people fell to the ground, and they could not lift them up again. After this nothing happened."

This buffalo robe sale flier reminds us that the significance of an object remains subjective and open to interpretation. For traders like I. G. Baker and T. C. Power, this document would have heralded progress, fortune, and so-called Manifest Destiny. At the same time, however, it symbolizes an unbridled, devastating assault on the economies, cultures, and sovereignty of Montana's tribal nations. *–JF*

British North-West Territory

Season 1877 Season 1877

BUFFALO ROBES

TRADE MARK REGISTERED.

THE UNITED COLLECTION FOR 1877 OF

T. C. POWER & BRO. AND I. G. BAKER & CO.

OF FORT BENTON, M. T.

Every Robe THIS SEASON'S CATCH, and specially selected for Canada.

UNQUESTIONABLY THE FINEST LOT OF BUFFALO ROBES EVER OFFERED IN THIS MARKET.

UNRESERVED AUCTION SALE

OF

A Collection of over 12,000 Selected Robes.

THE SALE WILL TAKE PLACE ON

Friday, 7th September,

In the Warehouse next door to T. JAMES CLAXTON & CO., St. Joseph Street., Montreal.

THREE (**3**) MONTHS' CREDIT, WITHOUT INTEREST,

WILL BE GIVEN ON ALL PURCHASES OVER $100.

The Robes will be open for inspection and Catalogues may be had three days before the Sale, on personal application or by letter. As there are arrangements with the Grand Trunk Railway for an extra cheap excursion from Toronto to Montreal on the 4th September, Fare $4.00, with corresponding low rates from all other points, good for 10 days, this will be a capital opportunity for getting a cheap trip and purchasing cheap Buffalo Robes. Those who were fortunate in purchasing Robes at the sale last year were well satisfied with the result, and as we intend making an established yearly Trade Sale, all may rely upon liberal treatment.

Sale at ELEVEN o'clock.

BENNING & BARSALOU,

Auctioneers.

MONTREAL, August 30th, 1877.

50. Square & Compass Branding Iron

ca. 1899, 42⅝" × 7½" × 6". Gift of the Montana Stockgrowers Association, x1967.08.07

Branding is a ubiquitous chore across Montana's cattle country. This image was taken on the Crow Reservation about 1894 by O. S. Goff. Bud Lake and Randy Brewer Crow Indian Photograph Collection, Lot 035 B03F0.07

By the time the first cattle arrived in Montana during the 1840s, the practice of branding livestock to show ownership was thousands of years old. Intended in large part to thwart theft, brands gained significance during the open-range era when herds belonging to different owners grazed together on public lands.

At first, Montana's territorial government authorized individual counties to record and regulate livestock brands. By 1872, however, the realities of open-range practices demanded reassessment of the statutes. In response to the new territory's burgeoning livestock industry, the 1871–72 legislative assembly created a general office for recording brands and marks, and mandated that the records be kept in a "book suitable for the purpose, which shall be free to the inspection of all persons interested." On February 10, 1873, the Poindexter and Orr Ranch in Beaverhead County became the first to register its brand with the entity destined to become the Montana Department of Livestock. A traditional symbol of the Masons, the Square & Compass brand appeared on the right hip of cattle and on the left shoulder of mules and horses.

Originally based in California, William Orr and partner Phillip Poindexter began wintering cattle in the Beaverhead soon after the beginning of Montana's gold rush. Poindexter served in the 1872 Territorial Legislature and promoted the construction of Montana's first railway, the Utah and Northern. Both families were integral in Dillon's founding and its establishment as Beaverhead's county seat. The partners were also among the first Montana ranchers to raise draft horses for the growing territory.

Although fifty-five other brands were also recorded on February 10, 1873, the Square & Compass was indisputably the first to be recorded in the current system. The Matador Cattle Co., located in Dillon, currently holds the brand, and Montana's original brand books, in use since 1873, continue to be held in trust by the Department of Livestock's Brand Division.

–ZAS

51. Evelyn Cameron's Camera

1903, 8⅝" × 10" × 18". Gift of the Estate of Janet Williams, Evelyn Cameron Collection, 1991.07.01

BORN into an affluent British family, photographer Evelyn Jephson Flower Cameron (1868–1928) came to eastern Montana with her husband, Ewen, in 1891 to raise polo ponies. When that venture failed and their savings disappeared with the collapse of the Stock Growers National Bank in Miles City during the Panic of 1893, the Camerons were forced to find new ways to support themselves. Ewen, an ornithologist, devoted his time to the study of Montana's birds, while Evelyn handled most operations on the family's small ranch, including cooking, gardening, selling produce, and taking in wealthy boarders.

Evelyn Cameron's most successful venture, however, began in 1894, when she purchased her first camera. Over the course of the next three decades, she produced what would become one of the most celebrated collections of Montana photography. Cameron photographed the people living on surrounding ranches and homesteads, charging twenty-five cents apiece for prints. Often traveling for miles to reach her subjects, she documented everything from the tarpaper shacks of homesteaders to XIT cowboys driving cattle across the Yellowstone River, and from shearers stripping sheep of their fleeces to farmers plowing the prairie. She also captured images of the isolated badlands of eastern Montana and of the birds and other wildlife her husband avidly studied.

Cameron purchased this camera—a five-inch by seven-inch Tourist Graflex manufactured by Folmer & Schwing—in 1905, affectionately nicknaming it "Lexie." She used a German-made Goerz lens. When not in use, the viewfinder and lens holder could be folded down and stored in the cowhide carrying case, an important feature for transporting fragile equipment by horseback. The photographer could adjust the aperture by manipulating knobs that widened or narrowed the space between the camera's two curtains. Twisting another knob wound up the tension of the shutter curtain take-up roller, increasing the shutter speed. This design allowed for shutter speeds as fast as 1/1000th of a second, making it possible for Cameron to capture clear photographs of fast-moving subjects like bucking horses.

A self-taught photographer, Cameron kept detailed records of her work in a diary, noting the aperture and shutter settings, lighting, and the type of negative she used. An entry written on October 12, 1908, describes a day spent photographing a neighboring family and their ranch:

> I took 2 exposures of 22 month old child holding pony, Mandan. Front view of house, Mrs Renn, sister Connie, child, dogs, pony front. Mrs Renn & Connie sitting on wolf hide on verandah. Saddled up. Took view with creek in, beef herd pasture, & one exposure of cattle crossing creek from Jim's back 1/25 4 film pack Sun hazey. Spoke to Cap as passed. Home 7:00.

Together, Cameron's photographs and diaries now comprise an unparalleled record of both her life and that of eastern Montana's ranching community during the first quarter of the twentieth century.

–*CE*

Cameron self-portrait, mounted on Trinket and holding "Lexie," ca. 1912. PAc 90-87 NB029E

GOLDEN ROD
VACUUM CLEANER
THE HUGRO MANUFACTURING CO.
CHICAGO

52. Hand-Operated Vacuum Cleaner

ca. 1912, 11" × 10" × 51". x1986.01.59

◈

Before the invention of the vacuum cleaner, homemakers or their servants cleaned carpets by sweeping them, sometimes after throwing down damp tea leaves or cornmeal to capture the dust. Even more laborious, spring and fall cleaning often required the shuffling of furniture so that rugs could be rolled up (after removing the tacks that held them in place), carried outside, and beaten on the clothesline, before putting the house back together again.

By the 1880s, the rise of industrialized manufacturing made carpet more affordable and increasingly common in middle-class homes. Around the same time, new evidence that bacteria spread disease fueled a fear of invisible threats lurking wherever dirt accumulated. Carpet sweepers—devices that combined a broom-brushing action with a dustpan—were effective for picking up large debris, but the problem of removing dust from thick, pile carpet remained. The answer, it turned out, was suction.

Inventors proposed a variety of ways to create a suctioning appliance, including bellows (which required a second pair of hands to operate) and hand-cranked fans. Devices like this Golden Rod vacuum cleaner, manufactured by the Hugro Manufacturing Co. of Chicago, used a third method: a plunger. To activate the suction, the user stabilized the machine with one hand while pulling up on the plunger handle with the other, like a syringe, which in turn sucked air and dust into the machine.

Hugro was one of over 250 "manual suction cleaner" manufacturers that came and went in the United States. Like its competitors, it primarily relied on door-to-door salesmen who worked on commission to land its product in the hands of homemakers. In 1912, Montanans could purchase a Golden Rod for nine dollars. The investment, according to a May 2, 1912, advertisement in the *Big Timber Pioneer*, was essential for health. While brooms and carpet sweepers "fill the air with dust-loaded dangerous disease germs," the ad warned, the "Golden Rod vacuum cleaner eats up the dust, makes your home sanitary, [and] increases the life of your carpet and your family."

Electric vacuums replaced hand-operated machines as electricity became increasingly common in the early twentieth century, yet some publications still promoted manual units alongside more advanced models, likely appealing to customers who, like many Montanans, lived in rural areas "where electricity is usually not available." With improved technology and ease of operation, the product's claims also became more elaborate: "With one of these machines, housecleaning will no longer be a nightmare. . . . The dust collected is said to be an excellent fertilizer."

Hugro promised that the Golden Rod was so easy to operate a child could use it and that the device would save purchasers "at least one hour's labor each day." While such claims were likely a bit exaggerated, hand-powered vacuums anticipated a fast-approaching future in which the Golden Rod's electric counterparts were so common as to be unremarkable. *–SAT*

53. Dressing Screen

ca. 1930, 72" × 1" × 60". 1984.103.01

◈

THIS screen was initially acquired by an antiques dealer from the estate of "Madam E. F. F.," owner of the Richmond Apartments in Butte's once-thriving, two-block red-light district. Allegedly used in a brothel as a dressing screen, the object is suggestive of the illicit past of a city that Montana historian Ellen Baumler described as "the widest open town in the wide-open west."

Indeed, the business of sex work in Butte boomed alongside the mining industry. By 1890, Butte counted six luxury parlor houses, numerous brothels, and hundreds of one-room closets, or "cribs," earning the town comparison to the much larger vice-ridden districts of San Francisco and New Orleans. The so-called public women caught the attention of potential customers by tapping on the ground-floor windows with thimbles, rings, knitting needles, and chopsticks.

In addition to the women and their clientele, various other individuals and institutions had an interest in the business of prostitution. The Anaconda Copper Mining Company, for example, recognized that it kept workers distracted and therefore less likely to organize. City coffers benefited from money paid by brothels in rents, fines, and protection fees. Wealthy businessmen also saw red-light real estate in the mining city as a lucrative investment.

Conversely, prostitutes themselves faced considerable risk and poor working and living conditions. In the years between 1910 and 1916, approximately one thousand women worked in Butte's red-light district at any given time, and many struggled to secure adequate food, housing, and access to reproductive healthcare. The business both peaked and began its decline, however, in 1916, when the rising threat of venereal disease prompted the federal government to crack down on prostitution. Shortly thereafter, the operation went underground—literally, in Butte's case—relocating to basements, alleyways, and tunnels filled with cribs.

Of course, brothels and parlor houses could be found in cities and towns across Montana. But in Butte, as Baumler writes, "prostitution was intertwined with other downtown businesses and was as much a part of the scenery as the steel headframes that loomed over the landscape." *–SAT*

Although Butte had Montana's largest and most notorious red-light district, prostitutes worked in almost every sizable community. These prostitutes, posing ca. 1905 with potential customers in Miles City, are wearing "Mother Hubbard" dresses, loose gowns designed to be worn without corsets. By the 1880s, these "easy access" dresses had become prostitutes' standard uniform.
Photograph from Robert C. Morrison Collection, PAc 95–70 Box 11 [18]

54. *Miners in the Stope*

1937, 20" × 24", by Paul Sample (1896–1974). Gift of Francis Kelley Wood, Mary Kelley Doubleday, and George Hepburn; Cornelius Kelley Collection, x1966.21.10

◈

The story of Montana is inseparable from the history of mining in Butte. By 1910, Butte was the largest producer of copper in North America and home to a population of more than ninety thousand people—fourteen thousand of them miners—making it the largest city between Minneapolis and Spokane.

While Butte called itself the "Richest Hill on Earth," it also garnered a reputation as the most dangerous mining district in the world. Accidents, cave-ins, and fires were common in mine shafts, and respiratory illness from inhaled dust caused long-term health problems for workers. Butte's miners unionized in the late 1870s, hoping to gain higher wages, better benefits, and safer conditions. During the early 1900s, the city was embroiled in many high-profile strikes and became nationally known as the Gibraltar of Unionism. *Fortune* magazine commissioned this painting from artist Paul Sample (1896–1974) for a 1937 feature article on the Anaconda Copper Mining Company. Titled *Miners in the Stope*, the painting unflinchingly depicts the physical demands on working miners.

While working on commission for *Fortune* magazine, Sample also captured this view: *Butte Hill as Seen from Butte City*. In 1988, MHS featured Sample's painting on a special Butte edition of its award-winning quarterly, *Montana The Magazine of Western History*.

Born in Louisville, Kentucky, in 1896, Sample volunteered for the U.S. Navy in 1917 after his first year at Dartmouth College. Following World War I, he returned to Dartmouth, where he gained notoriety as an intercollegiate boxing champ before graduating in 1921. Shortly thereafter, Sample contracted tuberculosis and spent the next four years recuperating in the Adirondacks, which led to his interest in art. He studied with Jonas Lie at the Otis Art Institute and then, in 1926, took a position at the University of California–Los Angeles as a professor of fine arts. In 1938, Sample became an artist-in-residence at Dartmouth College, where he remained until his retirement in 1962. In 1974, Sample died at his home in Norwich, Vermont.

Prior to the 1930s, Sample had been known as a landscape artist whose paintings portrayed scenes of rural New England, where he and his family often spent their summers. Prompted by *Fortune*'s commission, however, he turned his attention to the lives of industrial workers. *Miners in the Stope* illustrated the hazards mentioned in the January 1937 article, "Anaconda Copper." Today, the painting can be found in the Cornelius Kelley Collection at the Montana Historical Society Museum.

–*BS*

55. Smith Mine Disaster Message

1943, 12¾" × ¾" × 6". Gift of Elmer Anderson, 1985.38.01

At eight o'clock in the morning on Saturday, February 27, 1943, Emil Anderson and seventy-six other coal miners entered Smith Mine #3 near the community of Bearcreek. One hour and thirty-seven minutes later, employees close to the surface of the mine felt an enormous pressure in their ears, followed by a powerful gust of air filled with soot and debris exploding past them. Only three workers escaped from the mine. Within its depths, thirty men died instantly from the forceful blast and another forty-four would soon suffocate. Anderson was among this latter group. In the short time he had remaining, he used the materials he had available to leave his family this message in chalk on the lid of a dynamite box:

> It's 5 minutes pass [*sic*] 11 o'clock Agnes and children I'm sorry we had to go this way God bless you all. Emil with lots [of] kisse[s].

This deeply personal and tragic farewell serves as a reminder of the worst coal mining disaster in Montana's history. It is among the most poignant objects cared for by the Montana Historical Society.

The men who perished in the Smith Mine are part of a legacy of extraction that spans the state's history. Coal mining in Montana Territory began in the 1860s with small enterprises providing fuel to local families and businesses. Despite vast reserves, impetus for high-volume extraction lagged until the transcontinental railroads arrived during the

1880s and 1890s. Then, major coal mines developed along transportation routes at Bozeman Pass, Sand Coulee, and the Bull Mountains. Coal-rich lands south of Billings remained untapped until the federal government reduced the Crow Reservation in 1882. Within four years, businessmen staked mining claims and established the town of Red Lodge. By 1889, a railroad spur line transported the area's coal to market.

With two mines flanking the city, Red Lodge flourished, attracting immigrants from throughout Europe. The polyglot population included Scandinavians, Slavs, Germans, Welsh, and Irish. Emil Anderson, the youngest son of Finnish immigrants, spent most of his childhood in Red Lodge. His father and brothers also worked in the coal mines, and Emil began working in the mine in 1916, when he was just fourteen years old.

East of Red Lodge, over a steep divide, extraction of high-grade coal near Washoe and Bearcreek began in earnest when a railroad spur from Bridger was built in 1906. Production peaked during World War I, remained relatively steady through the 1920s and 1930s, and rose again during World War II.

The Smith Mine disaster in February 1943 did not halt the underground mining operations in the area. Wartime demand for high-quality coal and a few lucrative contracts kept area mines profitable through the mid-1940s. However, several factors—the end of World War II, the rising popularity of natural gas, railroads' conversion to diesel engines, the termination of railroad service to the area, and new strip mines in other localities—caused most of the area's mines to close by the late 1950s. The towns of Bearcreek and Washoe lost the vast majority of their populations, and Red Lodge transformed itself from a gritty mining town to an outdoor recreationists' retreat. Still, the hard work and sacrifices of the coal miners who once made their homes there remain evident on the landscape and in the community's memory. Artifacts related to the mines, like the delicate chalk writing on this wooden lid, provide a tangible link to this grueling and highly dangerous industry that was so central to Montana's development. *–KH*

56. A'aninin Quillwork Moccasins

ca. 1950, 10" × 3¾" × 5⅛", by Mabel Bradley (1903–1972).

Gift of E. E. MacGilvra, x1962.06.06 a-b

◈

Indigenous porcupine quillwork had almost died out when Mabel Bradley (1903–1972), an A'aninin (White Clay) artist from the Fort Belknap Reservation, made these beautifully decorated men's moccasins around 1950. The moccasins, carefully kept and likely never worn, represent the type of quillwork practiced for centuries by Native women prior to the introduction of glass beads from Europe. Beads, available in a wide variety of bright colors and easy to use, largely replaced quills among most artisans.

Quillwork, traditionally done by women in the winter months, was, and still is, a slow and exacting process. Once harvested from a live or dead animal, porcupine quills had to be washed to rid them of oil, etched in a solution so the dye would adhere to the quill, sorted by size, and then dyed. Plant dyes such as buffalo berries (red), blueberries (purple), yellow moss or wild sunflower (yellow), and wild grapes (black) provided vibrant colors. The artist softened each quill in her mouth, then pulled it between her teeth to flatten it. Two threads or pieces of sinew were used to sew parallel lines on a strip of hide. One end of the quill was tucked under the sinew, laid across the hide, and wrapped over the thread on the opposite side. When applied properly, the flattened and wrapped quills formed a lane of color with no holes or sinew visible.

For a more complex design, a highly skilled quill worker could use multiple quills at one time. In this method, called plaiting, two or more quills are folded and layered to form triangles, diamonds, or star shapes. The possibilities for design themes are limitless, and the quilled strips are durable and reusable. A decorated strip of hide could then be attached on top of a garment, often to cover seams. If the garment was damaged, the decorated strip could be removed and reapplied later. On these moccasins, the quills were applied directly to the deer hide, but the sole could be replaced and quills repaired to extend their life.

The Indian Arts and Crafts Act, passed in 1934, inspired a renewed investment in Indigenous peoples' traditional artistic skills and created a market for authentic, Indian-made products. From 1936 until 1942, Julia Ereaux Schultz (1872–1976), also of the A'aninin Tribe from Fort Belknap, led a Works Progress Administration program to revive the traditional material culture of the A'aninin and Nakoda Tribes. Schultz organized elderly women, who still retained the skills and knowledge of traditional designs, to share this information with younger women. Through classes, craft fairs, and even national exhibitions, women were able to sell their creations for profit, while preserving and perpetuating appreciation for these centuries-old traditions. Influenced by elders who preceded her, Mabel Bradley undertook a decades-long effort to revive the skill and artistry of quillwork. *–CB*

Montanans at Play

◈

Play constitutes more than simply fun and games; it reflects and influences the culture in which it is undertaken. Consequently, examining the ways in which earlier generations of Montanans spent their leisure time provides us with an important window into the past.

As with youngsters everywhere, play was a defining element of life for Montana's children. To a far greater extent than is the case today, however, play helped prepare younger generations for the roles they were expected to adopt in adulthood. Young girls hosted make-believe tea parties, played house, and carried dolls in toy cradleboards or baby buggies. Boys acquired the hunting skills they would someday need to feed their families by pursuing small game with child-sized bows and arrows and practicing with firearms.

Since the average family owned far fewer possessions of all sorts—and toys were no exception—children's play was defined to a much greater extent by their imaginations and the creative use of materials on hand. In addition, due to necessity and custom, youngsters of yesteryear were more likely to spend a significant portion of their time working. Once children completed their chores, however, parents commonly allowed them to venture forth without adult supervision, making unchaperoned explorations of their surroundings, whether rural or urban, a favored pastime.

Grown-ups, too, from earlier generations spent a greater percentage of their time working. At the end of the nineteenth century, for example, a standard workweek was almost sixty hours long. But even with less leisure time, recreation still offered important opportunities for relaxation and exercise, as well as escape from day-to-day routines and concerns.

While outlets for fun and enjoyment may seem a timeless human need, many aspects of play have evolved with changes in material and social conditions.

Under the watchful eye of timekeepers, competitors at Libby's Logger Days work the crosscut saw, while a crowd observes from packed bleachers, ca. 1960–1969.
Bill Browning, photographer.
PAC 2002-62- E1B-1089

(opposite) While copious snowfall hinders most means of travel, it provides a boon to winter recreation. Here, "Miss Forsyth" dons cross-country skis during her 1894 visit to Yellowstone National Park. F. Jay Haynes, photographer. Gift of Mrs. Isabel Haynes, Haynes Foundation Photograph Collection, H-03283

As soon as Montana communities grew large enough to field teams, organized sports became a cherished aspect of life across the Treasure State. In this ca. 1920 postcard, Polson football players face off against an un-pictured foe. Masse Photo Studio, photographer. Mulvaney Real Photo Postcard Collection, PAC 2013-50.1835

Surprisingly, although many spheres of public life became less restrictive along gendered lines with the passage of time, some activities in which women initially participated—rodeo bronc busting, for example—were later deemed off-limits when cultural attitudes decided they were too dangerous for female competitors. During the twentieth century, advances in technology gave rise to new forms of entertainment (motion pictures, radios, and computer games), rendered many activities safer (with helmets and other protective gear), and freed up more time for leisure activities through the invention of a great variety of labor-saving devices (washing machines, chain saws, and microwave ovens). Conversely, many activities that were formerly essential for survival—like hunting, fishing, weaving, and gardening—have, over time, lost their utilitarian necessity and become primarily recreational pastimes.

57. Nakoda Handmade Doll

ca. 1900, 17⅜" × 35½". Gift of O. C. and Edith Johnson and Don and Betty Johnson, 2013.20.07

◈

Like youth everywhere, Plains Indian children played with dolls that reflected—and often prepared them for—the grown-up world around them. Indigenous dollmakers used readily available natural materials to craft dolls and other toys in age-old designs. Later, they incorporated trade goods into traditional patterns. By the middle of the twentieth century, Indian dolls had also become popular as souvenirs collected by non-Indians, providing needed income for American Indian dollmakers.

Many of the particulars surrounding the maker and original owner of this Nakoda (Assiniboine) doll have, unfortunately, been lost to time. At thirty-six inches high, the doll is considerably taller than most traditional dolls, but even with so little known about her origin, she still conveys significant insights regarding Montana's past.

The detail with which she has been outfitted—including green cloth leggings that do not show—accurately reflect how Nakoda women dressed at the close of the nineteenth century. A red scarf covers her horsehair braids and frames the doll's carefully carved, wooden face. A black ribbon dress is wrapped at her waist with a tack-studded leather belt that features a drop made of tubular white glass beads. Her knee-length necklace is composed of round red beads and tubular white beads, and her moccasins are decorated in Nakota-style beadwork. This attention to detail continues on the back of the doll where the accessories that were traditionally carried by women are replicated in miniature—a small buckskin bag, a diamond-shaped umbilical pouch, a knife sheath, and a capped awl case.

The materials used in her manufacture—cotton and silk cloth, brass studs, glass beads, leather, straw, wood, and horsehair—indicate the supplies available in the sparsely settled region of northeast Montana at the turn of the century. Finally, the scarce detail that is known about the doll's history speaks to the role that trade with non-Indians played in reservation life: the doll's maker likely exchanged it for supplies with the donor's grandparents, O. C. and Edith Worthy Johnson, operators of Wolf Point's first general store, which served the nearby Fort Peck and Fort Belknap Reservations. *–SAT*

THIS IS A
OSTRICH
WILD MAN
COPYRIGHT, 1904, BY HARPER & BROS.

58. *Playing Circus*

1904, 8" × 10", by Fanny Cory Cooney (1877–1972). 2014.35.05

◈

In 1904, Harper & Bros. published a series of lithographs depicting children at play by Montana artist Fanny Cory Cooney (1877–1972). Part of that series, *Playing Circus,* pays homage to the creativity of the young impresarios while sympathizing with the plight of the less eager participants (a rooster masquerading as an ostrich, a tiger-striped dog, and a baby brother who, throughout the series, bears the brunt of his elder siblings' enthusiasm). Each scene was produced in at least two different versions, one of which included a descriptive verse. The poem for *Playing Circus* reads:

> We're planning for a circus—
> It's the nicest kind of play,
> We hope that some grown-ups'll come,
> 'Cause they have got to pay.
> The wild-man really howls because he thinks
> it isn't fun;
> And you just better wait until the tight-rope
> act's begun!

Because manufactured toys and games were rare possessions for earlier generations of Montanans, children relied heavily on their imaginations to make their own fun, using whatever resources were at hand. For those living on remote homesteads in sparsely populated regions, siblings, pets, and barnyard animals often served as their primary companions away from school.

No one better understood the world of children than Montana artist Fanny Cory Cooney. After graduating from Helena High School, Cooney ventured east in 1895 to study art and to work as an illustrator in New York City under the pen name F. Y. Cory. Her promising career was stalled, however, when Fanny, grieving the death of her sister Agnes, returned to Montana. In 1904, she married Fred Cooney and the couple settled on a remote ranch on the Missouri River, "27 miles from Helena . . . and 3 miles from anything."

Fanny's initial attempts to resume her career as an illustrator were frustrated by the demands of motherhood and ranch life. But as her children approached college age in the 1920s, she once again began working to bring in extra income, turning her talents—and her droll observations of her own children—into comics. Between 1926 and 1956, she drew three separate newspaper cartoon series, the most popular and longest-running of which was *Sonnysayings,* an internationally syndicated look at life through the eyes of an innocently mischievous, curly-headed boy who perpetually remained five years old.

Whether drawing *Sonnysayings* or scenes like *Playing Circus,* Cooney captured the blithe spirit of childhood in her work. As *The Critic* magazine noted in 1900, "She has fancy, brightness, and quaintness; she has the faculty which is not to be underestimated of focusing these qualities into timelessness and practical use. Her best pieces depict charming children, whose sweetness is tempered by mischievousness."

–KL

59. Fannie Sperry Steele's Saddle

1914, 26" × 21" × 38". Gift of Fannie Sperry Steele, x1970.06.01

◈

THIS saddle, stamped "World Champion Bucking Horse Rider" on the front of the cantle, was a gift to the Montana Historical Society from Fannie Sperry Steele (1887–1983). Fannie's husband, Bill, purchased the saddle from the Miles City Saddlery Company and had it specially tooled to commemorate her winning bronc ride at the 1914 Miles City Roundup.

Born on a homestead in the Prickly Pear Valley, Steele was destined to become a rodeo legend. Her lifelong love of riding began as a toddler, when her mother placed her on a horse for the first time and warned her not to fall. She grew up in the saddle, rounding up and breaking some of the roughest wild horses. During spontaneous riding competitions between neighboring ranches, Fannie demonstrated remarkable skill and tenacity on the wildest bucking broncs.

Steele's professional riding career began in 1904 at the Montana State Fair in Helena, where the teenager competed in high-speed relay races that required riders to change horses quickly. Afterward, Butte promoter Walter R. Wilmot signed Fannie and several other young women to ride relays across the Midwest. Wherever they competed, the so-called Montana Girls were popular with audiences. In 1905, at the Minnesota State Fair, Fannie won her first award—for "Meritorious Riding."

In 1907, the troupe of riders shocked spectators by sporting then-scandalous black riding bloomers during competition. That same year, Fannie rode in her first professional bronc contest in Helena, winning a gold medal. The *Helena Daily Independent* reported that "Miss Sperry showed what a Montana ranch girl can do when it comes to handling horses." Fannie always rode broncs "slick," which is without the stirrups "hobbled" (fastened together under the horse's belly), as she believed hobbling did not give the horse a fair chance and considered the practice unsporting.

It was during the first Calgary Stampede, held in 1912, that Fannie's fame as a bronc rider was secured. She drew a notorious horse, Red Wing, who had previously thrown and stomped to death rider Joe LaMar. Before a crowd of sixty thousand, Fannie rode Red Wing for the full eight seconds. The performance earned her the title of "Lady Bucking Horse Champion of the World," as well as a cash prize of one thousand dollars, a three-hundred-dollar gold belt buckle, and a beautiful saddle decorated with hand-tooled roses.

In 1913, Fannie married bronc rider and rodeo clown Bill Steele. The couple rode the rodeo circuit and performed with Buffalo Bill Cody in 1916 in Chicago. Fannie last competed in 1925, but she continued to ride exhibition broncs into her fifties. Bill and Fannie bought a dude ranch at Arrastra Creek near Lincoln, which she ran by herself for another twenty-five years after Bill's death in 1940. She was one of the first women in the state to receive a packer's license, and she guided hunting trips into Montana's backcountry well into her sixties. She passed away at the age of ninety-three. *–JBO*

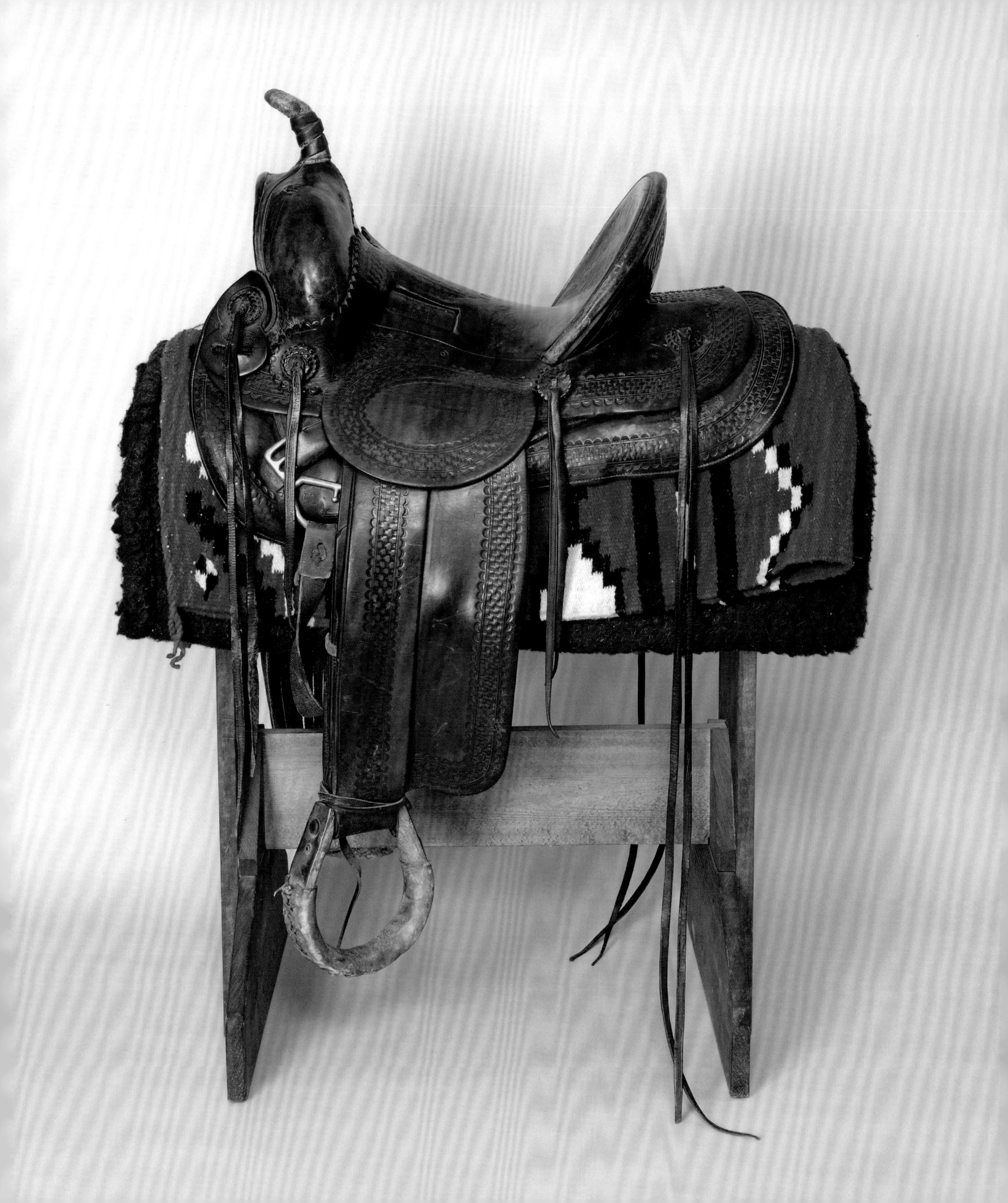

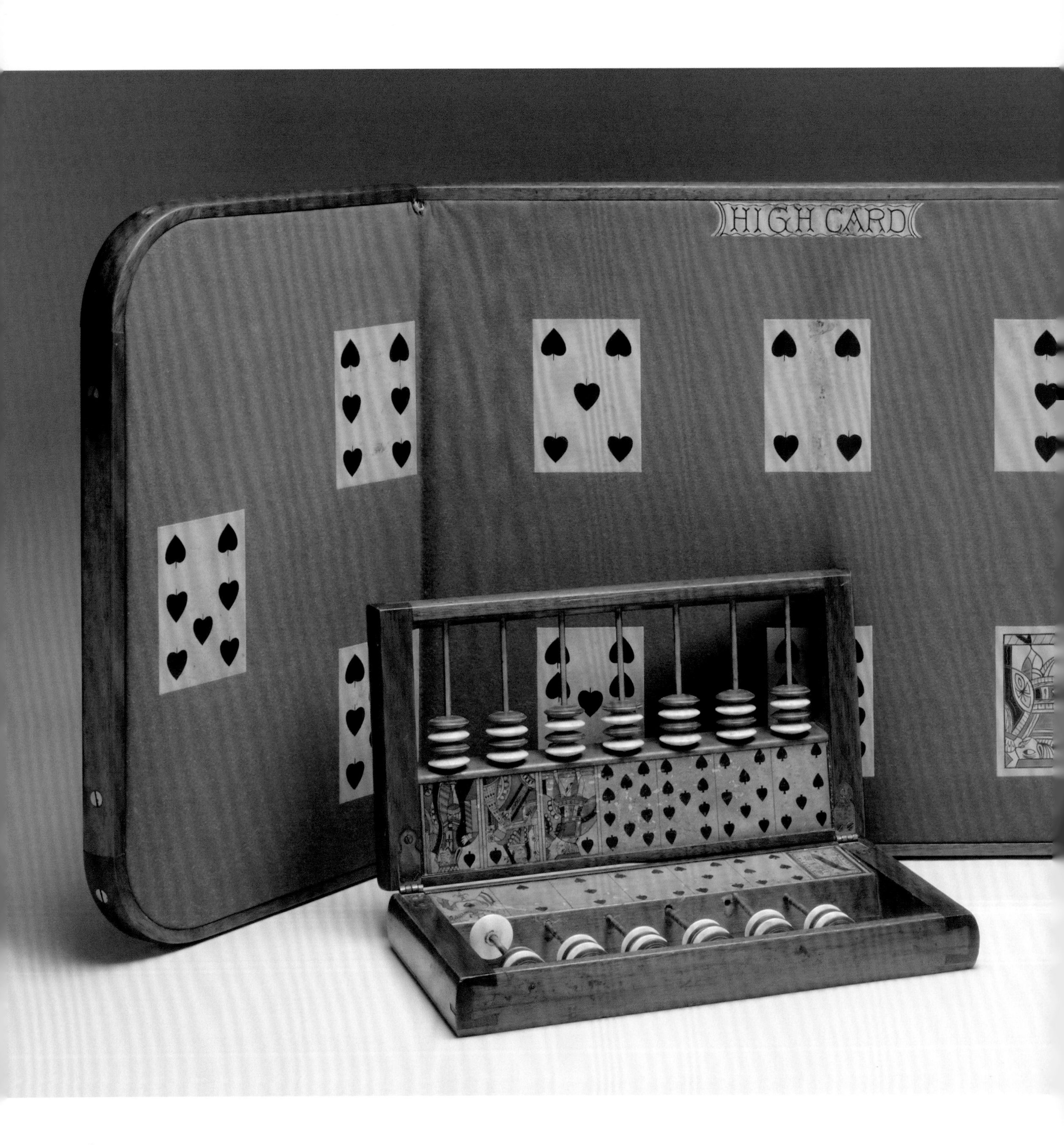
HIGH CARD

60. Faro Game Board and Casekeep

ca. 1920, 40" × 16¼". Transfer from the Attorney General's Office, Law Enforcement Department (now Department of Justice), x1925.03.01

WRITING about faro in 1894, John N. Maskelyne—an English magician who was ardently opposed to all serious forms of fraud—stated, "There is no game in which money is lost and won more readily. Above all, there is no game in which the opportunities of cheating are more numerous or more varied." Despite Maskelyne's misgivings, faro was the most popular game among gamblers in the West during the nineteenth century. Its play required a board, an abacus-like device known as a casekeep, and a fifty-two-card deck.

Although some early Montanans objected to gambling on moral grounds, it was not made illegal until passage of the state's 1917 gambling laws. At the close of 1918, the sale of alcohol also became another strictly forbidden vice. During Prohibition, many former saloons tried to maintain some form of business as soft drink parlors, pool halls, and cigar stores. Sometimes these establishments operated legitimately, but many were known as places to obtain an alcoholic beverage and partake in an illicit game of chance.

In May 1920, after an extensive raid in Miles City, the town's *Daily Star* reported, "Dragnet Spread over Local Underworld and Fourteen Gambling Places on Main St." Under the direction of Attorney General Sam C. Ford, the raid ultimately obtained "warrants for gambling in eleven cases, six warrants for bootlegging, and forty-eight warrants for prostitution." Forty-nine arrests were made. Among the items seized in the raid were this faro game board and casekeep, manufactured by A. Ball & Brothers, Chicago, Illinois. It was confiscated "from the old Montana Saloon," an establishment still in operation today. *–JBO*

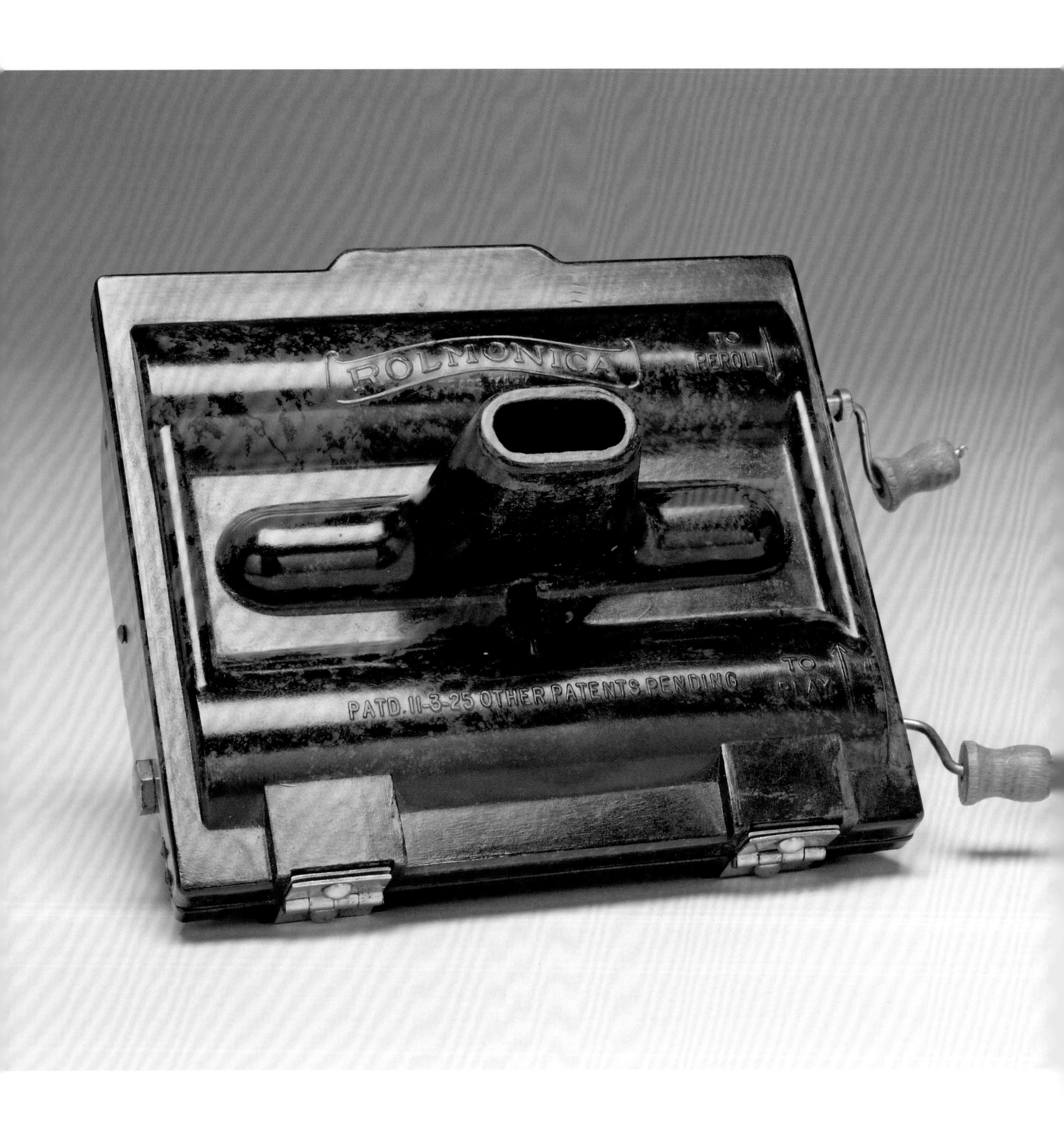
ROLMONICA
TO REROLL
PATD. 11-3-25 OTHER PATENTS PENDING
TO PLAY

61. Rolmonica and Music Roll

ca. 1930, 2¾" × 3¾" × 4". Gift of Kristine Hoverson Finch, 1997.24.31

◈

Music has long accompanied the human story, but until the invention of the radio and the phonograph, it generally required a live performer. Music boxes, which evolved from musical clocks, became popular during the early nineteenth century as the first mechanical instruments to rely on human ingenuity rather than musical expertise. Until the Industrial Revolution, however, music boxes were handcrafted and expensive, limiting ownership to the few who could afford them.

During the second half of the nineteenth century, new manufacturing techniques not only reduced the cost of music boxes but also produced a proliferation of novelty mechanical instruments. Many of these were elaborate, coin-operated machines intended for use at arcades and carnivals. Other devices were designed for personal use, allowing people of even modest means to enjoy music at home. Among the many new musical contraptions of this era was the Rolmonica.

Beginning in 1928, the Rolmonica Music Company of Baltimore, Maryland, manufactured this "automatic harmonica" that played a music roll, not unlike a player piano. The company touted that the device was "small in size . . . yet mighty in its finger-tickling, toe-tingling tune power." Anyone could play it, the promotion continued, "for all you have to do is insert a roll, and turn the handle while you blow."

Rolmonicas were a modified harmonica attached to a casing made of Bakelite, the first completely synthetic plastic. The Bakelite casing consisted of a mouthpiece through which the player blew and compartments for a roll of paper music. Two handles on the right side were used to unfurl and rewind the roll of music, which was perforated so that each hole resulted in the sounding of the proper note. The reeds on the harmonica allowed the player to produce sound by exhaling or inhaling, allowing for an uninterrupted melody. In the 1932 Montgomery Ward & Co. catalog, Rolmonicas sold for one dollar and came with four rolls of music; additional rolls came in sets of five at a price of forty-seven cents.

The Rolmonica in the Society's collection includes nine rolls of songs, with tunes such as "Hot Time in the Old Town" and "Love Song of the Nile." The instrument belonged to Kristine and Rhoda Hoverson, who grew up in the now-defunct community of Ollie. Their father, Alvin, operated a hardware store there that included a tin shop and Conoco gasoline pump. In a letter accompanying the donation of her prized playthings, Rhoda wrote, "I marvel that my parents, as little money as they had in those days [early 1930s], managed to provide us with such wonderful toys—we really had a lot of them and of good quality." *–KL*

62. John L. Fogarty's Stetson

1932, 16½" × 13½" × 7", illustrated by O. C. Seltzer (1877–1957). Gift of John L. Fogarty, x1966.29.01

◈

In December 1917, twenty-three-year-old Great Falls resident John L. Fogarty (1894–1984) set sail for France as a member of Montana's 163rd Infantry Regiment. In addition to fighting at Chateau Thierry and the Argonne Forest, Fogarty received favorable attention for his singing voice while serving overseas, and after the war he relocated to New York City to pursue a career in music. By the end of the decade, he enjoyed considerable renown as the "Montana Minstrel," a tenor specializing in light, lyrical ballads.

While Fogarty's performances on the stage ensured his popularity in the East, the burgeoning medium of radio also allowed his fans in Montana to share in his fame. In 1932, Fogarty's Montana friends wanted to give him a unique memento from his home state. They secured a round-crowned Stetson hat from Kaufman's menswear store in Great Falls. Acclaimed Western artist O. C. Seltzer—also a Great Falls resident—painted a simple scene on the front of the crown depicting two horses and the state seal on the brim. Seventeen Montanan brands were also added to the crown, presumably by Seltzer as well. To complete their keepsake gift, 277 of Fogarty's male friends and admirers—merchants, judges, cowboys, saloonkeepers, bankers, woolgrowers, clerks, newspapermen, politicians, and firemen—signed the top and underside of the hat's brim. Governor John E. Erickson placed his autograph prominently above the state seal.

"The Montana Minstrel" proudly displays his one-of-a-kind Stetson in this ca. 1932 photograph. 942–153

Once the signatures were added, the hat was shipped to New York and presented to the singer during "a Coast to Coast Broadcast over N.B.C." As part of the ceremony, Fogarty delivered a short speech and sang "In the Hills of Old Montana." The presentation thrilled fans listening back in the Treasure State, and the Stetson became Fogarty's most prized possession. "Every theatre that I played," he noted, "the hat got plenty of publicity."

After more than thirty years in show business, Fogarty retired in the 1950s. In 1966, concerned about the fate of his treasured Stetson, he decided that the Montana Historical Society would make a fitting home. "My thought in offering the hat," he wrote in a letter to the museum, "is that it will be in Montana long after some of us are gone. This is the first hat of its kind—some imitations have been seen, but none like the original. Rather than leave the hat with someone who don't appreciate my feelings about it, I thought that it would be in a place where it could be seen and appreciated for years to come."

–KL

O.C. SELTZER
1932
DAN CAMERON
THE GREAT SEAL OF THE STATE OF MONTANA
ORO Y PLATA

63. Dinosaur Gun

ca. 1936, 54¼" × 6½" × 9", by Thomas B. Larkin & the builders of the Fort Peck Dam. X2003.01.12

◈

CRAFTED during the 1930s by laborers constructing the Fort Peck Dam, this massive thirty-pound "dinosaur gun" stretches fifty-four inches from its butt to the gaping muzzles of its double barrels. Its stock is fashioned from a six-inch-wide fir timber, and the barrels are steel pipes one and one-half inches in diameter. While it does feature a simulated percussion lock at the breech of each barrel, the weapon is not a functioning firearm—nor has it ever been used to shoot a marauding dinosaur.

Four miles long and standing 250 feet tall when completed, Fort Peck Dam was constructed on the Missouri River in northeastern Montana by the U.S. Army Corps of Engineers during the trying times of the 1930s. It was designed to provide flood control and improve water quality while also generating electricity and providing employment as part of President Franklin D. Roosevelt's New Deal. The project employed more than ten thousand workers at its peak in 1936. Laborers from Montana and out of state flocked to the dam site, and soon eighteen boomtowns sprang up near the dam, with names such as New Deal and Cactus Flat.

Workers at Fort Peck Dam were eager to find amusement wherever they could, and they regularly spent their pay at the boomtowns' abundant bars and dance halls. Other recreational activities, however, focused on the unique geological history of eastern Montana. Searching for fossils became a popular pursuit for off-duty dam workers, and author Lois Lonnquist once wrote that "during one of the last hunts in October 1937 more than seventy autos full of hunters traveled to the badlands . . . and noted 'outstanding finds.'"

Near the dam site, the exposed Hell Creek Formation contained the fossils of such iconic giants as *Tyrannosaurus rex* and *Triceratops*, which were deposited during the Cretaceous Period some sixty-five to seventy million years ago. Local residents and visitors have long been fascinated by Montana's dinosaur remains. Both the Crows and the Blackfeet have oral traditions about discovering

giant fossils, and Ferdinand Vandeveer Hayden of the U.S. Geological Survey found fossilized teeth, bones, and shells near the mouth of the Judith River on an 1855 expedition.

Such enthusiasm for hunting dinosaur fossils in the Fort Peck Dam area likely inspired the fabrication of this compelling artifact, evidently manufactured for the amusement of the unknown builder (or builders) and his fellow workers. The fact that the dinosaur gun was made during the construction of Fort Peck Dam suggests evidence that dam builders, despite their toil, were able to indulge in a bit of humor and whimsy. *–VR*

Exhibiting the same sense of whimsy as the oversized "dinosaur gun," this 1937 postcard illustrates how Montanans used humor to cope with hardships during the Great Depression. 3½" × 5½". Coles Studio, photographer. Mulvaney Real Photo Postcard Collection, PAC 2013-50 EXAG.001

64. Royal Coachman, Artificial Fly

ca. 1950, 10" × 2½". Gift of the Penhale families of Butte: Matthew H. and Nellie W., Russell E. and Nellie A., 2009.22.45

◈

> In our family, there was no clear line between religion and fly fishing. We lived at the junction of great trout rivers in western Montana, and our father was a Presbyterian minister and a fly fisherman who tied his own flies and taught others. He told us about Christ's disciples being fisherman and we were left to assume, as my brother and I did, that all first-class fishermen on the Sea of Galilee were fly fishermen and that John, the favorite, was a dry-fly fisherman.
>
> —Norman Maclean, *A River Runs Through It*

To imagine Montana without trout fishing is a difficult proposition. It is the state's geographical good fortune to have some of the world's best trout habitat, and for many enthusiasts—from adventurous tourists to guides who make a living from the sport—Montana's culture and history are inextricably tied to its angling traditions.

One of the earliest observations on the sport of trout fishing in Montana comes from none other than Captain Meriwether Lewis, who commented on the talents of Private Silas Goodrich, fondly referred to as the "Izaak Walton of the expedition" after the famous author of the first-known text on fly fishing. Writing on June 13, 1805, near the Great Falls of the Missouri, Lewis observed that Goodrich caught a half dozen very fine trout.

Another early visitor, Rudyard Kipling, came to Montana in 1889 and was advised by a fellow traveler to visit "Yankee Jim" George, who owned a modest cabin on the Yellowstone River. Kipling's description of fishing the Yellowstone makes modern-day sportsmen and women green with envy:

> At the fortieth trout I gave up counting, and I had reached the fortieth trout in less than two hours. They were small fish—not one over two pounds—but they fought like small tigers, and I lost three flies before I could understand their methods of escape. Ye Gods! That was fishing, though it peeled the skin from my nose in strips.

Today, the fly-fishing industry is a significant driver of Montana's economy, accounting for approximately $400 million in annual consumer spending. Pick up any popular travel magazine and you can easily see the connection between Montana and the sport's steady popularity.

Fly fishing is often considered an art by its dedicated practitioners, most of whom recognize that casting a line into Montana's coldwater fisheries is a privilege that comes with responsibility. Regulations such as catch-and-release restrictions, seasonal limits, and closures of small streams during spawning periods are part of the conservation measures that protect the resource for future generations. Montana Fish, Wildlife & Parks, a state agency, is tasked with maintaining healthy fish populations in the state.

In recognition of the role that fishing has played in shaping Montana's identity over time, the Society possesses a collection of fly-fishing artifacts, from classic publications like *A River Runs Through It* to a fly reel made by tackle industry legend Charles F. Orvis. Such items are preserved and displayed with the knowledge that the delights of standing in a stream and presenting a small fly made from hair and feathers—like this hand-tied pattern used by Nellie Walker Penhale and donated to the Society by her granddaughter—will remain as much a part of Montana's future as its past. *–SAT*

Mar J. Woolley 1983

Montanans on the Move

◈

Due to Montana's vast size and varying topography, transportation has played an especially critical role in its history. For centuries, First Peoples traveled by foot, carrying their belongings—minimal by necessity—on dog-drawn travois. Beginning in the early 1700s, horses replaced dogs as the primary beasts of burden. People could now travel farther and faster, and, since horses could pull more weight than dogs, they could also acquire more possessions. Whether riding or working around camp, women carried their babies on their backs, securely bound in cradleboards, to free their hands for other activities.

By the early nineteenth century, the arrival of Euro-Americans set in motion changes that would forever alter life under the Big Sky. The first steamboat reached Fort Union on what is now the Montana–North Dakota border in 1832. More fur-seeking riverboats followed, traveling by 1860 as far as Fort Benton, "the world's innermost port." The upstream trip from St. Louis took two months or more, halving the time required to make the same journey overland. Passengers and goods unloaded in Fort Benton then traveled throughout the territory by stagecoach and freight wagon over rudimentary roads that followed trails used by Native peoples for centuries.

In the 1870s, railroads made the frontier even more accessible, providing safer and shorter passage from more populous parts of the country. With the 1883 completion of the Northern Pacific, the first transcontinental line to cross the Treasure State, Montana was at last fully connected to the outside world. The Great Northern and Milwaukee Roads followed, along with branch lines and short lines. By 1910, more than four thousand miles of track crisscrossed the state. Railroads transformed numerous aspects of daily life, opening up new, out-of-state markets for Montana's resources and bringing in everything from exotic foods to circuses and vaudeville acts.

Missed the Turn, 1983, 16" × 12", by Max J. Woolley (1916–2017).
Gift of Max J. Woolley, 2003.24.03

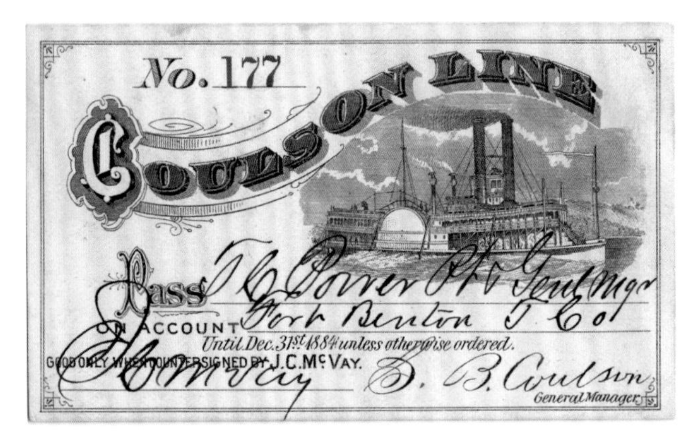

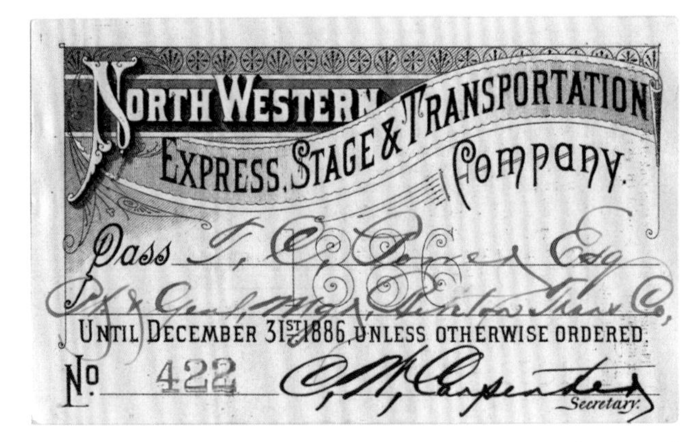

As evidenced by these passes issued to early Montana entrepreneur T. C. Power, stagecoaches and steamboats provided essential modes of travel for Montanans until they were supplanted by railroads in the late nineteenth century and automobiles in the early twentieth century. 1884 steamboat pass, 3⅝" × 2⅜", 1984.18.20; 1886 stage pass, 3⅞" × 2¼". Gift of Jane Power Tobin and her children, 1984.18.14

America's love affair with the automobile ultimately impacted Montana's built environment. The tipi-shaped design of Kramer's Wigwam Conoco gas station in Browning reflects the eagerness of Montana business owners to attract early automobile tourism. ca. 1930–1933. Gift of Mrs. Roy Cornelius, 940-436

Leaving from and returning to the state fair in Helena, Cromwell Dixon piloted the first flight over the Continental Divide on September 30, 1911. With such vast distances to cover—both within the state's borders and to other parts of the country—Montana benefited greatly from the advent of air travel. C & K, photographer. Gift of Mrs. Carl Holtman, PAC 941-848

During the twentieth century, automobiles completed the transportation revolution begun by railroads. By the mid-1920s, most middle-class families owned a car, which, unlike trains, operated at the individual's personal convenience. The success of automobiles, however, depended on drivable roads, which were slow in coming to the Treasure State. As early as the 1870s, bicyclists had begun a nationwide Good Roads Movement, calling for the construction of a network of adequate highways connecting America's cities. With the widespread use of motorized vehicles fifty years later, the movement gained momentum, ultimately culminating in the Federal Aid Highway Act of 1921 and the organization of a national highway system five years later. Even so, little improvement was made to Montana's roads until federally funded work projects built more than seven thousand miles of paved roads and thirteen hundred bridges during the Great Depression. While those who could afford it had long traveled to "pleasuring grounds" like Yellowstone National Park by railroad and stagecoach, personal automobiles and paved roads instigated a new era of leisure travel for the masses.

65. *A Trip to the States*

1867, 4⅜" × 5½", by John Allen Hosmer (1850–1907). Locker 917.8 H79T

◈

This slim, hand-sewn travelogue is not the oldest or most beautifully bound volume in the Montana Historical Society's rare book collection, but it is one of the most valued. Based on the diary entries of John Allen Hosmer, son of the first chief justice of Montana's territorial supreme court, Hezekiah Hosmer, *A Trip to the States, by Way of the Yellowstone and Missouri* recounts his family's journey from Virginia City in Montana Territory to Detroit, Michigan, in 1865. Produced in 1867 by Beaver Head News Print in Virginia City, it is credited as Montana Territory's second published book. The first copies sold for one dollar in gold dust. Aware of the publication's crudeness, Hosmer apologized to his readers in the foreword:

> I must now go to work and make a few apologies. My readers will notice, that in a great many places where there ought to be full stops, nothing appears but comma's [*sic*], my reason for this is, I had but one small font of type, and scarcely any capitals. . . . Secondly, I must make an apology for the register of the pages, having nothing but a little hand press, and being unable to print more than one page at a time, the register would very seldom print right. This is my first effort at writing. And having read the printed edition, I find a great many grammatical mistakes, which I must ask you to overlook.

The Hosmers first came to Virginia City in October 1864, and John studied under the tutelage of Thomas Dimsdale, author of *The Vigilantes of Montana*. The following year, John's father decided to return briefly to the states, during which trip teenage John kept a diary. By 1866, John was back in Montana working as a printer's helper for the *Montana Post*, the territory's first newspaper, and it was during this time that he edited, printed, and bound his book.

Due to the scarcity of even rudimentary printing presses in Montana at the time, publications prior to 1891 are extremely rare, and despite its myriad shortcomings, this booklet is considered a gem. As he mentions in his foreword, Hosmer's book was printed on a tiny press, one page at a time, with a limited number of typeset pieces. The front and back covers, stitched by Hosmer himself, consist of cardboard sheets, pasted over with butcher paper and wrapped in brown cloth. It is impressive, indeed, that the book ever came to print, and even more so that copies have survived.

With each passing decade, the historical value of this little book increases. While a 1963 *Billings Gazette* article estimated the book's worth at two thousand dollars, its value to Montana history today is incalculable, both as an example of early publishing in Montana and for its description of the trials of an overland journey through the region. Its pages depict cross-country travel through the eyes of a teenager and document an exciting chapter in the story of an extraordinary American family. –*RA*

A Trip to the States,

BY THE WAY OF THE

YELLOWSTONE AND MISSOURI,

BY J. ALLEN HOSMER,

With a Table of Distances.

VIRGINIA CITY, MON. TER.

BEAVER HEAD NEWS PRINT.

1867.

66. *Jerk-Line Twelve on the Old Freight Road*

1883, by L. A. Huffman. Gift of the Koster Family, 981-248

◈

For decades, Montanans relied on wagons to haul freight. Large wagon lines were the economic lifeblood of many western merchants and homesteaders, as each vehicle could pull as much as twenty thousand pounds of cargo from market to market. They were by no means a perfect method of transportation, however. Days spent driving wagons were long and slow, starting at dawn and often ending after dusk, and wagon trains only traveled between fifteen and twenty-five miles in a stretch. Rough road conditions and exposure to the elements were hard on the freighter, wagon, and animals alike. Nevertheless, freight "trains" were essential to Montana's development, serving new markets and bringing economic opportunities to communities across the territory.

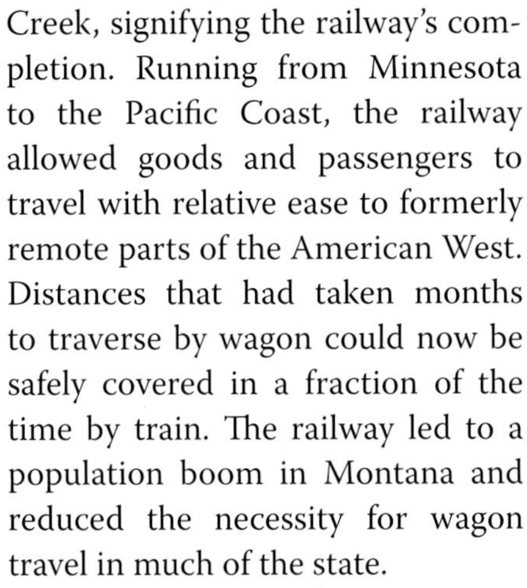

Photographer Laton Alton Huffman (1854–1931) came to Montana Territory via wagon in 1878. He served as post photographer at Fort Keogh before purchasing a studio in Miles City, where he continued to document frontier life. Huffman's affinity for Montana's wildness is apparent in this image, *Jerk-Line Twelve on the Old Freight Road, 1883*, which shows a twelve-horse team pulling freight between Miles City and Billings, surrounded mostly by open land. However, one can see Huffman was in the process of altering details he felt detracted from the image, most notably the pigs and haybales in the image's left-hand side. In later prints, these signs of civilization are removed, making the landscape appear more as it would have when Euro-American settlers first arrived in the area.

The same year Huffman captured this image, former president Ulysses S. Grant drove the Northern Pacific Railroad's ceremonial golden spike at Gold Creek, signifying the railway's completion. Running from Minnesota to the Pacific Coast, the railway allowed goods and passengers to travel with relative ease to formerly remote parts of the American West. Distances that had taken months to traverse by wagon could now be safely covered in a fraction of the time by train. The railway led to a population boom in Montana and reduced the necessity for wagon travel in much of the state.

Photographers have always dictated the version of reality their audiences see. In Huffman's case, he highlights—and, by editing the photo, creates—a romanticized vision of Montana's past. As historian John Mack Faragher explains, "The word 'myth' . . . [is not] a synonym for erroneous belief, but . . . the body of tales, fables, and fantasies that help a people make sense of its history. Like history, myth finds meaning in the events of the past. But unlike history, myth is less concerned with facts than with ideological essences." The myth that Huffman sought to perpetuate by removing signs of development from his photograph is evidence of his era's attachment to the notion that Montana was an "open" place—a place whose available land allowed for economic success through hard work and ingenuity. The wagon was the mechanism through which many Euro-Americans settled the frontier and attempted to make that myth a reality. *–AK*

67. Séliš Cradleboard

ca. 1880–1893, 14½" × 8" × 40". Gift of William A. Clark, x1900.03.13

◈

Throughout North America, Native peoples created a wide variety of baby carriers to carry their infants while traveling and to keep them out of harm's way while their mothers worked. Hard-backed cradleboards could be propped up against tipi poles and secured, while willow-frame baby baskets and soft, sling-like moss bags could be suspended from tripods. While designs took on regional styles and utilized different materials, they allowed babies, snug and comfortable, to be near their caregivers. Shoulder straps on the back of a cradleboard such as this one enabled the wearer to carry it like a backpack, and a third strap from the top of the cradleboard often wrapped around the mother's forehead to provide additional stability.

Most of Montana's Indigenous peoples used tall, high-backed cradleboards with a solid cottonwood frame covered in tanned buckskin to which a baby could be strapped safely in place and protected by a hood or shade. A simple chokecherry or willow hoop might circle the baby's head several inches from his or her face, providing extra protection and allowing the mother to attach attractive beads or to drape a cloth sunshade over the baby's head. Cradleboards were often decorated with quillwork, fringe, fur, and shells, making each one unique.

Like clothing, the decorative components of cradleboards reflect the influence of European trade and aesthetic sensibilities. As the fur trade moved west from the Great Lakes onto the northern Plains and into the Rocky Mountains, traders and their Métis employees brought new materials—such as glass beads, wool and velvet fabric, and metal bells—that could be used to decorate cradleboards. They also brought new design motifs, such as twining vines and floral patterns, then popular among French traders.

While intermarriage between traders and tribes and the increased mobility of tribes allowed for the exchange of both goods and designs, the overall style of baby carrier often remained identifiable by region or even by tribe. For instance, Cheyenne cradleboards typically feature a split-frame design with two long staves forming the support, while Crow-style cradleboards are identifiable by the series of individual belts or flaps that hold the baby in place.

This Salish cradleboard was donated to the Montana Historical Society by William A. Clark, who obtained it from the collection of Peter Ronan, the Indian agent on the Flathead Reservation from 1877 to 1893. The wood frame is covered with white buckskin, and its high, rounded top is fully beaded in a foliate design typical of the fur-trade era. A soft cloth hood protects the baby's head, while an attached buckskin sling laces up the front to hold his or her body. The addition of a beaded, red wool flap across the front would have added a layer of protection while also keeping the infant warm. According to Ronan's daughter, Mary, the cradleboard was "used for a chief's baby." *–LF*

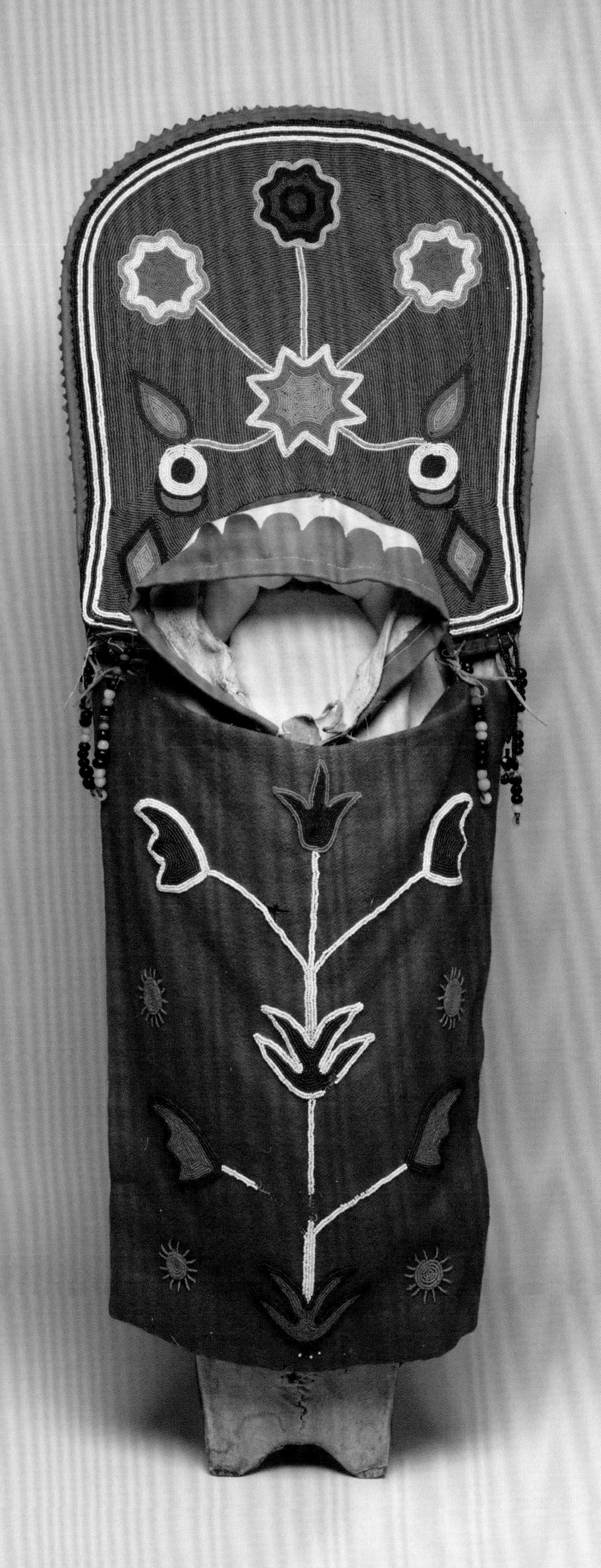

68. Reverend Edwin M. Ellis's Chainless Bicycle

ca. 1899, 59" × 40". Gift of Richard J. Dosker, 2002.45.01

◈

Chainless bicycles like this shaft-driven model made by Columbia enjoyed limited popularity in the United States during the 1890s. Reverend Edwin M. Ellis traveled over thirty-six thousand miles on this well-worn "war horse" while serving the Presbyterian Church in Montana. With no chain to get clogged with mud or tangled in weeds, Ellis's bicycle was perfect for the poorly maintained road system. The preacher outfitted himself with homemade gear suited for the task, including waterproof wading boots and chaps for crossing streams.

Reverend Edwin M. Ellis came to Montana at the behest of Dr. Sheldon Jackson, superintendent of Presbyterian missions in the western territory. His arrival in the Bitterroot Valley in 1884 began a forty-three-year career with the Presbyterian Church in Montana. He headquartered his activities in Stevensville, which had only "the thin shadow" of a failed Presbyterian Church when he arrived. He traveled across the Bitterroot on horseback, preaching in whatever venues were available—from schoolhouses to living rooms. When he wasn't preaching or visiting home missions, Ellis fundraised for church buildings and oversaw the valley's Presbyterian congregations. Eventually his diligent work paid off, and by the end of the decade Presbyterianism was flourishing in the Bitterroot Valley.

In 1891, the Presbyterian Church's Board of Public and Sunday School Missions recognized Ellis's efforts, making him Montana's first synodical superintendent of Sunday school missions. This required him to develop, supervise, and organize Sunday schools and churches across the state.

Ellis and his family relocated to Helena in 1892 for easier access to the railroad, which offered fast transit east and west. However, Ellis still struggled to access some congregations in more remote parts of the state. According to his daughter:

> [He] began to explore the possibilities of a bicycle. It could be taken inexpensively in the baggage car as far as he needed to go by train, and be immediately available with no waiting for hours or even days for a stage. If he were lucky enough to get a lift from some rancher, it could easily be hoisted into a wagon. . . . He would be free to go wherever he was needed.

Ellis left Montana for Michigan in 1923, officially retiring from his work with the Presbyterian Church four years later. He spent the rest of his life close to his children and grandchildren and died in Long Island, New York, in 1940. He left a legacy in Montana that lives on in the numerous churches that formed from his home missions and Sunday schools, many of which owe their origins in part to Ellis's chainless bicycle. *–AK*

69. John H. Voorhies's Pocket Watch

ca. 1903, 2⅛" diameter. Gift of J. Max Voorhies, x1971.26.01

◈

John H. Voorhies worked as a railroad conductor for the Northern Pacific Railway in Glendive at the turn of the twentieth century. He used this watch, which bears the Northern Pacific's red and black monad, to ensure that trains ran on time—a necessity for both safety and efficiency.

Montana's first trains covered distances in a fraction of the time previously possible on horseback. This change in transportation's speed and frequency demanded more consistent methods of time measurement. For much of the nineteenth century, everyday people used local time—based on a clock in a centralized part of a municipality—and solar time, using the sun's location. American railroad companies, however, used their own time measurements, as they required precision to coordinate the schedules of trains traveling cross-country through more than one hundred local time zones and fifty-three railroad time zones.

On October 11, 1883, a little over a month after the Northern Pacific completed its transcontinental line, delegates from railroad companies across the country met at the General Time Convention and established the Standard Time System. They divided the country into five time zones, each one hour ahead of the zone to its west. Standard Time was instituted on November 18, 1883, and adopted voluntarily by most cities nationwide.

Voorhies's "Conductor" plate from his uniform cap, ca. 1903. Gift of Max Voorhies, x1971.26.02

Standard Time made travel and communication throughout the country simpler for both transportation companies and travelers, but the new system had detractors who claimed that standardizing time was impractical in rural, agricultural areas. A January 4, 1884, letter to the *Helena Independent*'s editor complained that "it appears that the old jest of the man who claimed the possession of a watch which 'regulated the motions of the sun, moon and stars' has come true in Montana, the Northern Pacific railroad being the individual holding the watch." A week later, the *New North-West* reported that "a good many Helena citizen[s] are letting loose on bogus railroad time and setting their clocks to true solar time." Helena did not adopt railroad time until February 1885, and there were similar holdouts against Standard Time's "baneful influences" across the country.

Standard Time relied on the accuracy of the instruments used to measure it. Even though railroad companies had required periodic inspections of the watches used by their employees since the 1850s, inaccurate watches contributed to a number of catastrophic train accidents, leading to more stringent inspections of timepieces. In 1887, the General Time Convention required that all railroad watches be examined by a "responsible watchmaker every six months to ensure they did not run fast or slow by more than thirty seconds per week." By 1893, almost all U.S. railway companies adopted exacting standards for materials, sizes, and mechanical features of its employees' watches. As a result, manufacturers adapted their designs to meet these specifications.
–*AK*

HAMILTON WATCH CO.

17

I found a new wild garlic, or rather one new to my collection. The others would bring me their collecttions to name, which I was not always able to do, though I could give the family and genus.

We were startled by Miss Lillian Ehlert rushing into the camp crying "Look at me!; I am soaking wet!; I got into quicksand up to my waist!; the kids had to pull me out!" Her grip had to be taken from the boot of the coach so that she could change her clothes. The matron of the camp hung her wet skirt,etc., behind the range to dry. Miss Ehlert was very venturesome--always getting into trouble. Doctor named her the "awful girl" (orphan girl), and suggested that a guardian be appointed for her. Her sister said: "Well Doctor, I know no one so competent as yourself, and I will be only too glad to resign in your favor." But he said: "I have one orphan already to take care of,; meaning me.

As soon as Miss Ehlert's clothes were dry we resumed our journey, and shortly came to the Gibbon Falls, a very beautiful one as

70. Yellowstone Travel Journal

1903, 8⅜" × 10⅜". Gift of Bill Cooke, Hester Ferguson Henshall Journal, SC 1821

On August 10, 1903, naturalist Hester Ferguson Henshall and her husband, Dr. James A. Henshall, superintendent of the U.S. Fisheries Station near Bozeman, boarded a train for a weeklong excursion into Yellowstone National Park. Throughout their trip, organized by the Wylie Transportation Company, Mrs. Henshall jotted down notes and stories, read guidebooks, and painted flora and fauna, all of which were incorporated afterward into this sixty-one-page, leather-bound journal.

The train brought them from Bozeman to Livingston, where they admired the new, ornate

Northern Pacific Railway depot, and then took them on to Gardiner. There, they mingled with travelers from across the country and around the world, all looking for coaches, surreys, horses, and guides to take them into Yellowstone.

The Henshalls boarded a Wylie Transportation Company coach and entered the park, passing under the arch recently dedicated by President Theodore Roosevelt. Their experiences mirrored those of thousands of tourists who visited the park at the turn of the century. Touring companies shaped their itineraries and services to meet the needs and expectations of their Victorian-era, predominantly middle-class clients. Hester's journal describes the permanent campsite as "a group of tents arranged to form a small village," with amenities including large tents with wooden floors, comfortable beds, hot water for bathing, a stove stoked each morning by staff, and a separate dining tent.

Entertainment was also part of the experience, with evening music around a campfire and storytelling stagecoach drivers who enlivened travel from campsite to campsite. Concessionaires hawked curios and goods along the route, including guidebooks illustrated with photographs by F. J. Haynes, as well as beadwork and blankets. Guided hikes focused on expansive fields of wildflowers for sketching and pressing.

The route described by Hester would be familiar to modern travelers of the still-popular figure eight loop—from Mammoth Hot Springs to the Hoodoos, Gibbons Meadow, Old Faithful, the Punch Bowl, Yellowstone Lake, Grand Canyon Falls (today's Upper and Lower Falls of the Yellowstone), and back to Gardiner.

Throughout the journal, she not only describes the beauty of her surroundings, but also seems to relish poking fun at her travel companions:

> Next we came to a military fort where President Roosevelt quartered while touring the park. . . . Among us were some who viewed it as a religious devotee at a holy shrine, and almost held their breath as they gazed at the cot . . . it seemed to interest them more than the wonders of the park.

There was much in Henshall's experience that today's visitors would not share—like the feeding of bears or tossing handkerchiefs into geysers. But it is also true that what pulled her to the park still draws visitors today. Hester captures the lure of Yellowstone near the end of her journal after a visit to the Upper Falls:

> How can I describe the matchless wonder and beauty of it all[?] . . . I sat breathless; I could not speak. I did not want to talk, and did not want any one to speak to me; the tears ran unheeded down my cheeks . . .

With its engaging prose, colorful botanical sketches, and images clipped from guidebooks, Hester Henshall's journal provides a glimpse into early twentieth-century tourism and a view of Yellowstone on the cusp of major changes brought by the first automobiles in 1916. *–JF*

71. Good Roads Congress Delegate's Pin

1914, 2¼" × 3". Gift of David Hilger, 1978.08.12

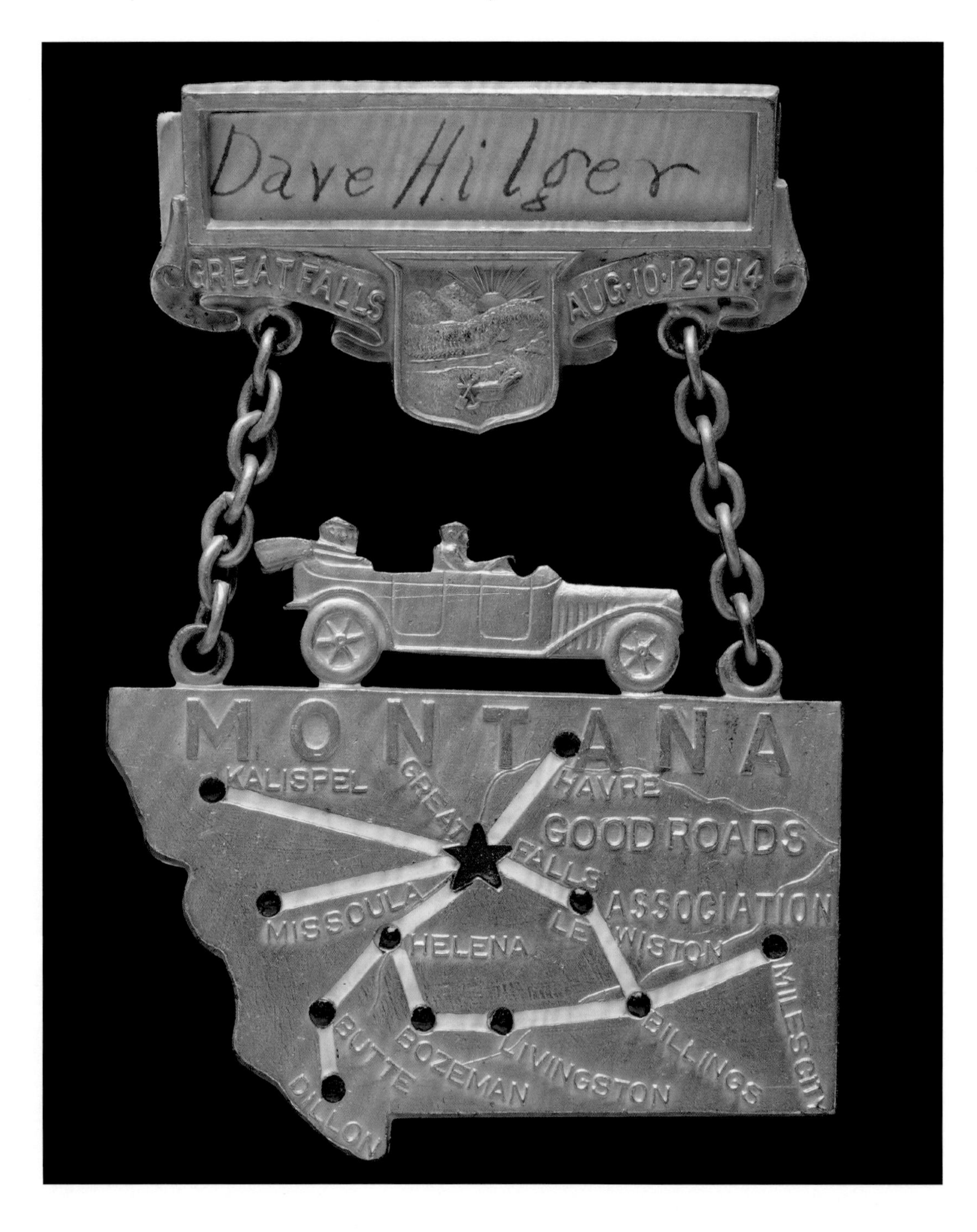

In August 1914, delegates to the Good Roads Congress sported smart gold pins as they fraternized with fellow road and automobile enthusiasts. Held in tandem with the Inter-Mountain Good Roads Congress at the newly constructed Rainbow Hotel in Great Falls, the week's events included a celebration of Montana's fiftieth territorial anniversary and its twenty-fifth anniversary of statehood. The organizing committee spared little expense, adorning Great Falls with decorative arches and electric displays. Delegates enjoyed boxing matches, dances, and various other entertainments during three days of lectures focusing on the physical networks that advocates hoped would knit together the far-flung corners of the state.

Difficulties with transportation had plagued Montana since its earliest territorial days. Because the Organic Act of 1864 did not provide for the taxation of citizens to fund infrastructure, the first territorial legislature granted licenses or charters to private companies for the operation of toll roads, ferries, and bridges. Maintenance, however, was virtually nonexistent, as it cut into the bottom line of the proprietor. By the 1880s, railways, not roads, dominated the state's transportation networks, and they exerted considerable economic and social influence on the towns platted beside the tracks.

Many goods and services, however, still required road travel, and communities struggled to raise funds for this much-needed infrastructure. Beginning in 1902, the federal government allocated Rural Free Delivery funds for the construction of post roads, but travel within and around most towns proved difficult. By 1910, the state prison in Deer Lodge had considered the use of convict labor outside prison walls for the improvement of road networks. Many trade and labor associations vehemently opposed the idea, as it would produce an unfair market, and the state board of prison commissioners disapproved of it on humanitarian grounds. Eventually, however, a compromise was reached, and convicts began the backbreaking work of laying Montana's roads.

Road improvements were primarily financed at the county level through property taxes and issuance of bonds. Counties generally adhered to state regulations for highway and bridge construction, but a centralized system was still needed. In 1913, the legislature passed a bill establishing the state highway commission, as well as the state's first motor vehicle registration law, which included license fees marked for road improvements.

The inaugural Good Roads Convention in Montana was organized in 1910 to discuss the logistics of road building. By 1915, delegates' most urgent concern was how to obtain sufficient funding for good roads. Montana Good Roads president, H. W. Brown, immediately drew attention to the need for federal spending.

The discussion was timely. Nationally, the Good Roads Movement gained traction after the construction of auto trails such as the Lincoln Highway from New York to San Francisco in 1913. The subsequent establishment of the American Association of State Highway Officials in 1914 added momentum to the national movement, as a bill drafted by the group eventually became the Federal Aid Road Act of 1916. This law established rules and regulations for federal and state partnerships in the construction and improvement of the nation's roads. It also provided federal funds that proved critical for building Montana's transportation infrastructure.

The Good Roads pin, with its touring car perched atop a state crisscrossed with enameled roads, symbolizes the optimism of Montanans intent on improving transportation across the state and the challenging reality of that endeavor. *–TT*

72. Lewis and Clark Bridge, Wolf Point

Photographed in 1930, as construction neared completion.

Montana Department of Transportation Photograph Collection, Lot 028 B08F11.1

◈

In February 1914, eager homesteaders arrived at Wolf Point expecting to cross the Missouri River on a bridge of ice. Instead, the river had thawed early that year, and because ferries could not run until April, the families were marooned on the north bank for weeks. Camped in tents and makeshift shacks, the stranded homesteaders dreamed of the day when a bridge could carry their families, farming equipment, livestock, and household goods to their new claims across the river.

The site had long been considered a strategic location. In 1860, an army engineer noted that it was the logical place for a bridge, but even after 1887, when the Great Northern Railway arrived, ferries remained the only means for crossing. The need for a bridge became even more apparent in February 1926, after two teenagers returning to McCone County after a Wolf Point basketball game attempted to cross the ice in their Model T. The car hit a hole and fell into the water, and the two boys drowned. The accident prompted renewed efforts, and years of lobbying finally came to fruition.

Construction on the three-span, Pennsylvania through-truss bridge began in 1929. The Missouri Valley Bridge and Iron Company of Leavenworth, Kansas, served as contractor. Built with state, federal, and private funds, the bridge spans 1,074 feet across the Missouri River, connecting residents to outside markets and Canadian neighbors. Straddling the McCone and Roosevelt county lines, it became the first free public crossing of the Missouri for 350 miles between Fort Benton, Montana, and Williston, North Dakota.

A crowd of fifteen thousand witnessed the opening celebration in 1930. Speakers included Montana's governor, J. E. Erickson, and Canada's minister of highways, A. C. Stewart. Bagpipe players, bands, and Indians in full ceremonial dress paraded across the bridge. Assiniboine tribal member Vera Smith offered remarks in honor of the occasion:

> Today, we weld this important link, joining in closer friendship, the north and south countries. In memory of the pioneers . . . who envisioned the spanning of the Missouri, to the present generation whose . . . efforts have made the long cherished dream a reality, and to future generations . . . as an incentive to greater development, we formally open and dedicate the Wolf Point Bridge.

To commemorate the 140th anniversary of the Lewis and Clark Expedition, officials in 1945 dedicated the park at the north end of the bridge to the explorers, and the structure then became known as the Lewis and Clark Bridge. Visible from a distance of fifteen miles, it appears as three prominent curves of gray against the prairie.

In the late twentieth century, when the bridge was threatened with demolition, the surrounding community rallied to ensure its preservation. Public efforts to save this and other historic Montana bridges led the Montana Department of Transportation to initiate an Adopt-a-Bridge program in order to facilitate the relocation or adoption of Montana's retired historic bridges. The Montana Historical Society accepted ownership of the Lewis and Clark Bridge in 1998. *–EB*

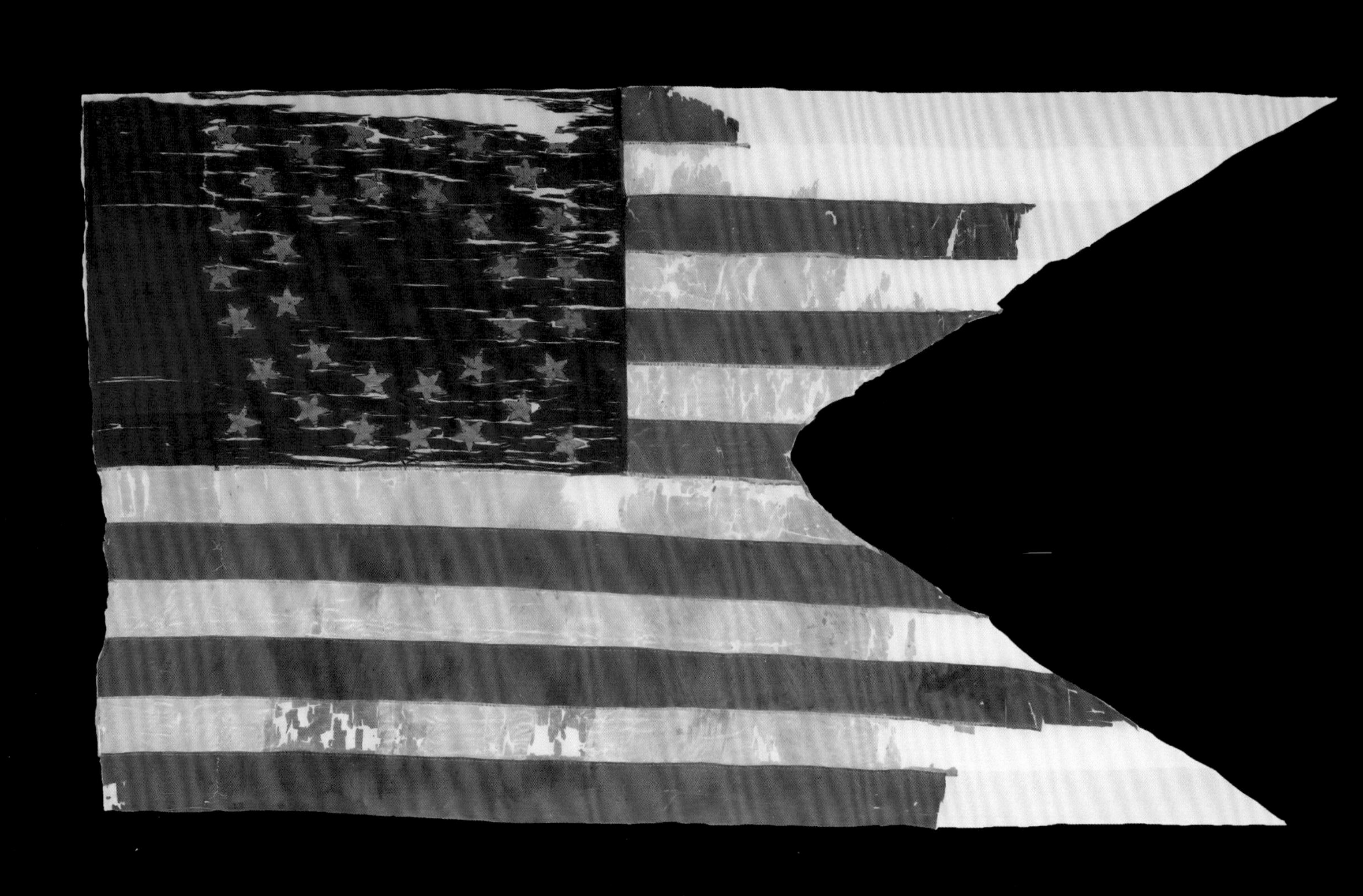

Montanans at War

◈

Conflict has been part of the Montana story since prehistoric times. For millennia, Indigenous peoples vied with each other to control territory and resources. The acquisition of horses and firearms by northern Plains tribes beginning in the 1700s altered traditional forms of warfare. At the same time, Euro-American expansion westward drove tribes from farther east into this region, creating new tensions and heightening old rivalries. After the Civil War, the U.S. Army turned its attention to the West, ushering in the era of the Indian Wars. During this period, tribal nations staunchly defended their homelands as non-Indians laid claim to more and more land, often in violation of treaty rights.

At the turn of the century, the Spanish-American War marked the United States' emergence as a world power. When President McKinley called for volunteers in April 1898, Montana's allotment called for the enlistment of five hundred soldiers. The state's national guard unit—established in 1887—immediately volunteered for service in its entirety. This group formed the nucleus of the newly established First Montana Infantry, United States Volunteers, whose ranks swelled to more than one thousand men almost overnight.

Shortly thereafter, World War I marked a time of great tumult in the Treasure State. Montana contributed a higher percentage of soldiers, money, and resources to the war effort than did any other state, while drought, labor unrest, influenza, and draconian sedition laws plagued the domestic front. Nationwide, more than ten thousand Indian men enlisted, despite the fact that the government classified them as "dependent wards" rather than American citizens.

Opportunities for women to join the military were more limited, but over two hundred Montana women served their country as Red Cross nurses, so-called

Cavalry Guidon, ca. 1876, 32⅜" × 24⅞". Gift of Grace E. Williams, X1955.08.01

This remnant of a ledger drawing likely depicts Cheyenne warriors attacking a Crow village. Drawn about 1885 with colored pencil and graphite on paper, it is attributed to White Bear (ca. 1867–1886), who is believed to have been Southern Cheyenne.
28¾" × 16½". Gift of Mrs. Francis Jergnes, X1961.16.03

In his ca. 1879 photograph labeled "Ft. Keogh MontGuard Mount in the Buffalo Coats," Miles City photographer L. A. Huffman captures what was too often a frontier soldier's worst enemy—extreme weather. 981–359

Like elsewhere in the Treasure State, the citizens of Cascade County awarded victory medals to their soldiers returning from World War I. This medal was presented to John L. Thurman, who served in the 166th Depot Brigade out of Fort Lewis in western Washington. 2½" x 5¾".
Gift of John L. Thurman, x1939.02.01

Hello Girls (telephone operators), and Navy yeomen. On the home front, men, women, and children grew more crops, cultivated victory gardens, bought liberty bonds, conserved food, and raised funds to support the war effort.

During World War II, Montana once again produced more soldiers per capita than almost any other state. Approximately 57,000 men from every Montana town, city, and reservation had served by 1945, and nearly 1,500 of them gave their lives to the war effort. Montana women also enlisted in all branches of the service, joining the nearly 400,000 women nationwide who volunteered. Because of its weather and topography, Montana itself proved a useful training ground for special operations during World War II. Additionally, its strategic location led to the establishment of the Army Air Corps's East Base (now Malmstrom) in Great Falls, and airfields for pilot training in Cut Bank, Glasgow, and Lewistown.

In wars from Korea and Vietnam to Iraq and Afghanistan, Montanans have continued to serve their country on the battlefield. Although it never led to combat between the superpowers, the Cold War, too, added to the military's presence in the state with the construction of two hundred Minuteman missile silos in the central part of the state. At the same time, throughout the twentieth century, other Montanans protested against these same conflicts—especially Vietnam—on ideological grounds. In 1970, Kathy Huppe gave up her Miss Montana crown to show solidarity with those who opposed the highly controversial war, and a photograph of Huppe, with a fist raised in protest, was printed on the cover of *LIFE* magazine.

During the conflicts known as the Indian Wars, the U.S. Army frequently relied on the services of Indian scouts, some of whom were enlisted and some of whom were hired civilians. Nakoda (Assiniboine) tribal member Chester Y. Arthur was a first sergeant with Company I of the Twentieth Infantry stationed at Camp Poplar River on the Fort Peck Reservation, between 1891 and 1894, when this photograph was taken. 957–84

73. Map of Canyon Creek Battle

no date, 11" × 8½", by Andrew Garcia (1853–1943). Gift of the Rock Foundation, 2013.29.04

◈

After the U.S. Army's defeat at the Battle of the Big Hole in 1877, the Nez Perce (Niimíipuu) fled east, passing through Yellowstone Park. The Seventh Cavalry pursued them, and they met on September 13, 1877, at Canyon Creek, a few miles north of present-day Laurel. Andrew Garcia (1853–1943), a private citizen working as a freighter for the army, was present during the event and later recorded his observations of one of the last battles of the Nez Perce War.

Garcia described the Canyon Creek Battle as "a running fight at first." Then, "using tactics similar to white men's warfare," Nez Perce warriors engaged the soldiers, delaying them while the women, children, and elderly made a dash to escape through the canyon. Many of the women had young children in cradleboards strapped on their backs and led older children by the hand as they fled. Little did Garcia know that his future bride, In-Who-Lise, was among the women retreating through the canyon that day.

During the battle, Colonel Samuel D. Sturgis sent a battalion commanded by Captain Frederick Benteen to flank the fleeing Nez Perce, while another commanded by Major Lewis Merrill approached from the opposite side. But the Nez Perce had the strategic advantage and hindered their advances with sustained fire. Another witness, Thomas A. Sutherland, recalled:

> Near the center of the valley was a dry creek at the bottom of a deep and crooked ravine between high perpendicular banks. . . . The warriors took possession of the different heights almost immediately and by their courage and good shooting baffled all the attempts of our men to get to the other end of the canyon through which the [horse] stock was being driven.

Nez Perce warrior Teeto Hoonnod stayed at the mouth of the canyon and continued to defend the position until most of the Nez Perce and their horses escaped. As evening fell and the troops withdrew, the warriors barricaded the opening of the canyon.

The Nez Perce's escape from Canyon Creek allowed them to reach the high plains near the Musselshell River, where they camped near present-day Molt. The next day, Sturgis and his men, joined by Bannock and Crow Indian scouts, hurried to catch up. A brief skirmish ensued, and the scouts captured many of the Nez Perces' horses, thus slowing them down on their flight north to Canada and setting the stage for their final encounter at Bear Paw later that month.

After his experience at Canyon Creek, Andrew Garcia drew this map featuring detailed annotations symbolizing troop movements and orientation during the battle. The red line that starts at the bottom of the map indicates the route the Nez Perce took, outlining the area where they camped the night before the battle (7), then continuing up to the canyon mouth. The oval areas outlined in red (22) denote the position of the Nez Perce sharpshooters. –*JBO*

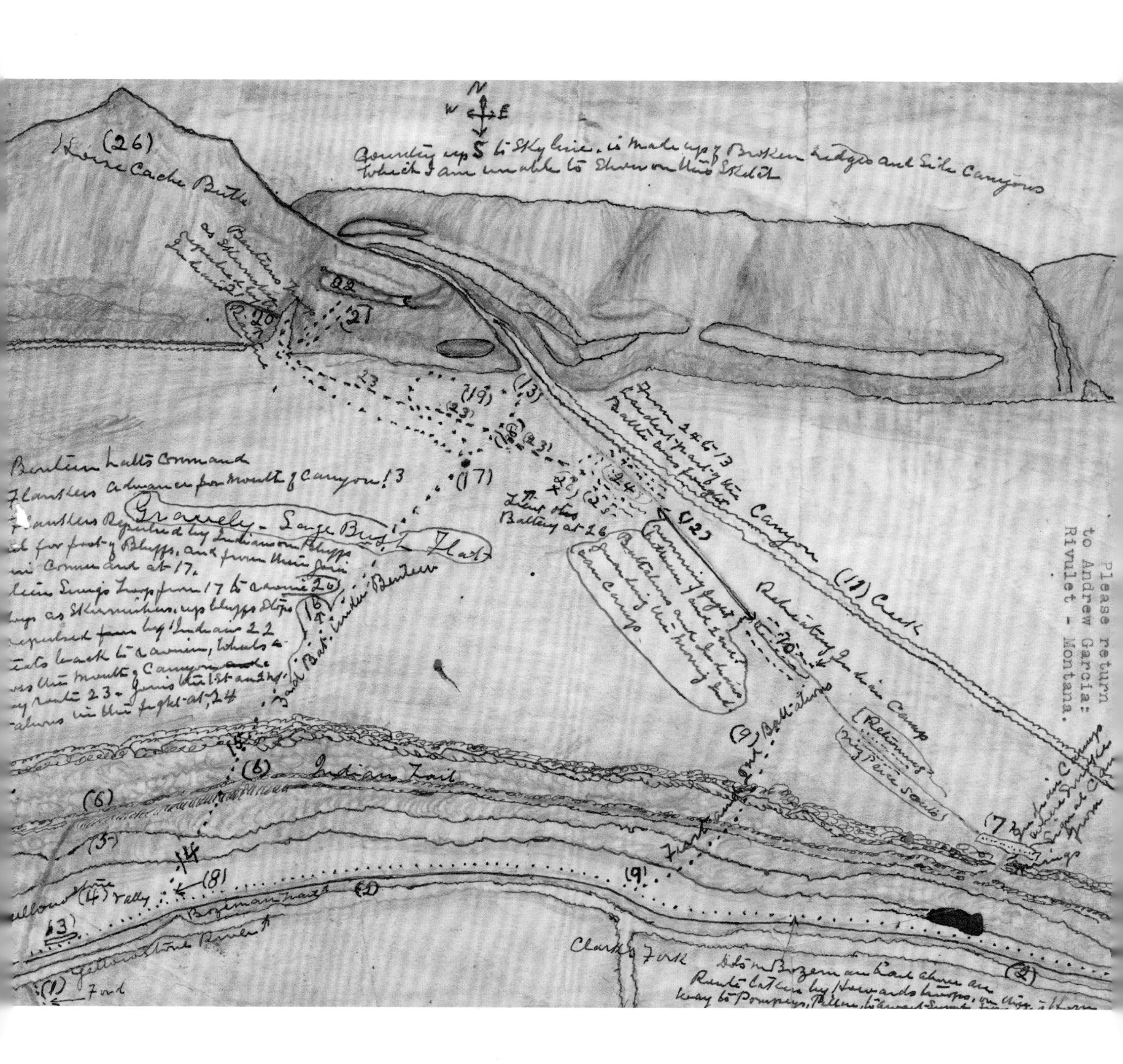
N
W
E
S
(26)
Horse Cache Butte
Country up S to Sky line, is made up of Broken Ridges and Side Canyons
Which I am unable to Show on this Sketch
Benteen halts Command
Gravelly - Sage Brush Flat
(17)
(19)
(13)
(12)
Canyon
(11) Creek
Indian Camp
Indian Trail
(6)
(8)
(9)
Clarks Fork
Yellowstone River
Ford
Please return
to Andrew Garcia:
Rivulet - Montana.

1st Montana Inft'y U.S.V.
ORO -Y- PLATA

74. Kessler Banner

1895, 60" × 48". Gift of Gay D. Stivers, x1942.02.01

◈

The use of flags to display allegiance dates back thousands of years. In fact, by the time the American colonists were ready to assert their independence from Britain, one of their first orders of business was to create a flag under which to fight. Like Old Glory, Montana's state flag can also trace its origins back to a colonial conflict: the Spanish-American War.

With the sinking of the *Maine* and subsequent declaration of war on Spain on April 23, 1898, the United States launched a multi-pronged assault at Cuba and at Spain's other far-flung possessions, including the Philippine Islands and Puerto Rico. To provide much-needed manpower, President William McKinley issued an appeal for volunteers. Montana's allotment called for the enlistment of five hundred soldiers. The state's national guard formed the nucleus of the newly established First Montana Infantry, United States Volunteers. Almost overnight, the regiment's ranks swelled to more than one thousand men, and Colonel Henry C. Kessler was placed in command.

In 1895, Colonel Kessler—a Butte resident and then commander of Montana's national guard—had a flag featuring the state seal made as a traveling trophy to be awarded to the "most efficient and exemplary company at the conclusion of the annual summer encampment." The men of the First Montana Volunteers chose that flag as their regimental colors, and Colonel Kessler had the words "1st Montana Inft'y, U.S.V." embroidered in silk floss across the top of the banner. As one historian noted, "This flag was taken to the Philippines in preference to a standard eagle-and-scroll infantry flag [because] the Kessler Banner was . . . sentimentally important to the regiment's men."

The Treasure State's soldiers had enlisted with the belief that they would be fighting for Cuban independence, but the First Montana Volunteers were routed to the Philippines instead. There, they found themselves battling the very people they had been sent to free from Spanish tyranny. Consequently, they petitioned for and were ultimately granted permission to return home. When the soldiers and their company flag arrived back in Montana on October 23, 1899, the Treasure State hailed her returning sons with a "reception and celebration at Butte, the likes of which had never been seen." To continue the fête, the Kessler Banner was proudly displayed at venues around the state.

In 1905, when the Montana legislature decided to select an official state flag, the Kessler Banner—minus the inscription across the top—was an obvious choice. The flag's design remained unchanged until 1981. Then, in order to distinguish it from similar-looking flags, Representative Mel Williams of Laurel sponsored a bill to add the word *Montana* above the state seal. Williams's wife Eugenia appliquéd a prototype to present to the legislature, lettering the flag just as the unidentified needle-worker had for Colonel Kessler in 1898. That flag is now included among the state's treasures, preserved by the Society for future generations. *–KL*

75. World War I Nurse's Uniform

1917. Gift of Mrs. John C. (Virginia) Harrison, x1963.11.01-06

◈

In June 1917, Virginia Flanagan of Great Falls was one of three Montana women selected during the first Red Cross call for nurses. Flanagan's army outdoor uniform consisted of a wool skirt and overcoat with a silk blouse, is pictured here, along with sturdy leather boots and gloves. The leather soles on her boots are so worn the interior lining shows through—a testament to the long hours Flanagan spent on her feet, nursing the wounded. Her photograph album documents her service, including joyful experiences in training and sorrowful moments tending patients during World War I.

As a child, Flanagan was an engaged member of Fort Benton's community. She rode floats in the Fourth of July parade, helped plan the town's Leap Year Ball, and performed in theater productions for Catholic Church benefits. Flanagan attended high school in Fort Benton and Dubuque, Iowa, and then moved to Great Falls, where she studied nursing and graduated from Columbus Hospital in 1911. When the United States entered the war, Margaret Hughes, supervisor of nursing for the American Red Cross, selected Flanagan, along with Violet Hodgson of Baker and Ellen Sterling of Missoula, to be Red Cross nurses. For more than two years, Flanagan served in the American Red Cross Nursing Service as one of the 170 Montana women who answered the call.

Flanagan's first year of service was spent at the Presidio of San Francisco and Camp Kearny in California, where she received battlefield training that included gas attack drills. In May 1918, Flanagan left for the front, where she joined medical units in France, including the American Red Cross Military Hospital No. 1 in Neuilly-sur-Seine, near Paris.

In spite of nursing's demands, Flanagan was able to travel around Europe during her service, and her album features scenic vistas of France, England, and Belgium, as well as snapshots of soldiers and nurses. Flanagan also documented the Great War's devastation, including cities in ruins and trenches filled with corpses of German soldiers. One photograph shows her and friends "gathering shells near Belleau Woods." She also collected buttons, medals, and pins from different servicemen's uniforms.

She was on leave in Nice when the armistice was signed on November 11, 1918, but she continued to care for the wounded until she returned to the United States on July 20, 1919.

Flanagan went back to Great Falls after the war, where she continued working as a nurse for several years. The 1930 and 1940 censuses list her occupation as "none" and stenographer, respectively. In 1958, Flanagan created a miniature replica of her hometown's namesake using adobe from the original fort and donated it to the local museum. Her model fort is currently on display at the Historic Old Fort Benton Trade Store.

Flanagan's uniform, photographs, and mementos are relics from a turbulent time in world history. They embody the willingness of Montanans to pull together to protect their families, communities, and country. In the face of violence and fear, men and women such as Flanagan risked their own safety and comfort to care for strangers halfway around the world. *–MO*

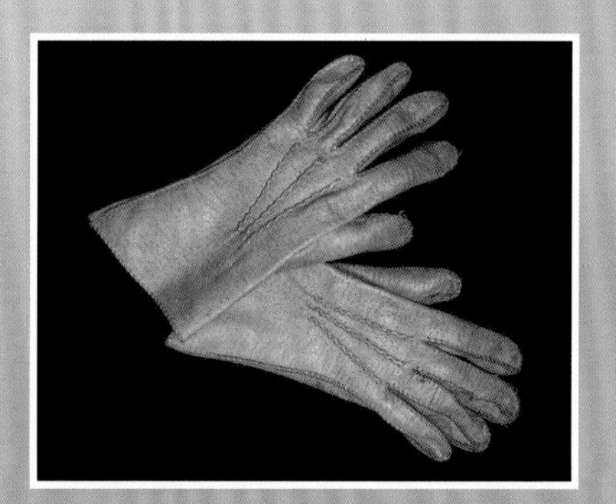

U.S.

76. Red Cross Quilt

1918, 81" × 82", by the Ladies Auxiliary of the United Commercial Travelers (UCT), Council 349, Cascade County. John Reddy, photographer. Gift of the Ladies Auxiliary to Council 349, Order of the United Commercial Travelers, x1982.71.01

◈

Embroidered on both sides of this quilt is an honor roll of over 1,300 names. Each name represents a supporter who contributed to the 1918 fundraising campaign for the Red Cross organized by the Ladies Auxiliary to Council 349 of the Order of the United Commercial Travelers (UCT), a fraternal benefit society founded by traveling salesmen at the end of the nineteenth century.

In 1911, the federal government recognized the Red Cross as the "official volunteer aid department of the United States," and World War I only made the organization more central to American interests. After the United States' entry into the war in 1917, the American Red Cross provided a myriad of services by furnishing an ambulance corps; staffing and equipping hospitals; distributing hand-knit or sewn sweaters, socks, and "comfort kits" to troops serving overseas; and providing clothing, tools, and other essentials to war refugees.

To make sure the Red Cross was up for the task, President Woodrow Wilson placed the organization under the American Red Cross War Council, which coordinated its relief activities and galvanized public support. A massive propaganda campaign ensued, and Red Cross membership exploded. In 1914, local chapters numbered just 107; by 1918 there were 3,864 chapters nationwide. By 1919, thirty-two million adults and eleven million children—roughly a third of the U.S. population—had joined the Red Cross.

Red Cross members volunteered their time, but they also raised funds, totaling over $400 million in 1917 and 1918. In Montana, they did this by canvassing house to house, hosting dances, publishing and selling cookbooks, and raffling everything from burros to quilts. This quilt was made for one such raffle.

Clara Roth, who brought the idea of a "quilt campaign" to the Cascade County UCT auxiliary, may have first read about the strategy in the women's magazine *Modern Priscilla.* In its December 1917 issue, the magazine promised that memorial quilts could fetch as much as $1,000 for Red Cross work. The magazine provided a pattern, created by Clara Washburn Angell, and detailed instructions, including a sample raffle ticket. It also made clear that "no Red Cross emblem or name can be used in announcements or advertisements of such affairs unless the entire proceeds are to be devoted to the Red Cross. The entire proceeds, not net or half."

The Great Falls quilters charged supporters twenty-five cents to have their names embroidered on the back of the quilt. The Malmberg family paid $100 for the honor of having their names on the large center cross. As recommended by *Modern Priscilla,* "one person whose hand-writing is plain and legible" (in this case, Mrs. R. B. Wilson) wrote all the names on the quilt, and another UCT auxiliary member embroidered them. Although technically illegal under Montana gambling laws, the auxiliary raffled the completed quilt, raising $1,060.80 in total for the Cascade County Red Cross. *–SAT*

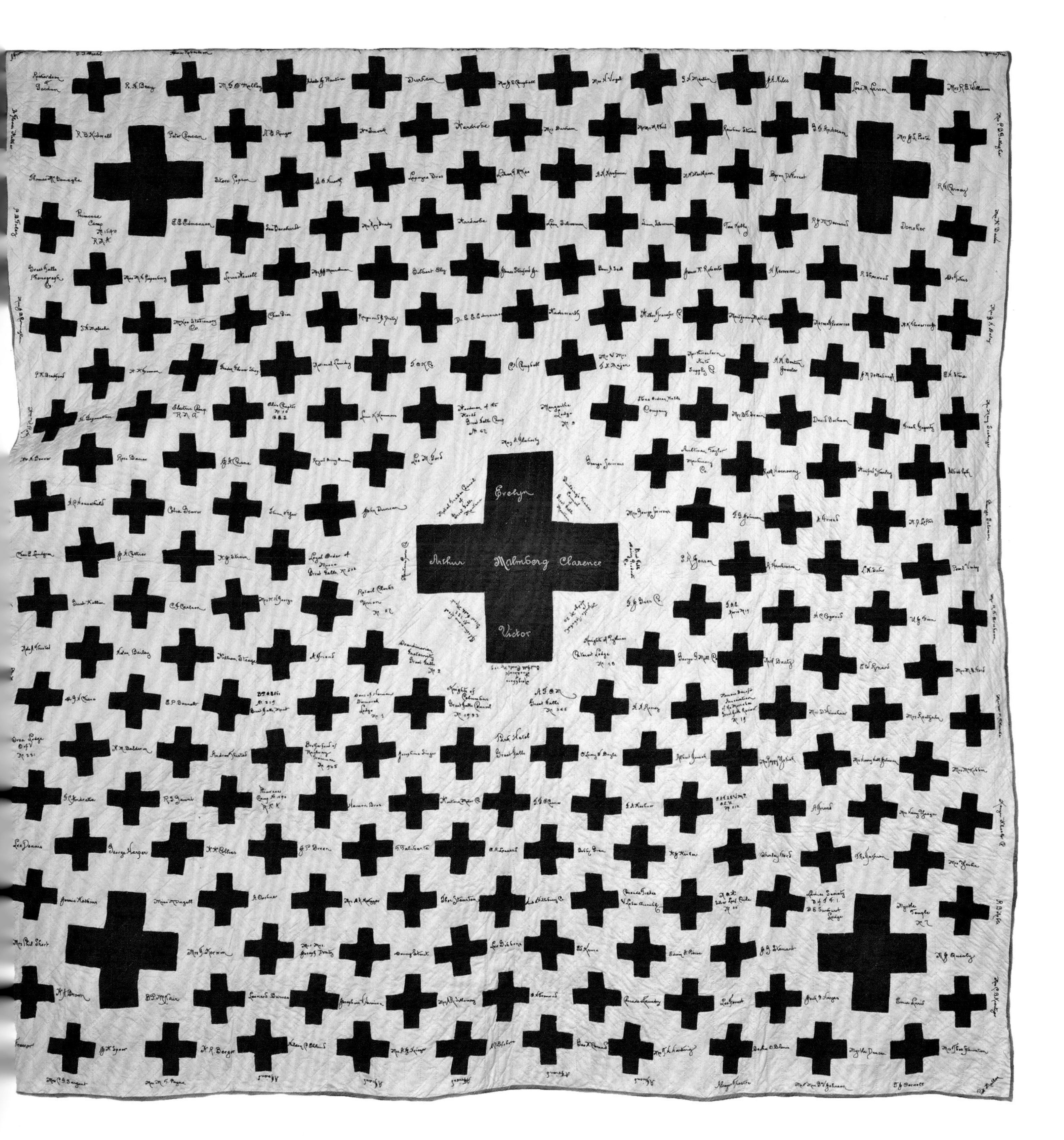
Evelyn
Arthur
Malmberg
Clarence
Victor

Beauchamp

77. *Kenya*

ca. 1943, 29" × 21", by John W. "Jack" Beauchamp (1906–1957).

From the estate of Eddie Barbeau, 1995.101.01

◈

Not all Montanans who served in times of war were human. Well into the twentieth century, the military employed horses and mules extensively to transport men and equipment. Lesser known are the sled and pack dogs that trained alongside their human counterparts at the War Dog Reception and Training Center at Camp Rimini during World War II.

Kenya, a Siberian husky, was one of approximately eight hundred sled dogs stationed at Camp Rimini between 1942 and 1944. He served as lead dog for a team that musher Eddie Barbeau (1908–1994) brought with him from Minnesota. Barbeau, who was of Ojibway and French Canadian descent, not only trained men and canines—he also served as a war dog purchasing agent, acquiring dogs from across the northern United States and Canada to train at Camp Rimini for military rescue operations in arctic climates.

Nestled in the mountains southwest of Helena, Rimini already had a storied past by the early 1940s, emerging first as a silver camp and later as an outpost for the Civilian Conservation Corps (CCC). When the U.S. Army needed a place to train dogs for use in World War II, Rimini's existing CCC structures, long winters, deep snow, and access to public lands offered the perfect site.

At Camp Rimini, soldiers learned to handle and care for their dogs properly, mastered winter survival skills, and helped design and build sleds, dog packs, dog harnesses, tents, sleeping bag covers, and other materials needed for use both at Rimini and in the field. After training, teams and drivers were relocated at strategic intervals along the two major Arctic flyways. A western route traveled from Great Falls to Ladd Field, Alaska, where Soviet pilots took planes bound for Siberian bases as part of the Lend-Lease Program. The North Atlantic route stretched from Presque Isle, Maine, to Great Britain by way of Newfoundland, Greenland, Labrador, and Iceland.

According to historian Karen Fischer, Arctic search and rescue squadrons saved 150 downed airmen, recovered 300 bodies, and salvaged millions of dollars in equipment over the course of the war. Despite its contributions, Montana's War Dog Reception and Training Center was short-lived. In the spring of 1944, the facilities at Camp Rimini were once again abandoned as servicemembers—both human and canine—were relocated to Camp Robinson, Nebraska. Although their time at Camp Rimini was brief, the men who trained there were deeply affected by the experience. Musher Stuart Mace later reminisced about the lifesaving purpose that united the soldiers:

> There was a great deal of satisfaction in doing something which was needed. . . . We were privileged to be participating in a process of saving lives rather than taking them. In wartime, this is a rare privilege.

–KL

78. "One Little Indian" Comic

1944, 7½" × 10¼", *Calling All Girls*. Gift of Ruth Ferris, PAM 4710

◈

THIS four-page color comic, "One Little Indian," celebrated the United States Marine Corps Women's Reservist Minnie Spotted Wolf (1923–1988) of Heart Butte. It focused on Spotted Wolf's life before she enlisted, on her family's ranch on the Blackfeet Indian Reservation, where she "did a man's job before the war." "Now," the comic exclaimed, "she's taking a man's place in the United States Marines." In the last panel, Spotted Wolf speaks directly to the readers, saying she's "happy and proud to be in the Marines, because . . . 'I want to help win the war.'"

The comic was published in *Calling All Girls*, a magazine that offered a lively mixture of fashion tips, clothing ads, and stories about female adventurers. In 1944, it presented an expansive view of women's opportunities while celebrating women and children's war work. "One Little Indian" fit right into the magazine's format and, despite its patronizing title, provided a surprisingly nuanced (though romanticized) portrayal of Minnie Spotted Wolf, one of the first American Indians to join the United States Marines Women's Reserve.

Born near Heart Butte, Minnie Spotted Wolf grew up doing ranch work, including herding horses, building fences, and driving trucks. According to her daughter, Gerardetta England, when Spotted Wolf tried to enlist at the beginning of the war, the recruiter discouraged her, saying, "The war was really not for women." Nevertheless, she persisted. In 1943, twenty-year-old Spotted Wolf reported to basic training at Camp Lejeune, North Carolina.

The military public relations team quickly embraced the private, spotlighting her as a symbol of feminine power and American unity. *Calling All Girls* took its information from the Marine Corps's public relations department. In fact, the image on the first page of "One Little Indian," which shows Spotted Wolf posed with a rifle in a Southwestern-style coat and cowgirl hat, matches one of the publicity photographs.

Spotted Wolf chose to enlist because she wanted to serve her country, but also to represent her family, her tribe, and all Native people. England recalled that Spotted Wolf didn't join "the military just for herself, but for the Indian people. She wanted others to know who she was and where she came from." In that effort, she was not alone: approximately 44,500 American Indians proudly served during World War II.

Spotted Wolf joined nearly four hundred thousand women who served during World War II. Because of her experience driving two-ton trucks back home, she became a heavy equipment operator as well as a driver for visiting officers in both Hawaii and California. Of the twenty thousand women serving in the Marine Corps, only a thousand stayed on after the war ended. Among them was Minnie Spotted Wolf, who served four years before returning home to Montana, where she became a schoolteacher and an active member of the Browning American Legion Post 127.

–MK

I'LL MISS THIS SORT OF THING WHEN I'M IN THE MARINES.
YOU'LL BE DOING PLENTY OF EXCITING WORK.
FOUR DAYS BEFORE MINNIE WAS TO LEAVE FOR BOOT TRAINING CAMP...
HE'S BADLY HURT! GET THE DOCTOR QUICKLY!
HE'S GONE, MINNIE.
PRIVATE MINNIE SPOTTED-WOLF OF THE UNITED STATES MARINE CORPS, WOMEN'S RESERVE, IS HAPPY AND PROUD TO BE IN THE MARINES, BECAUSE, SHE SAYS...
I SHOULD STAY AND HELP WITH THE RANCH.
NO, MINNIE. THE GIRLS AND I CAN MANAGE. YOUR COUNTRY NEEDS YOU MORE.
I WANT TO HELP WIN THE WAR.
26

79. Model of the Buckley Bomb

ca. 1943, 20" × 5½" × 7¾". Gift of Jim Buckley, x1907.02.01

◈

During World War II, a young man from Opportunity proved to be instrumental in the war effort through his creative design of a "bomb" that could drop thirty thousand leaflets over a radius of fifteen miles.

Previously a sheet-metal worker for the Anaconda Copper Mining Company, Technician Fifth Grade Jim Buckley put his unique skills to use when the U.S. Army's Psychological Warfare Division set out to develop a device that would distribute propaganda encouraging enemy soldiers to surrender. Looking back on his time as a member of the design team, Buckley told the *Billings Gazette* in 1995, "I was flying by my shirt tails." Unfamiliar with the mechanics of aircraft weaponry, Buckley improvised and cobbled together an apparatus by modifying a four-foot fuel tank from a British Spitfire aircraft. A series of bungee cords formed the bomb's internal mechanism,

enabling the pilot to trigger the apparatus's arming switch and release the surrender leaflets. "It was so simple," Buckley explained, "but that's why nobody else would have thought of it. If it had been high-tech, I wouldn't have been able to do a thing with it."

His prototype was successfully tested in 1944, and thereafter the "Buckley Bomb" was used over Germany and Japan. "I think it played a pretty important part," Buckley recalled. "A small part, but an important one."

A year after his discharge, Buckley received the Bronze Star in a Butte ceremony on May 11, 1946. Captain Eldon McLeod remarked to those in attendance that it was extraordinary that "Mr. Buckley did not receive [the award] for inflicting casualties on the enemy, but rather for saving thousands of lives by the ingenious invention of a bomb that proved to have disastrous effect on enemy morale."

In 1997, Buckley donated a model of the bomb, made of English cracker tins, as well as the device's design plans and his Bronze Star to the Montana Historical Society. When asked what he hoped future generations would remember about World War II, Buckley replied, "I think they should remember that it happened, and all of the different things that brought it to an end. I am proud that in a small way I was one of so many who helped." *–SAT*

80. Pat Blinn Letter to Betty Ann Gaston

1945, 4¾" × 8". Gift of the Pat Blinn Family, Pat Blinn Papers, MC 382

◈

AMONG the most heartfelt documents in the collections at the Montana Historical Society are letters written to and from servicemembers during wartime. For troops in the field, correspondence with loved ones provided an emotional lifeline, easing the burden of war's sacrifice and separation.

This letter, written in 1945 by John D. "Pat" Blinn, a Marine from Whitehall, to his childhood sweetheart, Betty Ann Gaston, shows how messages sent home from the front could convey far more than specific details about their sender's experiences in the war. In his many letters to Betty Ann, Blinn focuses on the mundane—in this case, the fact that he can't think of what to write. He keeps the letter light in tone, perhaps mindful of the censors, or to protect Betty from the horrors of battle, or even for a momentary reprieve from his surroundings:

> Hello Darling, I'm sitting on the edge of my fox hole as I write this. The guns are pounding away and to top it off I can't think of a darned thing to say. Pardon me while I light my pipe. Betsy, I feel like a heel. You've been so swell about writing and I've been so negligent. I haven't any excuse for not writing, that is what baffles me. Every time I get a blank piece of paper in front of me my mind gets just as blank. That psychiatry course you are taking will come in darned handy when we finally get together.

Despite the chatty tone of Blinn's letters, the war is clearly present, as loud as the chorus of pounding guns around him. His closing to this letter reminds us that there is much about his experience that went unsaid:

> Well Snooks I'm going to secure this—I've got some work to do.

Blinn returned to Montana after World War II, but, as was true for many servicemembers, the end of the war was a mixed blessing. He found it difficult to settle into civilian life and ultimately reenlisted in the Marine Corps. In October 1950, Blinn headed to Korea. As his unit prepared to ship out from Japan, he wrote Betty Ann:

> Take care of yourself Hon and don't worry—I'm still lucky.

On December 2, 1950, Blinn and his unit were engaged in the Battle of Changjin (Chosin) Reservoir in North Korea. Ordered to take his team and clear a nearby hilltop, Blinn was killed in action. In the chaos of the U.S. movement back across the 38th parallel, his body was not recovered.

For Betty, Blinn's letters—once tangible connections to her loved one far out of reach—became cherished reminders of their love story cut short.

–*JF*

All Honor To Their Names

PFC. JOHN D. "PAT" BLINN
Delta Delta (Purdue) 1951
U. S. Marine Corps
Killed in action in the Changin Reservoir area of Korea on December 2, 1950.

Following his death in the Korean War, Blinn was among those memorialized by his fraternity in *The Magazine of Sigma Chi*, March 1951. Gift of Jude Dorland Welter, MC 382

Iwo Jima
[March 14, 1945]

Hello Darling,

I'm sitting on the edge of my foxhole as I write this - the guns a pounding away and to top it off I can't think of a darned thing to say -

Pardon me while I light my pipe.

Betsy I feel like a heel. You've been so swell about writing and I've been so neglegent. I haven't any excuse for not writing that's what baffles me. Every time I get a blank piece of paper in front of me my mind just as blank. That psych course your taking will come in darned handy when we finally get together. Things are tough all over - even on Iwo Jima.

VIA AIR MAIL

PASSED BY NAVAL CENSOR

U.S. NAVY MAR 14 Calif

Miss Betty Anne Easton
435 McLeod Ave
Missoula, Montana
U.S.A.

[3/14/1945]

Walking Tours

GLACIER NATIONAL PARK

VACATIONS
$1. TO $5. PER DAY

Glacier National Park

Write for Free Walking Tour Booklet

H. A. NOBLE
General Passenger Agent
ST. PAUL, MINN.

NATIONAL PRINTING & ENG. CO., CHICAGO—NEW YORK—ST. LOUIS

Montana and the Nation

◈

Montanans take pride in the unique characteristics that define this place and its people—majestic mountains, wide-open spaces, extreme weather, abundant wildlife, independent spirits, and enduring ties to the land. At the same time, we also value the bonds that tie us—culturally and historically—to the rest of the nation. Nowhere are those ties more clearly demonstrated than in the collections of the Montana Historical Society.

Ever since Thomas Jefferson purchased the Louisiana Territory from France in 1803, Montana's history has gone hand-in-hand with that of the larger United States. The intrepid explorers Lewis and Clark spent more time in what is now Montana than in any other state on their storied expedition. Thereafter, the Treasure State's natural resources—including fur, minerals, timber, and even the land itself—helped fuel the national economy.

National events also gave shape to life under the Big Sky. The Civil War played a key role in the formation of Montana Territory and set the tone for its acrimonious early politics. Federal policy repeatedly expropriated Indian lands and attempted to suppress the traditional cultures of Native peoples. Franklin Roosevelt's New Deal funded everything from road construction to the Fort Peck Dam, and two world wars changed the lives not only of those who served overseas, but also those who did their part on the home front.

In turn, the Treasure State has left its own imprint on the larger country in a myriad of ways, for better and—at times—for worse. Montanans have elected such luminaries as Thomas Walsh, Jeannette Rankin, Mike Mansfield, and Lee Metcalf to Congress, as well as more controversial politicians like Burton K. Wheeler. In Washington, D.C., they influenced policy and exhibited leadership on the national stage. Political developments within Montana have also reverberated across the

Walking Tours, Glacier National Park, 1912, 14" × 21", by Joseph Scheuerle (1873–1948). Gift of Joe Scheuerle's grandson, Bill Grierson, and wife, Pat, 2017.75.04

In its role as Montana's memory keeper, MHS often serves as a repository for official gifts to the state. Governor J. Hugo Aronson attended the 1956 National Governor's Convention in New York where he received these baseballs signed by such legendary players as Jackie Robinson, Yogi Berra, Mickey Mantle, and Willie Mays. 10" × 5" × 4½". Gift of Governor Averell Harriman, x1969.14.27 a–d

Montana's official connection to the United States began with the Louisiana Purchase in 1803 and exploration of the territory by Lewis and Clark shortly thereafter. By the early twentieth century, the Corps of Discovery had assumed such importance in the public's mind that it became the most common theme for art commissioned for the new Montana State Capitol. *Lewis and Clark at Three Forks*, 1912, by E. S. Paxson (1852–1919), oil on canvas, 153" × 81". Capitol Art Collection, x1912.07.01

The completion of the Northern Pacific Railway's transcontinental line connected Montana to the rest of the nation by rail. This painting—which was commissioned by the Northern Pacific as a gift to the state capitol—depicts the celebration of this momentous event at Gold Creek on September 8, 1883. The two central figures are former President Ulysses S. Grant (holding sledgehammer) and Northern Pacific president Henry Villard. A delegation of Crow Indians, whose land the railroad crossed, watches from left foreground. *Driving the Golden Spike*, 1903, by Amédée Joullin (1862–1917), oil on canvas, 183" × 90". Capitol Art Collection, X1903.03.01

United States: for example, Montana's 1918 sedition law, which outlawed certain types of political speech in a clear violation of the First Amendment, served as the template for similar federal legislation that marked a dark moment in America's past. No less significantly, individual Montanans of all types of backgrounds—from industrial wheat farmer Thomas Campbell to scientist and inventor Jeff Holter—have made profound contributions to the nation and the world as a whole.

Since 1865, the Montana Historical Society has played a singular role in documenting Montana's relationship with the rest of the nation. It does so both because of its official capacity as an agency of state government and because Montanans and their descendants value the preservation of the Treasure State's wide-ranging and diverse history. The Society takes seriously its charge to hold in trust gifts to the people of Montana, whether they come from a foreign government, the president of the United States, or private citizens from around the country.

81. Iron Clad Loyalty Oath

1864, 8" × 12⅜". Montana Territorial Legislative Assembly Records, 1864–1865, LR-Terr 1

◈

THROUGHOUT the Civil War, the goldfields of the West drew men from both sides who hoped not only to strike it rich, but, more importantly, to evade the conflict's bloody reach. Once President Lincoln signed the act creating the Montana Territory on May 26, 1864, however, Montanans suddenly found themselves re-immersed in the wartime politics of the North and South.

Montana's first territorial governor, Sidney Edgerton—a staunch Unionist and member of the Republican Party—wished to ensure all territorial employees were loyal, and thus required they take an Iron Clad Oath (pictured here), swearing allegiance to the Union and attesting that they never carried arms against it. President Abraham Lincoln opposed such oaths, recognizing that if the nation was ever to be unified again, former Confederates would need a path to regain their full rights as citizens. Despite Lincoln's misgivings, however, such oaths became standard during and after the war.

In Montana Territory, the loyalty oath received a decidedly mixed reaction. Many council members were Union Democrats, loyal to the United States but unsympathetic to the Republican agenda. While these Democrats supported the Northern cause, they generally did not wish to punish former Confederates, nor did they advocate for equal rights—or even, necessarily, freedom—for African Americans. Predictably, they opposed oaths intended to exclude former Confederate supporters from public service.

After some posturing, however, most Democrats signed. Only one of their number could not: John H. Rogers, elected from Madison County to the territorial House of Representatives, was ineligible to serve under the oath's requirements. Rogers had fought in at least two engagements against Federal forces as an officer in the Missouri State Guard before resigning his commission and setting out for the goldfields of Colorado and Montana. He offered to sign an amended oath, striking the section on having never carried arms against the Union, but Governor Edgerton remained firm in his opposition to seating a man of such disloyalty. Rogers's fellow Democrats newly elected to the legislature initially refused to sign the oath in solidarity with him, but eventually he withdrew from the House and the rest signed.

Edgerton's unwillingness to allow Rogers to take his seat is indicative of the depths of the divide that spawned the war and was reinforced by the bloody conflict. As such, the oath—as well as Rogers's amended version—serve as physical reminders of a "house divided." Although hundreds of miles from the nearest battlefield, seeds of disunion found purchase in early Montana. *–RA*

[CJR —]

Introduced by E. De Leavitt

Council

Joint Resolution ~~No 7~~

In reference to the War.

Whereas, Our Country is now distracted by a gigantic Civil War, unprecedented in the annals of Civilized Nations, and in proportion to the magnitude of the present Conflict, the American Republic has arisen to the dignity and importance of the crisis, with an energy, and devotion of National Sentiment, and an Employment of blood and treasure unapproached in History, and, whereas, it is the special duty and pride of every Citizen of our Common Country to express his devotion to an unbroken Nationality. Therefore be it Resolved by the Legislative Assembly of the Territory of Montana, ~~Resolved~~, That we hereby renew our pledges ever entertained, of loyalty to the Union, and will ever "frown indignantly upon any attempt to alienate one portion of our common Country from another"; and as in this struggle, our present appeal to Arms may decide the fate of our Nationality, and the question of self Government in its present form, we will ever pray for the success of the Union, and the restoration of Constitutional Government, in the garuntee of battle thrown down by rebels in arms.

MONTANA
U·S·S·MONTANA

82. USS *Montana* Silver Service

1908, by Huber Brothers, and Reed and Barton. Gift of the United States Navy, 1997.81

◈

Following the Spanish-American War, a spirit of nationalism—combined with the recently realized need for a stronger navy—encouraged Congress to appropriate money for a new fleet of warships. An armored cruiser, the USS *Montana*, was one of twelve resulting vessels. In 1907, Montana's legislature appropriated six thousand dollars to fund the creation of a silver service for the new ship that would be sufficiently grand to "enable the officers of the vessel to entertain official guests in a manner befitting the dignity of the State [of Montana]."

Dillon's Huber Brothers jewelers secured the commission to have nineteen pieces hand-wrought by the Massachusetts firm of Reed and Barton. When completed, the highly ornate silver service was adorned with decorative motifs depicting both nautical themes and emblems of the Treasure State, including flora and fauna like the bitterroot and buffalo, as well as artworks by Charlie Russell and E. S. Paxson. The silver service comprises one large punch bowl with tray and ladle (left), one small punch bowl with ladle, two large serving trays, two fruit baskets (right), two five-arm candelabrum with shades, two compotes, two bottle holders, one coffee urn, and one humidor.

The official presentation took place at the Norfolk Navy Yard in Virginia on November 11, 1908. The silver remained on the USS *Montana* for use at gala receptions and banquets for officers and guests, including President William Howard Taft, who hitched a ride on the vessel for his visit to Panama in 1910. Eventually, it was placed aboard the USS *Helena* after the decommissioning of the *Montana* in 1921. In 1963, when the *Helena* cruiser was retired to the "mothball fleet," the silver returned to Montana on loan from the U.S. Navy for exhibit at the Montana Historical Society. The navy made the loan a permanent gift to the state in 1997.

These elegant symbols of pride in state and nation, produced over a century ago, impress present-day Montanans in much the same way they did in 1908. Ornate and expertly crafted, the silver represents the dignity of Montana's people, institutions, and history.

–SN

83. Jeannette Rankin's Shoe

ca. 1916, 9½" × 3" × 4⅞". Gift of John C. Board, 2006.01.01

◈

As the first state to elect a woman to federal office and among the first to grant women the right to vote, Montana maintains a long tradition of strong and politically active women. Jeannette Rankin (1880–1973) was one such figure. Serving two terms in Congress (elected in 1916 and again in 1940), Rankin believed that women instinctively understood the necessity of peace and equality, and she spent most of her career urging Montanans to work toward those ends by fighting against war and supporting social justice for all.

The oldest of seven children, Rankin attended the University of Montana in Missoula, the town of her birth, and received a degree in biology in 1902. After a trip to Boston, where she witnessed the horrible conditions of city slums, Rankin began her career as a teacher, seamstress, and social worker. In 1909, she attended the University of Washington and became involved in the women's suffrage movement. She continued to champion the cause when she returned to Montana in 1910, and women secured the vote in the Treasure State four years later.

Relying on her fellow first-time voters for support, Rankin ran for the House of Representatives on the Republican ticket in 1916 and narrowly won her seat. Shortly after taking office, she told her colleagues in

In 1985 Jeannette Rankin was inducted as Montana's second representative in Statuary Hall in the nation's capitol (Charlie Russell was the first). Terry Mimnaugh (b. 1955) was chosen over more than thirty other artists to execute the bronze likeness of Rankin. In addition to the one in Washington, D.C., this second casting of the statue now graces the Montana State Capitol in Helena. 33½" × 33½" × 112½".
Capitol Art Collection, x1980.41.01

the House, "I will stand by my country but I will not vote for war," thereby casting the first of her two votes against American involvement in both the First and Second World Wars. Her explanation of that initial vote resonates to this day:

> I have always felt that there was more significance in the fact that the first woman who was ever asked what she thought about war said NO and I believe that the first vote I had was the most significant act on the part of women, because women are going to have to stop war and I felt at the time that the first woman should take the first stand—that the first time the first woman had a chance to say no against war she should say it.

Between her terms in the nation's capital, Rankin continued her life's work of social reform, specifically as a pacifist and an advocate for workers. She developed a truly global perspective during her long life, remarking to a reporter in 1972, "I traveled around the world and stayed long enough to know how the Americans were dominating under-developed countries."

Rankin believed in simplicity in her domestic life, but she did allow herself occasional indulgences, including fashionable clothes and stylish shoes. Two statues of Jeannette Rankin—one casting in the National Statuary Hall in Washington, D.C., and the other in the Montana State Capitol—show Rankin wearing this gold brocade shoe now kept in the Society's collections.

While Rankin may have hoped for a more impactful legislative legacy, she nevertheless deserves credit for at least one far-reaching legal victory. In 1968, when Rankin was in her eighties and still a vocal advocate for peace and equality, she led a group of anti-war activists known as the Jeannette Rankin Brigade in a march through Washington, D.C., to protest the Vietnam War. The Brigade sued for being denied the ability to demonstrate on the grounds of the U.S. Capitol, and they won their case in 1972, securing that right for future protestors. Rankin died not long after in Carmel, California, in 1973. To date she remains the first and only woman from Montana to be elected to Congress. *–SAT*

84. Herman Bausch's Prisoner Description Sheet

1918, 8½" × 16¼". Archives Collection. Montana State Prison Records, MC 197, box 6

◈

During World War I, the persistent anxiety of war and notions of loyalty clashed, leaving communities across the United States torn. The prison record of Herman Bausch, who was jailed for sedition in 1918, captures this painful time in Montana's history.

In February 1918, Montana governor Samuel V. Stewart called a special legislative session to create a state council of defense, per guidelines provided by President Woodrow Wilson's National Council of Defense. As a result, the legislature charged the new Council of Defense to "do all acts and things not inconsistent with the Constitution of laws of the State of Montana, or of the United States . . . for the protection of life and public property . . . and toward the successful prosecution of [the] War." Montana's sedition law was one of the most punitive in the nation.

Initially, the Council of Defense concerned itself primarily with agricultural production aimed at supporting the war effort, but it quickly began focusing on promoting patriotic local meetings to boost morale and counteract anti-war sentiment originating from labor unions, radical farmers, and large immigrant populations. The resulting propaganda campaign led to a wave of hyper-patriotism that did not tolerate dissent. At rallies in communities across the state, mobs forced individuals perceived as "slackers" to kiss the flag. Schools and libraries burned German books, and people who were identified as radicals or of questionable loyalty were threatened and publicly ostracized. Ultimately, seventy-nine Montanans were deemed dissenters and imprisoned under the new law.

Herman Bausch, originally from Bavaria, was a naturalized American citizen who had purchased a small tract of farmland west of Billings in 1915. He married Helen Burg in 1916, and they had a child the following year. Soon after, Bausch ran afoul of the local Council of Defense for refusing to purchase war bonds. A group of local men threatened to hang Bausch in front of his wife and child if he did not purchase the bonds. When Bausch refused to acquiesce, the mob took him to the local Elks Lodge and interrogated him for hours. While detained, Bausch allegedly stated:

> I do not care anything about the Red, White and Blue; I won't do anything voluntarily to aid this war; I don't care who wins this war; I would rather see Germany win than England or France; I am not prepared to say whether or not Germany is in the right; We should never have entered this war and this war should be stopped immediately and peace declared; We should stop sending ships with supplies and ammunition to our soldiers; As far as I am concerned, I do not care if the Third Liberty Loan is a success or a failure.

This is My Country — This is My War

MEMBERSHIP CARD No. 17

Montana Loyalty League

"To Smash Hun Propaganda"

This is to Certify that

M Greenfield Chas D.

Having endorsed the principles and signed the pledge of the above organization is admitted to membership therein.

C. V. PECK, President — WILL A. CAMPBELL, Secretary

With the onset of World War I, Montanans were called upon to express their patriotism in a variety of ways. Helena newspaperman Charles D. Greenfield was not only a member of the Montana Loyalty League, but also a key player on Montana's Council of Defense. 4¼" × 2½". Gift of Charles Diggs Greenfield Jr. and Ann Greenfield Jancic, 1986.11.47

Bausch's responses to the abuse became the basis for his sedition conviction. He served twenty-eight months in the Montana State Prison. During his incarceration, his family suffered and his child ultimately died of dysentery. Released in 1920, Bausch returned to farming, but both he and his family dealt with the effects of this tragic time for many years. As his youngest daughter stated in a letter to Montana governor Brian Schweitzer in 1996, "The humiliating tactics and imprisonment of my father who lived a life of integrity, honesty and compassion fractured his American dream and negatively affected his entire life and that of his family."

The Council of Defense ceased active functioning when the armistice was signed in November 1918, although it was not formally dissolved until July 1921, after the United States had signed a treaty with Germany. In 2005, University of Montana law professor Jeff Renz and a group of law and journalism students launched the Montana Sedition Project, which researched all those convicted under the state's Sedition Act of 1917. Thanks to their efforts, all seventy-nine convictions were posthumously pardoned in 2006 by Governor Brian Schweitzer. –*JF*

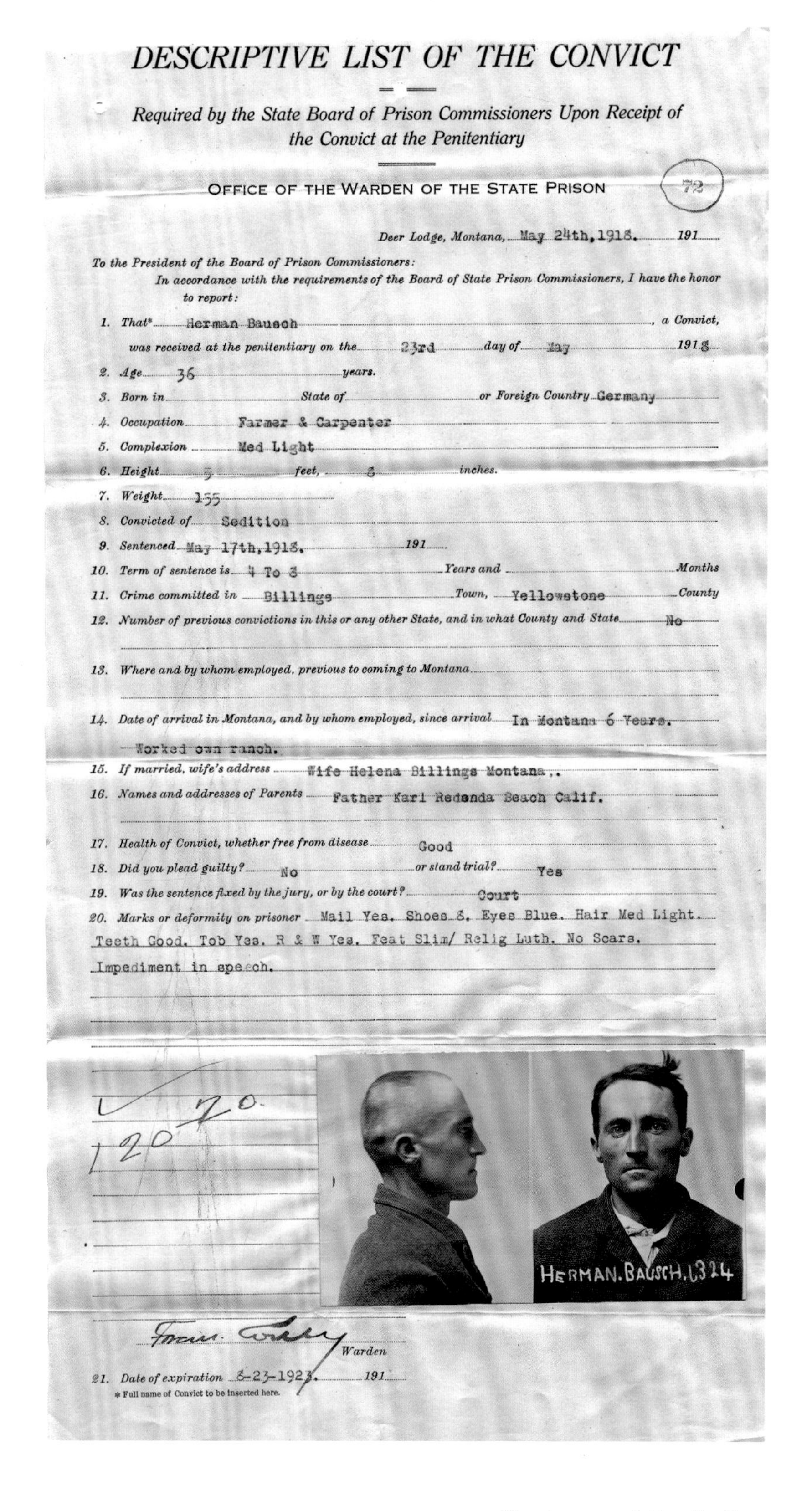

DESCRIPTIVE LIST OF THE CONVICT

Required by the State Board of Prison Commissioners Upon Receipt of the Convict at the Penitentiary

OFFICE OF THE WARDEN OF THE STATE PRISON (72)

Deer Lodge, Montana, May 24th, 1918. *191*

To the President of the Board of Prison Commissioners:

In accordance with the requirements of the Board of State Prison Commissioners, I have the honor to report:

1. *That** Herman Bausch *, a Convict, was received at the penitentiary on the* 23rd *day of* May *1918*
2. *Age* 36 *years.*
3. *Born in* ____ *State of* ____ *or Foreign Country* Germany
4. *Occupation* Farmer & Carpenter
5. *Complexion* Med Light
6. *Height* 5 *feet,* 8 *inches.*
7. *Weight* 155
8. *Convicted of* Sedition
9. *Sentenced* May 17th, 1918. *191*
10. *Term of sentence is* 4 To 8 *Years and* ____ *Months*
11. *Crime committed in* Billings *Town,* Yellowstone *County*
12. *Number of previous convictions in this or any other State, and in what County and State* No
13. *Where and by whom employed, previous to coming to Montana* ____
14. *Date of arrival in Montana, and by whom employed, since arrival* In Montana 6 Years. Worked own ranch.
15. *If married, wife's address* Wife Helena Billings Montana.
16. *Names and addresses of Parents* Father Karl Redonda Beach Calif.
17. *Health of Convict, whether free from disease* Good
18. *Did you plead guilty?* No *or stand trial?* Yes
19. *Was the sentence fixed by the jury, or by the court?* Court
20. *Marks or deformity on prisoner* Mail Yes. Shoes 8. Eyes Blue. Hair Med Light. Teeth Good. Tob Yes. R & W Yes. Feat Slim/ Relig Luth. No Scars. Impediment in speech.

[illegible] *Warden*

21. *Date of expiration* 8-23-1923. *191*

* Full name of Convict to be inserted here.

85. Miss Ishikawa, Japanese Friendship Doll

1927, 16⅛" × 33". Gift of the Prefecture of Ishikawa, Japan, x1928.01.01

Miss Ishikawa is one of fifty-eight friendship dolls presented to the children of America by the children of Japan in 1927 in appreciation for a similar gift given by the United States earlier that year. Miss Ishikawa and her companions were issued passports and first-class tickets for their voyage to San Francisco, and each traveled with a trunk packed with miniature lacquered furniture and personal items meant to make the dolls comfortable in their new homes. Each doll—known as *tôrei-ningyô* in Japan—had her own personal crest, which adorned her silk kimono and lacquered accessories.

Three years before the dolls crossed the Pacific, the U.S. Congress passed the Johnson-Reed Act, which limited immigration from some countries based on a quota system and banned almost all immigration from Asia. At the same time, Japanese Americans living on the West Coast were experiencing systematic discrimination and physical intimidation. As anti-Japanese sentiment grew in the United States and anti-American sentiment erupted in Japan, Reverend Sidney Gulick, a former American missionary, developed the idea of easing international relations by fostering friendship and cultural understanding between the two countries' children.

The friendship doll exchange began in 1927. As a goodwill gesture, members of Gulick's Committee on World Friendship Among Children shipped more than twelve thousand American dolls to Japan in time for *Hina Matsuri* (Doll Festival) on March 3, 1927. Called "blue-eyed dolls" by the Japanese, these tiny ambassadors were received with great appreciation and eventually were distributed to elementary schools and kindergartens throughout Japan.

In return, the Japanese government commissioned their own friendship dolls as gifts to the children of the United States. Each named for a Japanese prefecture, city, or colony, the dolls were intended to serve as symbolic diplomatic ambassadors. Upon the arrival of Miss Ishikawa and her peers in the United States, dignitaries and American families attended receptions in their honor.

The goodwill generated by the dolls, however, proved short-lived. Many of the children who participated in the doll exchange in 1927 became soldiers who fought one another in World War II. At that time, the imperial Japanese government mandated that the American dolls be destroyed. Today, few of the so-called blue-eyed dolls remain intact, and only forty-six of the fifty-eight Japanese friendship dolls still exist.

Miss Ishikawa joined the MHS permanent collection in 1928. She was first displayed in the basement of the state capitol, where the museum once resided, and over the years was featured in numerous exhibits. More recently, MHS's curators made the difficult decision to limit her public exposure due to concerns about her preservation. The doll's skin is made of *gofun*—a plaster-like material composed of ground oyster shells—which is highly susceptible to changes in humidity. In 1988, the doll was shipped back to Japan for exhibition and specialized conservation treatment. Despite precautions taken to acclimate her to the changing humidity, the restoration was not entirely successful.

In recent years, there has been a renewed interest in these goodwill dolls as historical artifacts and artistic expressions of cultural awareness. Organizations in the United States and Japan have planned reunions and homecoming exhibitions, as well as new doll exchanges. Meanwhile, however, the remaining American and Japanese dolls continue to represent the promise of friendship and peace among nations.

–AST

86. Campbell Farming Company Photograph

ca. 1935–1950. Gift of Phoebe Knapp Warren, Campbell Farming Company Collection, Lot 032 B1F07 09a,

◈

Dubbed the "Biggest U.S. Farmer" on the cover of *Time* magazine in 1928, Thomas D. Campbell developed dryland mechanized farming techniques on his Hardin farm that were emulated worldwide. This photograph captures the impressive scale of his eastern Montana farming operation.

A native of the Red River Valley in North Dakota, Campbell began working his family's expansive farm early on in life due to his father's poor health. As a young man, his aspirations led him to California, where he learned about innovative large-scale farming techniques.

In response to food shortages during World War I, Campbell developed a controversial plan to mechanize food production and lease large tracts of land on the Crow and Fort Peck Reservations in eastern Montana. By allotting reservation lands to individual tribal members, the 1887 Dawes Act had opened the door to the leasing of tribal land by non-Native people, which later spelled opportunity for people like Campbell.

With backing from financier J. P. Morgan, Campbell formed the Montana Farming Corporation and leased over 95,000 acres of land on the Crow Reservation, primarily from allotment landowners. The corporation was revolutionary in its extensive use of mechanization to produce wheat and other types of grain, but yields were paltry due to several years of drought. As a result, Morgan withdrew his support, and Campbell subsequently condensed the company's overall footprint to 50,000 acres of purchased and leased land and changed its name to the Campbell Farming Company. By the 1930s, Campbell had stabilized and expanded the company to include extensive land-grant holdings in New Mexico.

Despite its early challenges, the scale and productivity achieved by the Campbell Farming Company was unprecedented. A 1929 article in *The Scoop-Shovel*, an agricultural magazine from Winnipeg, Manitoba, reported that Campbell Farms was able to "plow 1,000 acres per day, seed 2,000 acres, harvest 2,000 acres, thresh 20,000 bushels of grain."

Campbell's industrialized dryland farming techniques were considered so cutting-edge that he was recruited as an advisor to the Soviet government in the early 1930s during the first of Stalin's five-year plans. Campbell also served in a similar capacity in Great Britain, Tunisia, South Africa, and Australia, and during World War II he enlisted in the U.S. Army and put his expertise to work improving mechanized military transportation.

In later years, Campbell faced harsh criticism for his use of allotment lands taken from the Crow Reservation. The loss of productive lands during this period has been among the causes of high unemployment and poverty rates on the reservation that continue to this day.

This photograph is part of an extensive collection of documents, photographs, and films related to the Campbell Farms operations in Montana and New Mexico, the Campbell family, and Thomas Campbell's international renown for innovative farming techniques. *–JF*

87. Big Medicine

b. 1933–d. 1959, 90" × 27" × 60". Gift of the United States Department of the Interior, x1961.24.01

The Treasure State is renowned for its abundant wildlife, but no single animal has gained more fame than Big Medicine, an extremely rare white buffalo that lived his entire life on the National Bison Range in western Montana. As noted by Montana historian Dave Walter, "Most Indian bands celebrated the white buffalo as a blessing. . . . The huntsman who killed a white buffalo brought honor not only to himself, but also his family and his entire band."

Big Medicine was born on May 3, 1933, in the worst years of the Great Depression. Initially named Whitey by Bison Range staff, he became known as Big Medicine as his fame spread throughout the nation, in recognition of his symbolic importance to America's Native peoples. "Just as brand-new President Franklin D. Roosevelt was creating New Deal programs to ease the country's economic and social woes," Walter observed, "the symbolism of the remarkable birth was lost on neither native nor Euro-American Montanans. . . . The idea of this majestic white animal—whether spiritual icon or remarkable curiosity—captured the imagination of a nation struggling to survive a collapsed national economy."

Prior to the mid-nineteenth century, the tens of millions of bison that roamed North America were a source of food, shelter, and spiritual significance for Plains Indian peoples. By 1883, the number of free-roaming bison numbered only in the hundreds. Their demise was due to the destruction wrought by hide hunters and federal policies that sought to end the Plains Indians' traditional way of life.

Fearing the extinction of the once-ubiquitous beasts, in 1905 a group of concerned citizens—including naturalist William Hornaday (1854–1937) and President Theodore Roosevelt (1858–1919)—formed the American Bison Society, which was dedicated to "the permanent preservation and increase of the American Bison." At Roosevelt's urging, Congress appropriated funds in 1908 to purchase land where "a representative herd of bison" could be maintained "to ensure the preservation of the species." The preserve, located on Montana's Flathead Indian Reservation, was stocked with thirty-four animals from which most of the Bison Range's stock—including Big Medicine—would descend.

A bison's normal lifespan is approximately twenty years, but Big Medicine—who was given singular care and a special diet—lived to be twenty-six. He spent most of his later years in the Bison Range's smaller exhibition pasture, where he received individual attention from both the public and his caretakers. As a *Great Falls Tribune* reporter noted in 1959, "Like all older buffalo bulls, Big Medicine remains apart from the herd. . . . His spirit and strength for fighting have given way to grazing alone in quiet contentment. . . . He is one of the most photographed animals in the world. People seem to sense an air of mystery about him and gaze in awe at his shining white coat and his crown of dark brown hair. 'Big Medicine,' an appropriate name for a magnificent animal." –*KL*

88. *Woman*

ca. 1950–1952, 10" × 14", by Willem de Kooning (1904–1997).

Gift of George and Elinor Poindexter, Poindexter Collection, x1960.05.01

This painting by Willem de Kooning (1904–1997) was the first of many works of modern art given to the Montana Historical Society by George and Elinor Poindexter. George was a third-generation Montanan who grew up in Dillon, and his family was affiliated with the Poindexter & Orr Ranch in Beaverhead County. George left Montana to become a highly successful businessman in New York City. There, he and his wife owned and operated the influential Poindexter Gallery, which featured works by artists representing the New York School of Abstract Expressionism—a defining art movement of the mid-twentieth century.

In 1960, George and Elinor decided to donate their extraordinary collection of art—ninety-eight paintings and one photograph—to the Montana Historical Society. The entire collection came in installments over a period of years, with Willem de Kooning's *Woman* as the first arrival, followed by other modern masterpieces by artists such as Jackson Pollock, Franz Kline, Richard Diebenkorn, Sonia Gechtoff, and Robert DeNiro, father of the famous actor by the same name. Explaining his intention for the donation, George Poindexter wrote:

> I hope that the pleasure they [these paintings] have given me will be shared by the people of my native state. . . . I have been collecting these pictures for ten years and I love them all. My reason for giving them away is because my whole family were always Montanans at heart and I'd like to do something for the state. I believe the collection is good enough and varied enough to have an effect on Montana's cultural climate.

The Society's ninety-nine-piece Poindexter Collection contains numerous masterworks of Abstract Expressionism, including this untitled oil on canvas by Franz Kline.
1951, 42" × 25". x1974.04.04

Upon mailing *Woman* to the Montana Historical Society in 1960, Poindexter wrote to director Michael Kennedy in December, "Two or three days ago I turned the little de Kooning lady over to the shipper . . . you should have it shortly. . . . I don't have to tell you that you are getting a good picture." Willem de Kooning was one of the most important artists of the twentieth century, and his *Woman* series secured him as a central figure, alongside Jackson Pollock and Franz Kline, in the New York School of Abstract Expressionism.

The Poindexters' gift to Montana provides a lasting resource of inspiration and art history for the state. Countless Montanans have viewed this collection over the years, and since 1960 it has been shown in sixty-one exhibitions in fourteen states, ranging from New York to California. Today, the works are frequently shown to Montana high school and college art classes, and researchers and artists from all over the country come to appreciate the collection.

–JBO

89. Holter Heart Monitor

ca. 1962. 16" (with strap) × 7" × 3". Gift of Joan Treacy Holter, Holter Research Foundation Collection, 1985.53.39

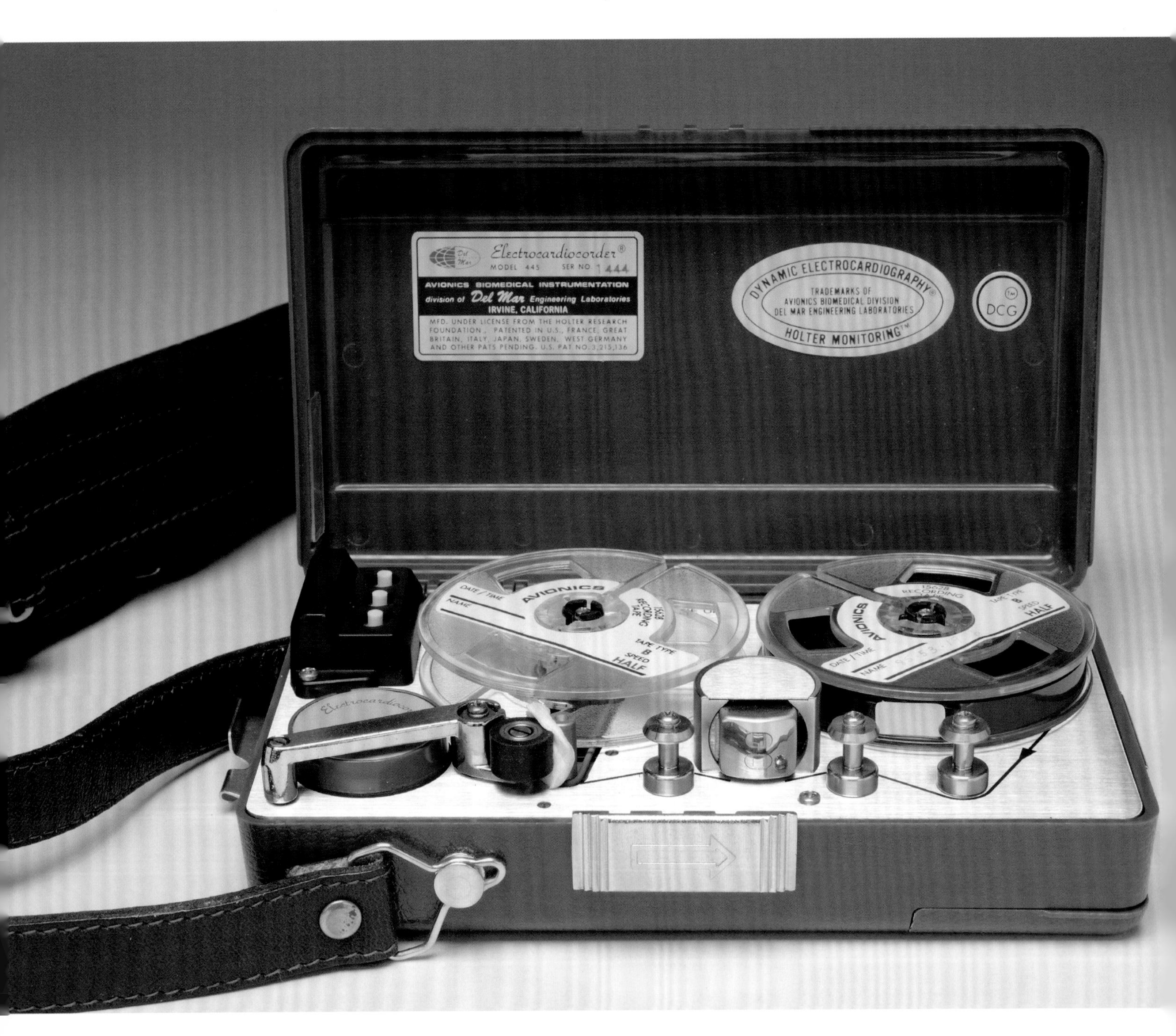

To the untrained eye, this apparatus resembles a reel-to-reel recording system from the 1960s, but careful examination and some context yield a different story. The development of this ambulatory electrocardiogram (AECG)—also known as the Holter heart monitor, named after Helena native and biophysicist Norman Jefferis "Jeff" Holter (1914–1983)—revolutionized the study and treatment of human and animal heart disease.

Known as the father of ambulatory and long-term cardiography, Jeff Holter came from a long line of industrious Montanans. His grandfather, Anton Holter, was also a tinkerer and an early entrepreneur, and his parents, Norman and Florence, embodied the family's values of hard work through the operation of their hardware store located near Last Chance Gulch. At an early age, Holter found a mentor in pharmacist Emil Starz, who encouraged his interest in science and technology. After graduating from Helena's Carroll College in 1931, Holter's educational pursuits took him to the University of California–Los Angeles and the University of Southern California for degrees in physics and chemistry, followed by graduate work at the University of Heidelberg, the University of Chicago, and the University of Oregon Medical School.

In the early 1940s, Holter joined the U.S. Navy, eventually becoming a senior physicist tasked with studying the effects of atomic bombs detonated underwater. Through this work, Holter developed disdain for the country's reliance on nuclear weaponry, and not long after his service in the South Pacific he returned to Helena to establish the Holter Research Foundation, initially located in the back of his parents' hardware store (and, later, in an abandoned train station nearby).

Holter's goal for the foundation, as vague as it was ambitious, was to "follow whatever idea appears most likely to lead us to things not previously known." From the outset, he embraced the abstract possibility of innovation: "We have no idea what we might be working on a year from now. It could be anything from outer space to bird feathers."

With his partner William Glasscock, Holter developed a prototype for his most significant invention: a system for recording and observing the action of the heart. While the technology to perform such measurements already existed among stationary machines, Holter's creation was revolutionary in the fact that it was small enough to be carried alongside the patient, recording a subject's heart during regular activity. Holter's original apparatus was cannibalized for parts in the development of subsequent models, and eventually a mass-market version like this one entered commercial production in 1962.

Holter resisted the opportunity to capitalize on his monitoring device, believing that "science and business don't mix." Indeed, such freedom from the structured world of university or government research enabled him to think outside the box. "Serendipity and coincidence," Holter expressed, "play a large part in what anyone does in life . . . the formation of ideas follows a quite circuitous path and often leads to results never originally visualized or planned. Research should never be conducted to prove a point but rather to discover the unknown." Holter and Glasscock went on to make further advancements in science and technology.

Much more compact than their predecessors of the 1960s, contemporary versions of Holter's invention now weigh less than most cell phones and can be concealed easily under a patient's clothing. Holter heart monitors still bear the name of their creator, however, and today they are used in cardiology wards around the world.

–SAT

90. Lee Metcalf Letter to Edwin S. Graf

1964, 8" × 10". Gift of Donna Metcalf, Lee Metcalf Papers, MC 172, box 355

◈

For twenty-five years Lee Metcalf (1911–1978) represented the people of Montana in Washington, D.C., first as a representative (1953–1961) and then as a senator (1961–1978). A February 1964 letter from Metcalf to constituent Edwin S. Graf of Stevensville hinted at the pivotal role Metcalf would play in the passage of the Civil Rights Act later that year. In response to a letter from Mr. Graf, he wrote:

> The Civil Rights Bill . . . as I see it simply tries to give our colored citizens the same opportunity to vote, for their children to attend decent schools, and opportunity to have available public accommodations. . . . I do not hold myself out to be an expert on the Civil Rights Bill. I am going to participate in the debate, listen carefully and try to analyze and read the material that is presented. . . . I do know that if I were a Negro and treated as I can see Negroes are treated here in Washington, D.C., I would be protesting, I would be marching, and I would be sitting in, too.

In August 1960, then–U.S. Representative Lee Metcalf (center) meets with Democratic leaders: (left to right) President John F. Kennedy, National Democratic Party Chairman Henry M. Jackson, Senate Majority Leader Lyndon B. Johnson, and Assistant Majority Leader Mike Mansfield. U.S. Senate Democratic Photograph Studio, photographer. Gift of U.S. Senate Historical Office, Lot 031 B16F1 01

As it turned out, Metcalf's deft work as the U.S. Senate's permanent acting president pro tempore helped end a seventy-five-day filibuster by anti–civil rights senators and cleared the way for a full Senate vote on the bill on June 19, 1964. The bill passed the chamber that day, and President Lyndon B. Johnson signed it into law on July 2, 1964.

For Metcalf, the bill's passage was part of a political trajectory that followed that of President John F. Kennedy's administration. From Metcalf's participation in what was known as the Democratic Study Group (credited with securing Kennedy the Democratic nomination in 1960), to his work on various New Frontier and Great Society programs, he maintained a close political connection to Kennedy-era progressive social issues. Senator Metcalf was considered a leading federal legislator for social welfare, Indian affairs, water and land resource management, conservation and wilderness protection, education, and poverty legislation in the 1950s through 1970s. His legislative involvement included work on the Clean Air Act of 1963, Wilderness Act of 1964, Economic Opportunity Act of 1964, Indian Civil Rights Act of 1968, National Forest Management Act of 1976, Montana Wilderness Study Act of 1977, and Surface Mining Control and Reclamation Act of 1977.

By the 1970s, Senator Metcalf's health was failing. On January 12, 1978, he died in his sleep from a heart condition. President Jimmy Carter observed that Metcalf's death "stills a voice that had long spoken up for preserving the great wilderness areas of this country. He was a friend of working people and family farmers and an early sponsor of legislation for

15 February 1964

Zip Code 20510

Mr. Edwin S. Graf
Box 5
Stevensville, Montana

Dear Mr. Graf:

I have received your letter of 10 February.

I am making a request to the Internal Revenue Service to expedite payment of your income tax refund. As I told you, I have taken up with the Department of Labor the employment problems being given to the people of Ravalli County by importation of domestic labor from the Southwest.

The Civil Rights Bill is a complicated and voluminous bill, passed by a substantial majority in the House of Representatives after one of the longest debates in history. As I see it, it simply tries to give our colored citizens the same opportunity to vote, for their children to attend decent schools, and opportunity to have abailable public accommodations--rights the Anglo-Saxon people have had since the establishment of English Common Law. I have read about cases that arose in fourteen and fifteen hundred where an innkeeper or a tavern owner who holds himself out to accommodate the public could not turn anyone away without good and sufficient reason, so this is a part of the basic tradition of Anglo-Saxon people.

I do not hold myself out to be an expert on the Civil Rights Bill. I am going to participate in the debate, listen carefully and try to analyze and read the material that is presented. I see no reason why we shouldn't continue this Anglo-Saxon relationship of public accommodations and public facilities for all citizens. I know of no drive on to move Negroes into every community although I deplore the fact that Negroes are insisting that they be driven by bus into areas away from where they live such as New York and Chicago. I know of no attempt to have Negroes imported into such areas as Montana.

Judy

Civil Rights - opposed

clean water, federal aid to education and reclamation of strip-mined land. His loss will be deeply felt."

This letter and the thousands of similar constituent letters, reports, legislation, speeches, and photographs within MHS's Metcalf Collection allow visitors to the Society's archives a chance to explore the political challenges facing Montanans and the nation in the 1960s and 1970s. Many of these issues continue to be relevant to present policy debates about civil rights and environmental protection. *–JF*

91. *Montana—A Buried History*

1976, 95½" × 47½", by James Todd (b. 1937). John Reddy, photographer.

Gift of the Montana Federation of Teachers in memory of Perry Melton, 1984.63.01

◈

In 1976, Montana joined the rest of the United States in celebrating the nation's two-hundredth birthday. Tasked with organizing the state's commemoration, the Montana Bicentennial Administration (MBA) noted that the upcoming anniversary offered a "once-in-a-century opportunity to make a better America." By June 1975, the MBA announced that almost fifteen hundred projects had been proposed, making Montana "third in the nation in the number of Bicentennial projects being planned."

Montanans celebrated the bicentennial in a variety of ways: installing "living logos" in public and private flower beds, refurbishing local museums, writing county history books, selling commemorative medals, and traveling to Billings to view the American Freedom Train, a twenty-two-car-long rolling exhibition of historical documents and artifacts that toured the country in 1975–1976. For its part, the executive council of the Montana Federation of Teachers (MFT) commissioned Missoula artist James Todd to

create this mural depicting the history of labor in the Treasure State.

An artist, labor activist, and University of Montana professor, Todd was a natural choice for the commission. Describing his completed work, Todd noted that *Montana—A Buried History* "concentrates largely upon what I believe to be some of the major events and transitions in the labor and corporate history of the state. My interpretation of this history is partisan and selective, and does not pretend to be a complete or detached overview." Todd saw his approach to the subject matter as serving an important purpose: "I attempt to symbolize events and connections, which I believe are frequently ignored and sometimes even repressed." In addition to portraying Montana's labor heritage, Todd also focused his attention on "our Native Americans whose culture was destroyed as a price for the industrialization of Montana."

Stylistically, Todd based his mural on Chinese revolutionary art of the 1970s. The top portion of the painting depicts a realistic contemporary landscape, offering an aboveground view of the state, while the lower two-thirds of the painting showcases a variety of significant characters in Montana history. Among those depicted are Captains Meriwether Lewis and William Clark, fur traders, gold miners, Indian warriors from the Battle of the Little Bighorn, railroaders, "Cowboy Artist" Charlie Russell, the victims of the 1917 Speculator Mine disaster, and suffragist Jeannette Rankin. The painting also represents significant historic events, including the hanging of union organizer Frank Little, the World War I–era Sedition Act, the U.S. military's establishment of missile sites across the state, the declining fortunes of family farms, as well as the protest movements that championed Indian rights and environmental protection.

In Todd's artwork, the invisible past is interwoven with the tangible, cultural objects that are literally buried, such as gold, bones, mine shafts, and missile silos. To weave the threads of this heritage together, the artist chose the motif of the coyote. According to Todd, the coyote is "shown three times running throughout the margin of the picture. He is the Coyote of Indian legend, and symbolizes the underlying spirit of the open nature with which we are blessed."

–KL

Montana Imagined

◈

Art performs the obvious function of making the world a more beautiful and interesting place. It also serves as an important form of communication. For eons, Plains Indian men crafted symbolic records on stone in the form of petroglyphs and pictographs, the meaning of which would have been clear to their contemporaries but are now often enigmatic. They also chronicled their individual war deeds on hide and maintained communal winter counts to document tribal histories. Women decorated parfleches with painted geometric patterns and adorned clothing with embroidered quillwork designs as well as stone, bone, and shell beads. After contact with Europeans, Indians adeptly incorporated new materials—most notably glass beads of all shapes and sizes—into time-honored practices.

Nineteenth-century newcomers to the region relied on their own artistic traditions to create works that conveyed their impressions of this place and its peoples. In the 1830s, artists like Karl Bodmer (1809–1893) and George Catlin (1796–1872) traveled up the Missouri River as members of scientific expeditions and began a tradition of Native American portraiture that continues today. Likewise, Euro-American artists were drawn to Montana by its spectacular scenery, abundant wildlife, and frontier mystique. Many, like Bodmer and Catlin, came only for short sojourns; others, like Great Falls "Cowboy Artist" Charles M. Russell (1864–1926) and Helena landscape painter Ralph E. DeCamp (1858–1936) were enraptured by the Treasure State and made it their permanent home.

Individual pieces of art arrived in Montana in various ways. Immigrants brought with them works of artistic merit or sentimental significance for their own personal enjoyment. Collectors, like Helena saloonkeeper August Fack, imported pieces from Europe and other parts of the United States to display in galleries, business establishments, and private clubs. To these collections, they soon added the works

The Rosebud River, 1928, 83" × 42", by Ralph E. DeCamp (1858–1936). Capitol Art Collection, x1928.06.03

In his 1988 oil painting, *White Bears and White Cliffs*, Helena artist Robert F. Morgan (1929–2015) relegates the subject of the painting—the Lewis and Clark Expedition—to the distant background, focusing instead on Montana's majestic wildlife and incredible scenery. 95 3/16" × 72¼". 1988.103.01

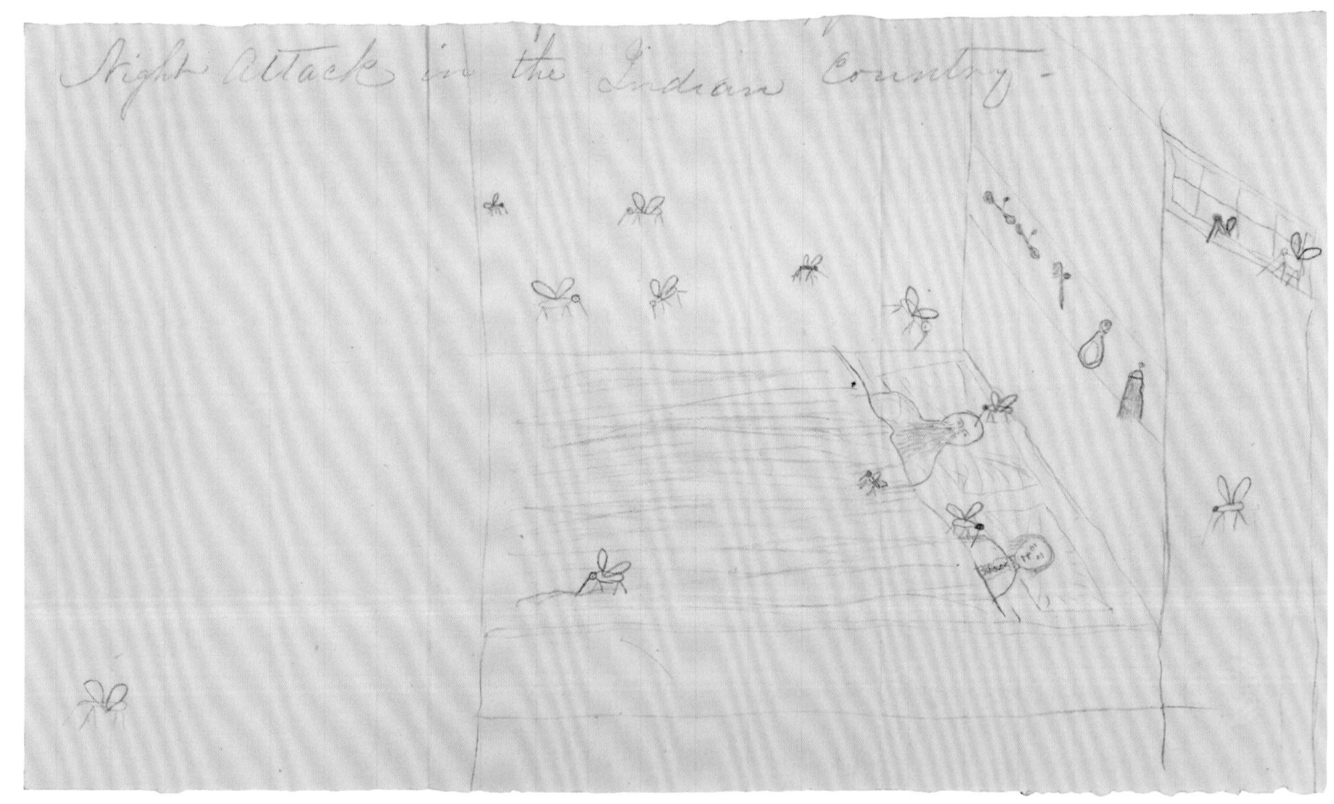

By titling her ca. 1867 sketch *Night Attack in Indian Country*, Elizabeth Chester Fisk (1846–1927) played upon stereotypical fears held by many non-Indians in Montana Territory. The subject of the drawing, however, depicts a much more common plight: a night made sleepless by swarms of mosquitoes. 8" × 4¾". Fisk Family Papers, 1983.95.02

Joe Halko's (1940–2009) 2009 bronze sculpture, *Headed for the Highwoods*, captures one of Montana's most celebrated animals, a regal bull elk, craning his neck to scan his surroundings. John Reddy, photographer. 10½" L × 5½" × 11¾". Rendezvous Legacy Collection, 2009.41.01

of Montana artists as well. And beginning with the founding of the Society in 1865, museums across Montana joined in the pursuit of collecting and exhibiting works of art for the public's benefit.

Throughout the twentieth century, art proliferated under the Big Sky. Montana-born artists joined those who continued to be drawn to the Treasure State from elsewhere. While some Indian artists continued to practice traditional Native art forms, others, like William Standing (1904–1951) adopted classic Euro-American techniques in painting and drawing. Still others, including Blackfeet sculptors John L. Clarke (1881–1870) and Jay Laber (1961–2019), mastered approaches uniquely their own. In addition to paintings and sculptures, Montana artists—both Indian and non-Indian—also created cartoons, poems, and songs to express their perceptions of life in the Treasure State. Together, these creative traditions provide us with a set of shared symbols that help us understand and appreciate our past, our present, and one another.

92. *Odalisca*

1875, 28" × 18" × 51", by Cesare Lapini (1848–1893). Gift of Mrs. William (Elizabeth) Walker, x1987.04.01

◈

In 1875, the Italian artist Cesare Lapini sculpted *Odalisca*, a classically styled tribute to odalisques, female slaves or concubines from the Ottoman empire. Balancing on her left toes, she lifts both arms lithely over her head while holding one end of the billowing veil that drapes her body. Her left hand, now broken below the wrist, once held the intricately carved handle of a feathered fan behind her head. Around the turn of the century, Helena art collector and proprietor August Fack (1856–1917) acquired the white marble statue for $7,200. *Odalisca* commanded a prominent place at Fack's saloon among C. M. Russell paintings and other impressive works of art.

Although rumored to have never seen the captivating marble statue prior to his purchase, Fack likely acquired it from Lapini's Florence gallery on one of his buying trips to Europe. Fack was a German immigrant and proud naturalized American citizen, and his elegant saloon, the California Wine House, was a longtime Main Street fixture among Helena's wealthier residents. At a time when women did not patronize such businesses, Fack opened his wine house exclusively to them on a special "Ladies' Day" each year so that they, too, could enjoy his fine art collection, including the alluring *Odalisca*.

Curator Bob Morgan and an unidentified colleague stock the bar in preparation for the 1969 opening of the Society's Territory Junction exhibit. *Odalisca* receives pride of place on the historic back bar, which came from the Mint Saloon in Great Falls. MHS B11 TerrJct

When Fack retired in 1913 due to poor health, he transferred the California Wine House to Harvey Fister and William Barworth, who also purchased his extensive art collection. After Prohibition forced closure of the establishment in 1918, Fister and Barworth acquired the former Grand Central Hotel at 10 North Main Street. In 1919, they changed its name to the Harvey Hotel and moved the art collection there, where *Odalisca* continued to attract admirers.

In the early morning hours of July 16, 1928, a fire swept through North Main Street, and many of the city's commercial buildings—including the former wine house and the Harvey Hotel—were destroyed. Caught in the blaze, *Odalisca* fell through the burning hotel floors and landed in the basement. Although she was rescued from the ruins, her flawless white marble was blackened and smudged, the handle of the fan and her left hand were broken, and the tips of three fingers were missing from her right hand.

For a time, she resided in the Walker Paint Company store on Park Street, but in 1961 Helena's *Independent Record* proclaimed that "Odalisca is destined to become a homeless woman unless Mike Kennedy takes her into his bosom and gives her a home in the historical library." It was an offer the Society's director couldn't refuse. Today, the marble statue and her journey offer a small glimpse into Helena's past. Though scorched by fire and missing pieces, she remains a romantic, dancing figure captured eternally in mid-step. –*RH*

ODALISCA

93. White Swan's Robe

ca. 1880, 70" × 80", by White Swan (ca. 1850–1904) and unidentified artists.

Gift of Isabel Haynes, 1978.38.105

◈

In a centuries-old tradition, Plains Indian men painted narrative scenes on buffalo robes, hides, and tipis to chronicle their personal feats, memorializing and making public their heroic deeds. White Swan (ca. 1851–1904), a young Apsáalooke (Crow) warrior who served as a scout for the U.S. Army during the 1876 Battle of the Little Bighorn, painted the lower half of this magnificent robe circa 1880. A prolific artist, he often depicted events from the famous battle in his works. On this robe, however, he illustrates his exploits in intertribal warfare. Here, among other heroic deeds, he is shown counting coups on his enemy and stealing a gun in hand-to-hand combat.

A different artist, possibly another Crow warrior and U.S. Army scout known as Curley (ca. 1859–1923), painted the battle scene on the robe's upper half. While Curley's contribution cannot be verified, the unique composition of several of the warriors' feet, arms, and faces resemble warriors in ledger artwork attributed to Curley, and some evidence indicates that he and White Swan were related. Additionally, photographer F. J. Haynes photographed Curley wearing the robe in 1883, although Haynes may have simply been using it as an attractive studio prop for the portrait. Another possibility is that two different artists worked on the upper part of the robe, suggested by the stylistic differences in the rendering of some of the warriors' faces. The third artist may be Bird Far Away, as an image of a now-lost tipi liner that belonged to Medicine Crow shows similar shading of the horses as on the White Swan robe. This treatment of the horses imparts a more realistic three-dimensionality rarely seen in art of this kind.

Ashishishe, known as Curley, a Crow scout who served in the Seventh Cavalry under Lieutenant Colonel George Armstrong Custer, wears White Swan's robe in this ca. 1883 portrait. F. Jay Haynes, photographer. Gift of Mrs. Isabel Haynes, F. Jay Haynes Collection, H-00936

The robe's two panels are made of soft buffalo hide, separated by a beaded band. The band features red, pink, dark blue, light blue, yellow, white, green, and turquoise glass beads, and is made of a different piece of hide from the rest of the robe—possibly a remnant from an older hide that was recycled and retained for its beauty. The beadwork features the hourglass-with-broken-circle motif typically employed by skilled Crow women. *–JBO*

94. *When the Land Belonged to God*

1914, 72" × 42½", by Charles M. Russell (1864–1926). X1977.01.01

◈

TODAY, nothing better captures perceptions of Montana's colorful past than the work of the "Cowboy Artist" Charles M. Russell (1864–1926). In every respect, Russell belongs to Montana, and to most citizens of the Treasure State he still merits the accolade of "magnificent." As poet and author Grace Stone Coates succinctly wrote in 1936, "OF COURSE Russell was glorious—who doesn't think so?"

Dramatic in both scale and visual impact, *When the Land Belonged to God* exemplifies Russell's genius. To those unfamiliar with his beliefs about "the West that has passed," the painting stands as an immense and masterful depiction of wildlife. Set on the Missouri River at daybreak, the scene depicts a regal bull pausing momentarily amid a small group of bison that have just emerged from the water and climbed a rocky knoll a few miles downstream from the town of Fort Benton. A seemingly endless stream of buffalo trails down the far hills and cross the river behind them. Hungry wolves and a bison skull and skeleton serve as reminders of nature's adversity in an otherwise Edenic setting.

More importantly, however, the painting functions as a testament to Russell's belief in the superiority of life in Montana before it was forever altered by the arrival of miners, farmers, fences, and boosters. Russell's fondness for the West as it had been was unmistakable in most of his paintings, but no place is it more stunningly portrayed than in this masterwork. As a reporter for the *New York Times* observed in 1911, "It is necessary to remember that historical documents in art mean the record not merely of facts and incidents but of the spirit of a vanishing time. Mr. Russell has preserved the spirit of the vanishing old West to a remarkable degree."

In 1969, Russell expert Frederic G. Renner lauded *When the Land Belonged to God* as "the greatest of all Russells." Helena's famed Montana Club—a private gentleman's association that for many decades

played a key role in both the social and political life of the Treasure State—had commissioned the painting. It was installed in a prominent location in the club's reading room in 1914 and, ultimately, became the association's most prized possession. When financial difficulties forced the club to sell the painting in the mid-1970s, the state purchased the masterpiece, leading Governor Tom Judge to observe: "The work of Charlie Russell and a handful of other artists and writers has kept those of us who were not fortunate enough to know the Old West firsthand from forgetting her. . . . His paintings—their color, drama and size—bring home to us forcefully the dreams of independence and reverence for nature which underlie the quality of life we Montanans work hard to nurture and defend."

–KL

E. Lochrie

95. *Cecile Boy*

1934, 11¾" × 17¼", by Elizabeth Davey Lochrie (1890–1981). Gift of the artist, 1979.12.29

◈

Butte artist Elizabeth Davey Lochrie (1890–1981) was a renowned portraitist specializing in Native American subjects. In 1979, she gave many of her works to the Montana Historical Society's collections. The subject of this piece, Cecile Black Boy—whose name in the Siksika language was *Noomohtsiistaapitapi Sstaniiniki* (Tobacco Pod Woman)—collected hundreds of Blackfeet stories for the Montana Writers' Project from 1939 to 1942. Her work to preserve this heritage is remarkable, and she is representative of the people whom Lochrie most enjoyed painting.

Born in Deer Lodge, Lochrie attended the Pratt Institute in Brooklyn, New York, and an art school taught by Winold Reiss in Glacier National Park. She also attended Stanford University, where she learned the art of painting murals. Her talents as a muralist were noted by Montana governor Joseph Dixon, who commissioned her in 1923 to paint a series of murals for the children's ward at the Montana State Tuberculosis Sanitarium at Galen. Lochrie's friend, Helen Clark, called her a "historian with a brush," in part because she took the time to include biographical and cultural information on the backs of her paintings. In Lochrie's essay, "Montana: An Artist's Paradise," she argues that people who find "a creative outlet experience a greater joy than the average person."

Lochrie's passion for painting Montana's people and places shines unquestionably through her work. This particular piece showcases Lochrie's talent and honors Cecile Black Boy and other tribal members, past and present, who have worked to preserve Native cultures. *–SAT*

In 1979, advancing age forced Elizabeth Lochrie to relocate to California to live near her daughter. Before leaving Montana, she donated her entire studio collection to MHS. It contained completed paintings, photographs, book illustrations, and study sketches like this one, which depicts Alan Crooked Arm (top), Ties His Knees (bottom left), and Frank Going (bottom right). ca. 1925, 12" × 18". Gift of the artist, X1979.14.782

96. "Memories of the Range"

no date, 8" × 10", by Dominick John "D. J." O'Malley (1867–1943).

Gift of the O'Malley Family, Dominick John O'Malley Papers, MC 186

◈

Born as campfire entertainment for late nineteenth-century cattle drivers in the American West, cowboy poetry is best known for its vivid storytelling, wry humor, and lamentations for a lost way of life. The most popular and compelling early cowboy poetry came from those who actually rode the range, like the author of this poem, Dominick John "D. J." O'Malley, also known as the N Bar N Kid White. From the 1880s until his death in 1943, O'Malley published poetry and prose extolling the glory days of the open range.

O'Malley was born in New York City in 1867, the son of a Civil War veteran who died following complications from surgery in 1869. Margaret O'Malley, his mother, then married Charles H. White, also a soldier, who transferred to Fort Keogh, Montana Territory, in 1871. White was discharged in 1881, but soon thereafter abandoned his family, who never heard from him again.

That year Margaret and her children moved to Miles City, where Dominick started work as a horse wrangler for the Niedringhaus brothers of St. Louis, Missouri, owners of the Home Land and Cattle Company, operating as the N Bar N Ranch. Between 1881 and 1896, O'Malley drove cattle from Texas to Montana and worked as a horse wrangler, on the range crew, and as a representative or "rep"—a cowboy who worked roundups with neighboring ranches.

Over his lifetime D. J. O'Malley was credited with writing many poems, but likely produced far more than we know. The most well-known include "A Cowboy's Death," "Cowboy's Soliloquy," and "After the Roundup." The latter was set to music and distributed as "When the Work is All Done This Fall," and was recorded by various artists including Carl T. Sprague and Marty Robbins:

> After the roundup's over, after the shipping's done,
> I'm going straight back home, boys, ere all my money's gone.
> My mother's heart is breaking, breaking, breaking for me, that's all;
> But with God's help I'll see her when the work is done this fall.

Most of his work, like this poem, focused on his years with the N Bar N and the end of the open range:

> I Long for the Brakes of Sunday Creek
> for the Flats on the Little Dry
> . . . I think of the days on the wide open range.
> Good days now long gone by
> but when happy and free as a human could be
> I rode for the N bar N.

After leaving the N Bar N in 1896, O'Malley served as a special deputy sheriff in Rosebud County, a deputy inspector for the Montana Stockgrowers Association, and a guard at the Montana State Prison. In 1911, he moved to Wisconsin, where he operated a raspberry farm and worked at the Gillette Rubber Company (later UniRoyal) from 1927 to 1941. O'Malley died on March 6, 1943.

His writings live on not only as a glimpse of life on Montana's open range in the late nineteenth century, but also as an important contribution to the various expressions of cowboy culture still popular to this day. *–JF*

Memories of the range

By D. J. O'Malley N bar N Kid

I long for the brakes of Sunday Creek
For the flats on the Little ~~Dry~~ Dry
Thoughts of the Sage brush on Porcupine
Oft causes me to sigh
And I think of the days on the wide open range
Good days now long gone by, but when
Happy and free as a human could be
I rode for the N bar N

I oft think of Cowboys who rode with me there
On the roundup we rode each spring
A gay careless crew, brave hearted and true
Their friendship was as a steel ring
But where are they now? They have crossed the divide
All have dis-appeared from Mortal ken
Of that gay happy crew 'twould be hard to find two
Who rode for the N bar N

97. *Trophy Hunters*

1930, 53" × 15½", by Earl E. Heikka (1910–1941).

Gift of J. W. Bowman in memory of Mr. and Mrs. Carlos Ryan, x1974.15.01

THIS sculpture by Earl E. Heikka (1910–1941) vividly portrays a party of hunters returning from a high-country quest for big game. The lead horseman, with his gear arranged precisely on his mount, guides the five-horse pack string while his companion on the fifth horse, sensing danger, pulls his rifle from its scabbard. Accurate details such as the hunters' clothing, the weapons, and the packhorses' loads—which include a bear head and skin, a stove and provisions, a bighorn ram's head, and a full moose rack—make *Trophy Hunters* an exceptional rendition of this slice of Montana life.

The details Heikka portrayed in *Trophy Hunters* came from real-life experience. With his closest brother, Mike, Heikka spent the late 1920s working for a well-known hunting and fishing outfitter, the K Bar L Ranch, northwest of Augusta. Emil Klick, who helped establish the K Bar L in 1927, said Earl "noticed things about the animals, how they looked and how they were packed—things most kids his age would never pay any attention to, and few older folks would either."

Earl Heikka's short, tumultuous life makes his artistic accomplishments even more impressive. Born in Belt, Earl was one of six children of Finnish immigrant parents. The family moved to Great Falls in 1912, where Earl's father died three years later, leaving his mother in serious financial trouble. Young Earl lived with his older sister and her husband in Laurel and later Lewistown for seven years. During this time, he first showed his talent as a sculptor, modeling animals from mud for the couple's sons. In 1923, he returned to Great Falls, but high school proved overwhelming to the shy boy, who was afflicted with a stammer. He dropped out of school at about the same time that his sculptures were first publicly displayed at a local store. Heikka worked as a taxidermist at Great Falls Sporting Goods while his fame as an artist spread, and eventually he received commissions, invitations to national shows, and his own sculpture exhibit in Los Angeles. When his brother unexpectedly died in 1935, however, Earl's downward spiral began. He battled alcoholism and depression, committing suicide in 1941 at age thirty-one.

Despite having no formal training as a sculptor, Heikka produced appealing figures by applying Marblex, a water-based, air-drying clay, to the strong frameworks he expertly crafted. Joe Halko, one of Montana's most renowned sculptors, commented that Heikka's sculptures seldom, if ever, experienced cracking. "He had a method for successfully drying his models which we don't fully understand," Halko once said, attributing the mystery to "absorbent materials he used around the armature on the inside, then drying the clay slowly so that all the moisture was gone by the time he added the finishing touches." Another Montana master sculptor, Bob Scriver, was convinced that Heikka's experience with taxidermy led to the "strong inner structures which are basic to good taxidermy and, of course, to good sculpture." Despite his short life, Earl Heikka produced over two hundred pieces that are today recognized as some of the best sculpture representing the American West.

–SN

98. *Mountain Goats*

ca. 1950, 12" × 11" × 18½", by John Clarke (1881–1970).

Gift of Lorraine Scriver, Bob Scriver Collection, 2000.15.868

◈

Deprived of the ability to hear and speak after suffering from scarlet fever at the age of two, celebrated sculptor John L. Clarke (1881–1970) was known in his native Piikuni (Blackfeet) language as *Cutapuis*, the Man Who Talks Not. Although he was proficient in both Indian and American Sign Language, Clarke communicated most powerfully through his carvings, especially those that depicted the wildlife in and around Glacier National Park. *Mountain Goats* is a masterwork carved from a single piece of cottonwood, which Clarke skillfully rendered into the texture of animal hair and rock cliffs using a variety of tools and techniques.

Clarke, holding his sculpture of a cow elk, shares a smile with his daughter Joyce, ca. 1933. PAc 76–18.22

Clarke was born in Highwood in 1881, a grandson of Malcom Clarke, whose death was pivotal in the events that led to the 1870 massacre of more than two hundred Blackfeet people. As a child, John was sent to schools for the deaf during the same period that many other Native children were forcibly removed to boarding schools. While his tenure at these institutions—some as far away as North Dakota and Wisconsin—separated him from family, it also gave him skills for living a productive and creative life.

In 1913, John returned to Montana and set up a small studio in Midvale (now East Glacier), carving the animals he knew best from his childhood rambles and forays afield hiking and hunting. Clarke's patrons included President Warren G. Harding, railroad magnate Louis W. Hill, John D. Rockefeller Jr., friend and colleague Charles M. Russell, and countless visitors to Glacier National Park, who revered his unique ability to capture the anatomy and spirit of the animals he loved. People admired his kindness, too, and were captivated by the strength and gentleness of his hands.

Sadly, much of Clarke's work was destroyed in a house fire in 1962. His work lives on, however, in the pieces that remain in the collections at the Montana Historical Society, such as these mountain goats, gracefully perched on a rock face. *–RJW*

99. Stan Lynde Cartoon

1975, 16¾" × 11¾", by Stan Lynde (1931–2013).

Gift of the Stan and Lynda Lynde Trust, 2012.34.210

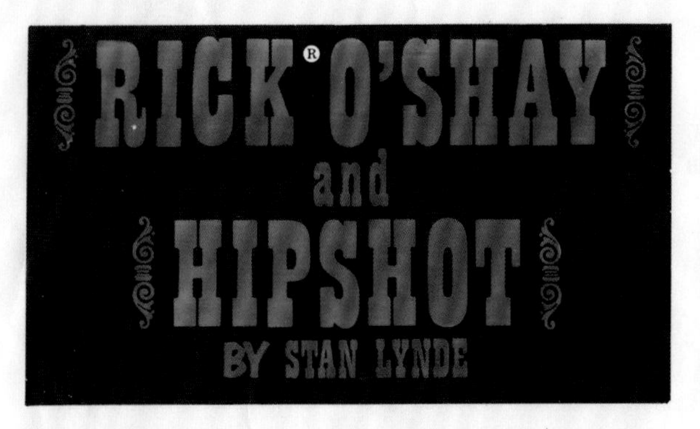

To Dad and Mom, with love, from Stan

GROWING up during the Great Depression on a sheep ranch near Lodge Grass, Stan Lynde (1931–2013) was familiar with both Montana's natural beauty and its harsh realities. Inspired by the cartoons of the 1930s and 1940s, Lynde began drawing comics in elementary school, and during the Korean War he developed strips for U.S. Navy publications. His most famous work was the nationally syndicated *Rick O'Shay*, which followed the lives of characters in the fictional Western town of Conniption and ran for twenty-three years. *Rick O'Shay* attracted commercial and critical acclaim for its humor and its ability to celebrate the Old West while satirizing romanticized stereotypes of it. By some estimates, the strip attracted fifteen million daily readers at its peak.

As a child, Lynde knew he wanted to be a cartoonist and shared the simple aspiration of most budding artists. "I used to hope that people would like my drawing," Lynde said, "but first, I hoped they wouldn't have to ask me what I'd drawn." When a teacher destroyed a notebook of Lynde's *Willy the Kid* cartoons after discovering it circulating about his classroom, the young artist became more dedicated to his craft. He was first published in his sophomore high school yearbook, the *Golden Eagle*, and during his service in the navy he received payment to produce the cartoon *Ty Foon*, an original daily strip for the *Marianas Mariner* and *Our Navy* magazine.

In April 1958, Lynde's *Rick O'Shay* comic strip debuted in the *New York Post*. The cartoon ran until 1981 (though Lynde no longer created it after 1977) and appeared in roughly one hundred papers. Following the comic's success, Lynde created five more comic series that, like *Rick O'Shay*, often conveyed his social and political commentary, including *Latigo*, a daily strip published nationally from 1979 to 1983, *Grass Roots*, a regional weekly strip in which Lynde addressed issues facing the people of the West, *Pardners*, a two-part graphic novel, and *Chief Sly Fox* and *Rovar (Bad) Bob*, magazine comic strips published in Sweden. Before his death in 2013, Lynde had created more than nine thousand daily and weekly comic strips, numerous oil paintings, a memoir (*Rick O'Shay, Hipshot, and Me*), and an eight-volume illustrated Western mystery series featuring U.S. deputy marshal Merlin Fanshaw.

Lynde drew this untitled pencil sketch in 1995 as an illustration for *The Bodacious Kid*, the first novel in his eight-volume series of Western mysteries featuring U.S. deputy marshal Merlin Fanshaw. 6" × 9". Gift of the Stan and Lynda Lynde Trust, 2012.34.298.1

In 1991, a fire in Lynde's Billings home destroyed the house and most of its contents. Among the few surviving possessions was a box of original *Rick O'Shay* comic strips. In 2012, the Stan and Lynda Lynde Trust donated more than one thousand items spanning Lynde's career—including many *Rick O'Shay* strips—to the Montana Historical Society's collections. They offer visitors a look into the creative process of a gifted and prolific artist who was deeply influenced by his Montana roots. *–AST*

100. *Symbol of the Pros*

1982, 144" × 78" × 204", by Robert M. Scriver (1914–1999). Gift of Lorraine Scriver, Bob Scriver Collection, 2000.15.60

◈

This sizable bronze sculpture epitomizes the classic sport of bronc riding, an event in which man and beast are pitted against each other in an eight-second whirlwind of muscle, fury, and bone-wrenching action. Robert MacFie Scriver (1914–1999) completed this monumental work as a proposal for acquisition by the Professional Rodeo Cowboys Association (PRCA). It was modeled loosely after that organization's logo, which features a horse named Sea Lion being ridden in the traditional style by Bill Ward.

Scriver was born on Montana's Blackfeet Reservation, where his family operated a mercantile company in the community of Browning. Growing up amid vast plains and towering mountains, the young Scriver was influenced by the geography, people, and animals of the Glacier National Park area, as well as by the romance of the Wild West. As an adult, he devoted his talents to music and taxidermy before becoming one of the nation's most celebrated sculptors of Western life. He is remembered especially for his magnificent renderings of Montana wildlife, rodeo cowboys, and traditional Blackfeet culture.

Largely self-taught, Scriver opened his first major exhibition at his studio in Browning in 1961 to critical acclaim. Greater national recognition soon followed, along with an ever-growing audience of admirers and collectors. Scriver later opened his own bronze foundry and museum to showcase his work as a taxidermist and sculptor, and in 1968 he began his series devoted to the daring men and women of the rodeo. In the early 1970s, he added to his repertoire with a series of sculptures depicting the culture and traditions of the Blackfeet people.

In *Symbol of the Pros*, completed in 1982, Scriver's bronc wears PRCA-approved rodeo gear such as a heavy wool-protected halter; a thick, square-woven hack rein attached to the halter; a regulation saddle with a high pommel; and the wool-covered flank strap, loosely attached to encourage the horse to kick higher. The rider wears regulation blunt-roweled, unlocked spurs. The bronze was cast in New York and exhibited in front of Scriver's museum in Browning before being relocated to the east lawn of the Montana Historical Society in 2000.

Scriver died at work in his Browning studio in 1999. Following his death, his widow, Lorraine, inherited not only his life's work but also the daunting task of ensuring that her late husband's legacy be properly preserved. While art museums across North America coveted the world-class collection, Lorraine determined that these masterpieces rightfully belonged where they could be treasured by those who know Scriver's work best—the people of Montana. In March 2000, she presented the Montana Historical Society with a three-thousand-piece collection comprising bronzes, plaster sculptures, taxidermy mounts, and Western memorabilia. As a result of Lorraine's generosity, Scriver's artistry will continue to enrich the lives of Montanans, and all lovers of the West, for generations to come. *–JBO*

101. *Swift Fox*

2004, 22" × 27", by Jay Polite Laber (1961–2019). 2005.17.01

◈

On May 31, 1805, near present-day Great Falls, Captain Meriwether Lewis recorded in his journal the sighting of an unfamiliar animal: "I saw near those bluffs the most beautifull fox that I ever beheld, the colours appeared to me to be a fine orrange yellow, white and black."

Although unknown to early explorers, the swift fox (*Vulpes velox*) held spiritual significance for many of Montana's Indigenous peoples. By 1918, however, predator extermination efforts had eradicated the buff-colored canid from Montana's short-grass prairies, and only some fifty years later, swift foxes were believed to be extinct in Montana.

The other Laber sculpture in the Society's collection—*Warning, Road Hazards Ahead* [detail]—is also made of rusted car parts. Measuring 156" × 108" × 108", however, it is more typical of Laber's monumental works than the comparatively diminutive *Swift Fox*.

In the mid-1990s, efforts to revive populations of the species began when ten Great Plains states formed the Swift Fox Conservation Team. In 1998, the Blackfeet Tribe, Defenders of Wildlife, and the Alberta-based Cochrane Ecological Institute began returning swift foxes to the Blackfeet Reservation. The Assiniboine and Sioux Tribes of the Fort Peck Reservation in eastern Montana began a parallel reintroduction in 2006. These efforts have proven largely successful, and the swift fox has once again become well established in parts of the Montana prairie. In this sculpture, commissioned by the Montana Historical Society for an exhibit on Lewis and Clark, Blackfeet artist Jay Polite Laber (1961–2019) captured the animal's essence with surprising methods and materials.

Born on the Blackfeet Reservation, Laber was greatly influenced by the tragedy of the disastrous 1964 flood, when his family's home was wiped out and many Blackfeet tribal members perished. Years later, using the ruined cars that had washed up along the riverbed as his medium, Laber created the iconic, larger-than-life warriors on horseback that now greet visitors when entering the Blackfeet Reservation. Central to Jay's oeuvre was the practice of making use of what is available in the surrounding environment. By repurposing pieces of rusted automobiles and other metal objects he found on the landscape, Laber sculpted vibrant works and dynamic celebrations of Piikuni culture. In the case of the swift fox, his sculpture symbolizes the resurrection of the species back from the brink. Crafted from junked car parts and discarded barbed wire, Labor's scrap-metal *Swift Fox*—known as *Senopah* in Blackfeet—is paused, alert to its surroundings, and ready for action.

–*JBO*

About the Authors

◈

Rich Aarstad is Montana's State Archivist. A Montana native, Rich grew up in Libby, where timber was king and cowboys were something you read about in Louis L'Amour Westerns. He received his bachelor's and master's degrees at the University of Montana. Rich is the father of one son, the grandfather of two precocious granddaughters who call him "Bump," the devoted walking companion of cow dog Teddye Blew, and the humble husband of Kim—his partner in crime.

Ellen Baumler earned her PhD in English, classics, and history from the University of Kansas. Until her retirement in 2018, she was the longtime Interpretive Historian at the Montana Historical Society and co-curated the museum's award-winning exhibit, *Forgotten Pioneers: The Chinese in Montana*. Ellen received the Governor's Award for the Humanities in 2011 and is the author of numerous books and articles.

Jennifer Bottomly-O'looney is the Senior Curator/Museum Manager at the Montana Historical Society. She has been with MHS for many years and has curated numerous exhibits. Her writings include *Montana's Charlie Russell: Art in the Collection of the Montana Historical Society* with coauthor Kirby Lambert and *Charles M. Russell: The Women in His Life and Art*, with coauthors Joan Carpenter Troccoli, Brian Dippie, Emily Crawford Wilson, and Thomas Petrie.

Christine Brown is a Historical Specialist in the Montana Historical Society's Outreach and Interpretation Program. She researches and writes about Montana's built environment. She coauthored *Hand Raised: The Barns of Montana* with Chere Jiusto, published by the Montana Historical Society Press in 2012.

Christy Eckerle worked as an Assistant Editor and Photo Editor of *Montana The Magazine of Western History* for eight years. A fourth-generation Montanan, she lives in Clancy with her husband and two children.

Laura Ferguson, MA, is an Associate Editor for *Montana The Magazine of Western History* and the Montana Historical Society Press. She is a contributing author to *Beyond Schoolmarms and Madams: Montana Women's History* (MHS Press, 2016) and lives in Helena with her husband, Mike Jetty, and two daughters.

Jodie Foley was born and raised in Missoula, where she studied history as an undergraduate and graduate student at the University of Montana (Go Griz!). Foley came to the Montana Historical Society in 1990 to work as an Archives Technician and worked her way up to Oral Historian, Archivist, and ultimately State Archivist, a position she retired from in 2020. She has contributed essays to *Montana The Magazine of Western History*, *Women's History Matters*, and the popular series *Jerks in Montana History*. She also served as the president of the Council of State Archivists.

Kate Hampton is the Community Preservation Officer at the Montana Historical Society's State Historic Preservation Office, where she works directly with local community preservation programs to document and preserve their cultural resources. She also directs the nationally recognized Identifying Montana's African American Heritage Resources projects, which identify, research, and document resources and places throughout the state associated with African American history. For more than a quarter century, Kate has studied and written about Montana's important places and the architectural landscape that make the state unique and tie its history to the rest of the nation.

Rowena Harrington is a Museum Registrar at the Montana Historical Society.

Roberta Jones-Wallace was born and raised in Helena and is a graduate of Montana State University. She is an Exhibit Specialist at the Montana Historical Society.

Martha Kohl has worked at the Montana Historical Society since 1995, most recently as a Historian with the Outreach and Interpretation Program. She is the author of *I Do: A Cultural History of Montana Weddings*, which was published by the Montana Historical Society Press in 2011.

Alex Kurki is the Assistant Program Officer at Cultural Vistas. He previously served as an intern at the Montana Historical Society.

Kirby Lambert has been with the Montana Historical Society since 1985, serving in a variety of capacities, most recently as the Outreach and Interpretation Program Manager. He is the coauthor of *Montana's Charlie Russell: Art in the Collection of the Montana Historical Society* and *Montana's State Capitol: The People's House*, and is a regular contributor to *Montana The Magazine of Western History*.

Susan Near served the Montana Historical Society as Director of Museum Services, Curator of Collections, Museum Registrar, and Development & Marketing Officer until her retirement in 2017. A thirty-five-year staff veteran, Near curated over twenty major MHS museum exhibitions ranging from Western art to decorative arts, conducted material culture research, presented programs on a broad range of historical collections, and led the expansion of in-house MHS fundraising functions. She coauthored *Montana's State Capitol: The People's House*, authored several pieces for *Montana The Magazine of Western History*, and contributed the Montana essay for three editions of the *Encyclopedia of Local History*.

Margarete "Maggie" Ordon is an Interpretation Planner at Newfields in Indianapolis, Indiana. She previously served as Curator of History at the Montana Historical Society, where she interpreted and developed the historical collections at Montana's Museum and the Original Governor's Mansion. She also worked at the Helen Louise Allen Textile Collection at the University of Wisconsin–Madison and with the Wisconsin Decorative Arts Database. She earned her PhD and MS in design studies and a certificate in material culture from the University of Wisconsin–Madison, and her BA in Letters from the University of Oklahoma.

Vic Reiman served as Museum Technician at the Montana Historical Society for seventeen years before retiring in 2019. His special interests include nineteenth-century firearms and the history of the Montana cattle industry.

Brian Shovers retired from the Montana Historical Society Research Center as the Library Manager in 2014. He started at MHS in the fall of 1993 as a Reference Historian. Shovers launched his career in history during his ten-year tenure in Butte, where he studied mining history and served as president of the Butte Historical Society. He is the president of the Montana chapter of the Society for Industrial Archeology and has written a number of articles for *Montana The Magazine of Western History* on a variety of topics.

Zoe Ann Stoltz serves as the Reference Historian for the Montana Historical Society, combining her two passions: the people and history of Montana. After growing up in eastern Montana and raising three daughters in the northwestern corner of the state, Zoe Ann pursued her dream of becoming a public historian. To this end, she graduated from Mount Holyoke College in Massachusetts and earned her master's degree in history from the University of Montana. She has been the MHS Reference Historian for over a decade. Her current projects include introducing students to the thrills of research, as well as a study of the MHS cookbook collection, Montana foodways, and Montana livestock brand histories.

Tammy Troup is the Cataloging and Metadata Coordinator at Bucknell University. She previously served as the Montana Historical Society's Digital Services Manager.

Amanda Streeter Trum is the Curator of Collections at the Montana Historical Society. She completed an Archaeological Field School in Kenya through St. Lawrence University, earned a master's degree in museum studies from the University of Florida, and has interned at the National Museum of American History in Washington, D.C. She has worked for the Montana Historical Society since 2007.

Stephenie Ambrose Tubbs lives in Helena and works with conservation and preservation organizations around the state.

Further Reading

◈

Black, George. *Empire of Shadows: The Epic Story of Yellowstone.* New York: St. Martin's Press, 2012.

Bottomly-O'looney, Jennifer, and Kirby Lambert. *Montana's Charlie Russell: Art in the Collection of the Montana Historical Society.* Helena: Montana Historical Society Press, 2014.

Cheney, Roberta Carkeek. *Names on the Face of Montana: The Story of Montana's Place Names.* Revised edition. Missoula: Mountain Press Publishing Company, 1996.

Dillon, Mark C. *The Montana Vigilantes, 1863–1870: Gold, Guns and Gallows.* Logan: Utah State University Press, 2013.

Egan, Ken, Jr. *Montana 1864: Indians, Emigrants and Gold in the Territorial Year.* Helena: Riverbend Publishing, 2014.

Elofson, Warren M. *Frontier Cattle Ranching in the Land and Times of Charlie Russell.* Montreal: McGill-Queens University Press, 2004.

Fritz, Harry, Mary Murphy, and Robert Swartout, eds. *Montana Legacy: Essays on History, People, and Place.* Helena: Montana Historical Society Press, 2002.

Hanshew, Annie. *Border to Border: Historic Quilts and Quiltmakers of Montana.* Helena: Montana Historical Society Press, 2009.

Hoxie, Frederick E. *Parading Through History: The Making of the Crow Nation, 1805–1935.* New York: Cambridge University Press, 1995.

Kohl, Martha, ed. *Beyond Schoolmarms and Madams: Montana Women's Stories.* Helena: Montana Historical Society Press, 2016.

Kohl, Martha. *I Do: A Cultural History of Montana Weddings.* Helena: Montana Historical Society Press, 2011.

Lambert, Kirby, Patricia Mullan Burnham, and Susan R. Near. *Montana's State Capitol: The People's House.* Helena: Montana Historical Society Press, 2002.

Lopach, James J., and Jean A. Luckoski. *Jeannette Rankin: A Political Woman.* Boulder: University Press of Colorado, 2005.

MacDonald, Douglas H. *Montana Before History: 11,000 Years of Hunter-Gatherers in the Rockies and Plains.* Missoula, MT: Mountain Press Publishing Company, 2012.

Malone, Michael, Richard Roeder, and William Lang. *Montana: A History of Two Centuries.* Revised edition. Seattle: University of Washington Press, 1993.

Martin, Dale. *Ties, Rails, and Telegraph Wires: Railroads and Communities in Montana and the West.* Helena: Montana Historical Society Press, 2018.

McDermott, John D. *Red Cloud's War: The Bozeman Trail, 1866-1868.* 2 vols. Norman, OK: Arthur H. Clark Company, 2010.

Oberdorfer, Don. *Senator Mansfield: The Extraordinary Life of a Great American Statesman and Diplomat.* Washington, DC: Smithsonian Books, 2003.

Robison, Ken. *Montana Territory and the Civil War: A Frontier Forged on the Battlefield.* Charleston: The History Press, 2013.

Russell, John C. *Treasure State Tycoon: Nelson Story and the Making of Montana.* Helena: Montana Historical Society Press, 2019.

Schwantes, Carlos A. *Long Day's Journey: The Steamboat and Stagecoach Era in the Northern West.* Seattle: University of Washington Press, 1999.

Smith, Duane A. *Rocky Mountain Heartland: Colorado, Montana, and Wyoming in the Twentieth Century.* Tucson: University of Arizona Press, 2008.

Smith, Norma. *Jeannette Rankin: America's Conscience.* Helena: Montana Historical Society Press, 2002.

Steel, Volney. *Bleed, Blister, and Purge: A History of Medicine on the American Frontier.* Missoula: Mountain Press Publishing Company, 2005.

Swibold, Dennis L. *Copper Chorus: Mining, Politics, and the Montana Press, 1889–1959.* Helena: Montana Historical Society Press, 2006.

West, Elliott. *The Last Indian War: The Nez Perce Story.* New York: Oxford University Press, 2009.

Index

◈